THE REMINISCENCES OF
Rear Admiral Harold B. Miller
U.S. Navy (Retired)

INTERVIEWED BY
Dr. John T. Mason, Jr.

U.S. Naval Institute • Annapolis, Maryland

Copyright © 1995

Preface

The late Min Miller was a gifted storyteller, the kind of individual who could mesmerize an audience as he recounted his adventures. To a degree, that quality has been captured in the oral history that follows. Unfortunately, the reader can't see Admiral Miller's gestures, hear the inflections in his voice, or see the twinkle in his eye. Even so, his love for the Navy--and particularly naval aviation--is manifest in the pages that follow.

Miller got his wings only a few years after the Navy's first aircraft carrier, the Langley, was commissioned in the early 1920s. He served in one of the ship's squadrons in the late 1920s. Indicative of the versatility of naval aviators of the era, he flew in battleship and cruiser floatplanes, as well as in flying boat squadrons. But the tours of duty that really set him apart from his contemporaries came in the early 1930s when he was pilot of the tiny Sparrowhawk fighter that operated from flying aircraft carriers. These were the huge rigid airships Akron and Macon. Miller was in the crew of each at the time of her loss, the Akron in 1933 and the Macon in 1935. The oral history includes an engrossing account of the Macon's loss.

Another interesting theme is Admiral Miller's long involvement with writing and public relations. In the 1930s he did what were essentially oral history interviews with naval aviation's pioneers and wrote the first overall account of the Navy's entry into the air age. He and his first wife wrote numerous magazine articles, and he was later a driving force in setting up Training Literature in the Bureau of Aeronautics during World War II. This section not only enhanced training within naval aviation but also served as an effective propaganda arm for selling the program. Because of the success of those efforts, Miller was made Pacific Fleet public relations officer in 1944 and greatly improved the Navy-media relationship. That led to a spot promotion to rear admiral far ahead of his contemporaries and the head public relations billet in the Navy. After his retirement from active duty, Admiral Miller did public relations work for TWA, Pan American, the American Petroleum Institute, and Hofstra University.

In addition to the contributions of Admiral Miller himself, two other individuals did a great deal to facilitate completion of this transcript. Since the admiral did not get a chance to review the transcript, his widow, Mary Louise, and younger son, Barry, undertook that task on his behalf. They have been enormously helpful in providing editing suggestions, footnote annotations, and material from the admiral's files to nail down specific points from his memory. I have also done some of the editing and annotating, with their blessing. A small amount of the material has been moved from one place to another in order to improve the continuity of the story.

My predecessor, Dr. John Mason, initiated the project by conducting the interviews for this oral history shortly before his own retirement in 1982. Much more recently, Ms. Ann Hassinger of the Naval Institute's history division has made a significant contribution through her diligence in the overall process of printing, proofreading, and overseeing the binding of the completed volumes.

Paul Stillwell
Director, History Division
U.S. Naval Institute
October 1995

REAR ADMIRAL HAROLD BLAINE MILLER
U.S. NAVY (RETIRED)

Harold Blaine Miller was born in Newton, Iowa, on 4 January 1903, son of Abraham K. and Nora Belle Vanscoy Miller. On 10 June 1920 he entered the U.S. Naval Academy, Annapolis, Maryland, after attending Westlake School for Boys in Los Angeles, California. As a midshipman at the Naval Academy, he participated in lacrosse and boxing. Graduated and commissioned ensign on 5 June 1924, he was subsequently promoted to the rank of rear admiral on 18 April 1945. He was transferred to the retired list of the U.S. Navy in that rank on 1 December 1946.

After graduation from the Naval Academy in June 1924, he joined the USS California (BB-44) and served as a junior officer in that battleship until February 1926, when he was ordered to the Naval Air Station, Pensacola, Florida, for flight training. Designated naval aviator on 17 November 1926, he joined Aircraft Squadrons Battle Fleet in February 1927 and had duty successively with Observation Squadron One, aviation unit of the USS West Virginia (BB-48), and Fighting Squadron Two, based on the USS Langley (CV-1). From January 1930 to June 1932 he was on duty at the Naval Air Station, Pensacola, first as a flight instructor, later as ground school instructor. While in that assignment he received a letter of commendation from the Secretary of the Navy in May 1930 for aiding in the rescue of a pilot who had crashed his seaplane in the water.

Transferred to the heavier-than-air unit of the airship Akron (ZRS-4), he flew planes on and off that dirigible until her loss off the coast of New Jersey in April 1933. He next had duty in connection with the pre-commissioning detail of the airship Macon (ZRS-5) at the Naval Air Station, Lakehurst, New Jersey. He served with planes attached to that airship from her commissioning, 23 June 1933, until 12 February 1935. He was on board the Macon that day when she was lost off Point Sur, California. Ordered to the Naval Air Station, Sunnyvale, California, he served there until June 1935, when he had duty with Scouting Squadron Nine, aviation unit of the heavy cruiser Northampton (CA-26), later of the heavy cruiser Salt Lake City (CA-25).

From April 1937 until June 1938 he served with Patrol Squadron 16, attached to the seaplane tender Thrush (AVP-3) and later to the tender Teal (AVP-5), which operated in the Alaskan area during much of this period. In June 1938 he was transferred to Patrol Squadron Five as executive officer and in May 1939 assumed command. During his served with Patrol Squadron Five, which was redesignated Patrol Squadron 33, operating in the Central American and Caribbean areas, his squadron won the Schiff Trophy for maximum flying time with minimum accident rate.

In June 1940 he reported as aide and flag secretary on the staff of Commander Carrier Division One (Rear Admiral Arthur L. Bristol) and was attached to the flagship, USS Saratoga (CV-3). He continued staff duty when Admiral Bristol became Commander Aircraft Scouting Force, and until February 1941 was attached to the flagship Hulbert (AVP-6). In March 1941 he became and aide and flag secretary to Commander Support Force, U.S. Atlantic Fleet (Rear Admiral Bristol), and from October 1941 until February 1942 commanded the flag unit of the Support Force.

He was awarded the Legion of Merit with the following citation:

"For exceptionally meritorious conduct in the performance of outstanding services to the Government of the United States as Aide and Flag Secretary on the Staff of the Commander of the Task Force, U.S. Atlantic Fleet, from March 3, 1941, to February 22, 1942. Largely responsible for the details of the establishment and organization of the Task

Force, [he] achieved distinctive success in developing close cooperation between units of the United Nations engaged in escort and anti-submarine operations in the North Atlantic. Captain Miller's brilliant executive ability and wide experience were essential factors in the planning, indoctrination and training of the composite forces and their subsequent success in the protection of our convoys and in the punishing offensive campaign against encroaching submarines by the Task Force."

Reporting next to the Navy Department, Washington, D.C., he organized and served as Head of the Training Literature Section, Training Division, Bureau of Aeronautics, from March 1942 until November 1943. He then reported for duty as naval attaché and naval attaché for air and assistant U.S. naval attaché, American Embassy, London, England. There he had additional duty with the Commander U.S. Naval Forces in Europe. He was detached in September 1944 for duty as public relations officer on the staff of the Commander in Chief U.S. Pacific Fleet.

"For exceptionally meritorious conduct . . . as Public Relations Officer on the Staff of the Commander in Chief, U.S. Pacific Fleet and Pacific Ocean Areas, from September 9, 1944, to April 12, 1945 . . . " he was awarded a gold star in lieu of the second Legion of Merit. The citation continues: "During this period Captain Miller worked tirelessly to build a Public Relations section capable of meeting the rapidly expanding need for press, radio and pictorial coverage of the Army, Navy, Marine Corps and Coast Guard activities in the Pacific Ocean Areas. The establishment of the Advance Headquarters of the Commander in Chief . . . at Guam necessitated the creation of many new facilities for the accommodation of War Correspondents accredited to the theater, and for the expeditious transmission of their written and pictorial material. This task was accomplished with outstanding efficiency, resulting in the moving of unprecedented volume of news material in record time, resulting from the assault and capture of Iwo Island and positions in the Ryukyu Islands. Through his devotion to duty and farsighted planning, representatives of the world press, and through them the American people, were supplied news of the Pacific war and of their Navy with maximum speed and in great volume . . ."

On 23 April 1945, with the accompanying rank of rear admiral, he became Director of the Office of Public Relations, Navy Department, and on 18 June 1945, his title was changed to Director of Public Information. He served in that capacity until relieved of all active duty on 31 July 1946, pending his retirement on 1 December of that year.

In addition to the Legion of Merit with Gold Star and his special Letter of Commendation from the Secretary of the Navy, Rear Admiral Miller held the American Defense Service Medal with Bronze "A;" the European-African-Middle Eastern Campaign Medal; the American Campaign Medal; the Asiatic-Pacific Campaign Medal; and the World War II Victory Medal.

After retirement Admiral Miller became vice president of Trans World Airlines. Later he became director of information, American Petroleum Institute, and still later director of public relations, Pan American World Airways.

In 1928 he was married to Miss Jean Dupont of Berkeley, California; their daughter Joan was born on 4 April 1931 at Pensacola, Florida. His second wife, to whom he was married in June 1946, and who died in February 1952, was the former Mrs. Mary Whately-Smith, widow of a British Army officer. In December 1953 Miller married Miss Mary Louise McGee of Kansas City, Missouri. Their first son, Harold Blaine Miller, Jr., was born on 1 June 1956. Their second son, Barry McGee Miller, was born on 23 October 1957. Admiral Miller died 15 May 1992 at Overland Park, Kansas.

CHRONOLOGY OF EVENTS, NAVY CAREER OF REAR ADMIRAL HAROLD B. MILLER

Updated 10/95

1920 - 1924	Midshipman, U.S. Naval Academy, Annapolis
1924	Graduation, USNA.
1924 - 2/26	U.S.S. CALIFORNIA [battleship], San Pedro/Long Beach, CA.
2/26-1927	Student, USNAS Pensacola, FLA 　　Designated Naval Aviator 11/17/26 (Naval Aviator No. 3322).
2/27 - 1928	U.S.S. WEST VIRGINIA [battleship] 　　Observation Squadron 1.
1928 - 12/29	U.S.S. LANGLEY [aircraft carrier], San Diego, CA. 　　Engineering officer, Fighting Squadron 2.
1929 - 1932	Instructor, USNAS Pensacola. 　　Flight instructor, then ground school instructor (engines).
6/32 - 1933	U.S.S. AKRON [rigid airship], Lakehurst, NJ. 　　Assigned to HTA (Heavier-than-Air) unit. Squadron of 8 F9C2 aircraft. Akron lost April 1933, off coast of New Jersey.
1933 - 6/35	U.S.S. MACON [rigid airship], Moffet Field, Sunnyvale, CA. 　　Senior Aviator, HTA Unit. Duty with precommissioning detail; Macon commissioned 6/23/33. Macon crashed 2/12/1935 off Point Sur, CA. Remained on duty at NAS Sunnyvale 2/35 to 6/35; worked on perfecting a navigation homing device.
6/35 - 4/37	Scouting Squadron 9. 　　U.S.S. NORTHAMPTON [cruiser], San Pedro, CA, then U.S.S. SALT LAKE CITY [cruiser].
1936	Went to NYC for several months to write <u>Chronology of Naval Aviation.</u>
1937	*Navy Wings* published.
4/37 - 6/38	Patrol Squadron 16, Martin Flying Boats. 　　Attached to seaplane tender THRUSH and later seaplane tender TEAL, operating much of the time in Alaska.
6/38 - 5/40	Patrol Squadron 5 (later designated 33), PBY's, Coco Solo, Panama. 　　Served as XO until 5/39, then became C.O. Squadron operated throughout Central America and Caribbean. Won Schiff Trophy for low accident rate.

PERSONAL CHRONOLOGY

Parents

Father — Abraham Kimball Miller. Born 11/12/1874, in Pittsburg, Indiana, or Winchester, Indiana. Died 12/17/54, Los Angeles, CA.

Mother — Nora Belle Vanscoy Miller. Born Sept. 7, 1881, Newton, Iowa. Died 12/21/34, Los Angeles, California (cancer).

Married 11 September, 1899, Murphy, Iowa
Divorced 25 June, 1913, Los Angeles, California

Personal

1/4/1903 — Born, Newton, Iowa. Lived in Newton and Los Angeles, California. In Los Angeles, CA.

"Schools attended"

7/07 - 5/13	Main Street, Los Angeles, CA	
9/13 - 5/17	Slagel Dell School, Newton, IA	
9/17 - 2/18	Westlake School for Boys, Los Angeles, CA	
2/18 - 6/18	Poly High School, Los Angeles, CA	
6/18 - ?	Westlake School for Boys, Los Angeles, CA	

1920 — USNA appointment from Henry F. Osborne.

1928 — Married Jean Dupont.

4/4/31 — Joan Miller (Ingalls) born.

5/29/46 — Divorced Jean Dupont.

6/13/46 — Married Mary Emery Hodgkinson

2/13/52 — Mary Hodgkinson died (suicide).

8/20/52 — Baptized Roman Catholic by Maurice Sheehy.

8/23/53 — Confirmed (Confirmation name Christopher).

12/28/53 — Marrried Mary Louise McGee in Kansas City, MO.

6/26/54 — Joan Miller married Ronald Boyd Ingalls.

6/1/56 — Harold Blaine Miller Jr. born, New York, NY.

10/23/57 — Barry McGee Miller born, New York, NY.

5/15/92 — Died, Overland Park, Kansas.

Different Addresses:

6717 Willow Lane, Shawnee Mission, KS (1986-1992)
116 North Woods Rd., Manhasset, NY (10/1/56 - 86)
200 East End Avenue, NY, NY (1/54 - 10/56)
110 West 57th Street, NY, NY (1/53 - 1/54)
117 East 35th St., NY, NY (?)
10 Elm Street, Pelham Manor, NY (1950 - 1952)
300 East 57th St., NY, NY (1948 - 1950)
2500 Que St., NW, Washington, DC (1946 - 1948)
36 Paradise Walk, London, England (1943-1944)
Alexandria, Virginia (1942-1943)
Norfolk, Virginia (1941)
Coronada, California (1940-1941)
Coco Solo, Canal Zone (1938-1940)
Seattle, Washington (1935-1938)

Authorization

The U.S. Naval Institute is hereby authorized to make available to individuals, libraries, and other repositories of its choosing the transcripts of four oral history interviews concerning the life and career of the late Rear Admiral Harold B. Miller, U.S. Navy (Retired). The interviews were recorded by Admiral Miller on 6 April 1981, 4 May 1981, 11 May 1981, and 8 September 1981 in collaboration with Dr. John T. Mason, Jr., for the U.S. Naval Institute.

The undersigned does hereby release and assign to the U.S. Naval Institute all right, title, restrictions, and interest in the interviews. The copyright in both the oral and transcribed versions shall be the sole property of the U.S. Naval Institute. The tape recordings of the interviews are and will remain the property of the U.S. Naval Institute.

Signed and sealed this 5th day of September 1995.

Mary Louise Miller, for the estate of
Rear Admiral Harold B. Miller, USN (Ret.)

Interview Number 1 with Rear Admiral Harold B. Miller, U.S. Navy (Retired)

Place: Admiral Miller's home, Manhasset, New York

Date: Monday, 6 April 1981

Interviewer: Dr. John T. Mason, Jr.

Q: Admiral, I'm delighted to have discovered you through our mutual friend Hanson Baldwin.[*] Now I hope that we will have a series dealing with your very eventful naval career and post-naval career, you being a man of many parts. Would you begin, sir, in the proper way of a biography--by telling me the date of your birth and the place and then something about your family's background and your early education.

Admiral Miller: I'm an Iowa farmer, basically. I was born on a farm in Newton, Iowa, on January 4, 1903. I grew up around that area for a while. Those were the days when the Iowa farmers were going back and forth between California and Iowa. When I was a child in arms, we did the California route back and forth several times.

Q: What was the reason for that?

Admiral Miller: California was welcoming and inviting people, and that accounts for always having an Iowa fair out there, which was heavily attended by these Iowa folks who knew each other. It was a great migratory movement out there in those days.

---

[*] Hanson W. Baldwin was a Naval Academy classmate of Miller. Following several years of naval service, Baldwin began a distinguished career as a newspaperman. His oral history is in the Naval Institute collection.

Q: Does this indicate that the farmers in Iowa were pretty affluent?

Admiral Miller: I doubt that they felt that they were. They may have been running away from the farm even that early, but I guess there's a part of that. They had the means to do it, and quite often they were captivated by the California climate and just stayed out there. We sort of went back and forth, I suppose. It depends on what my group is. I was appointed to the Naval Academy from California, or I could be an Iowa farmer--whichever fits best.

Q: I see.

Admiral Miller: My brother stayed on the farm with my grandparents. I went with my mother back to California until I was about 12 or 13. I should point out that I remember clearly my mother taking me down to San Pedro when the big fleet was in. That was the round-the-world cruise.

Q: That was the one that Roosevelt sponsored.*

Admiral Miller: Right, in 1908.† I was only five years old, but I distinctly remember seeing the ships out there. Later on, she took me down a time or two and we went aboard--I'll never forget--the old USS Yorktown, a gunboat.‡ I began to get somewhat interested in seagoing things, but with no idea of any followup on the thing.

---

* Theodore Roosevelt was President of the United States during the around-the-world cruise of the Great White Fleet from 1907 to 1909.
† The fleet visited San Pedro from 18 to 25 April 1908.
‡ A veteran of the Spanish-American War, the Yorktown was commissioned in 1889 and remained in service until 1919.

When I was back on the farm in Iowa, I was going to a one-room country school. We had a wonderful teacher. One day I was going through the encyclopedia, and I came across Annapolis. For the first time, I realized it wasn't Indianapolis at all; it was Annapolis. My interest was very much aroused, and I decided then and there that I just had to have an education of some sort if I were going to try to go to Annapolis. I had a good crop of pigs that year; my granddad would give me the runts, and I had about $400.00 in the bank.

Q: You were a wealthy boy.

Admiral Miller: I was well off, indeed. I wrote my mother that I was coming out, so I climbed on the train and went to California. That was 1917.

Q: Your father, I take it, had died?

Admiral Miller: No, my folks had been divorced. I never saw much of my father at any time.

Q: I see.

Admiral Miller: She happened to know this old professor, George Gardiner, who had a small school, Westlake School for Boys. It had about 20, or perhaps 25, students of all ages.

Q: This was in California?

Admiral Miller: In Los Angeles, at Westlake Park. He happened to be an aspiring young man in Georgia for the Naval Academy but was never able to make it. So he had a deep interest in me, who was also trying to make it. He pumped me full. I didn't have time to go to high school on this, but he certainly compensated for it. I had all the Greek and Roman roots, I had English, I had history, I had math from algebra right on through solid trig and everything else. I didn't know anybody or how to get an appointment.

Q: How long a time were you under his tutelage?

Admiral Miller: About 18 months. It really was solid work, I must say. Then, of course, I had to get an appointment, and I wrote to the two senators. One was Hiram Johnson, I remember, and I don't even remember who the other was.[*] There was no particular response, of course. Then we had a congressman, Henry Z. Osborn.[†]

Q: This was before Joe Crail, then?[‡]

Admiral Miller: Yes. I remember that name Crail. The great day came for the examination. To get the appointment, you had to take an examination that was almost the same as the entrance exam in those days. I remember they had an even 100 applicants there. I stood number one in this thing. That was my appointment.

Q: I would think so. Your tutor was pretty good, wasn't he?

---

[*] Hiram W. Johnson, a Republican, served in the U.S. Senate from 1917 until his death in 1945.
[†] Henry Z. Osborne, a Republican, represented California's tenth congressional district (Los Angeles County), 1917-23.
[‡] Joe Crail, a Republican, represented California's tenth congressional district, 1927-33.

Admiral Miller: He was great.

Q: Did he use examinations?

Admiral Miller: I had sent for all of those; I had all the books of exams. Oddly enough, my papers somehow or other must have been returned to me, because they ended up on the farm in Iowa. A cousin of mine sent them to me a couple of years ago, and I went through these things. He commented, "I don't know how you ever got through those." I got 100 on this and 100 on that, and it just worked out beautifully. Of course, that permitted you then to take the examination for the Naval Academy. That worked out quite well.

The first contact I had officially with the Navy was a set of orders to report to the submarine base at San Pedro. They had one there in those days. I went for a fitness exam, and I think that is the first set of orders I have in my files.

Q: This was being given at the behest of the academy?

Admiral Miller: Right, right. I had some concern about the physical exam, oddly enough, because when I was a kid there on the farm, we were sledding down a hill, and I had a little fellow on top of me. I didn't make the turn at the bottom of the hill, and we hit a stump. My thighs were hanging over the rear of the sled, and this tore my left leg right down to the kneecap, just tore it open. I've got a scar twice as big as the palm of your hand. The question was whether the scar had adhered to the muscle and was immobile or whether it became skin again and was perfectly flexible. That's the way it turned out. A good old country doctor had taken care of me very properly. So I had no physical problems at all.

Q: Was your mother delighted at this turn of events?

Admiral Miller: Oh, she supported me all the way through. She, I'm sure, never had much in the way of school, of course, or anything like that, but she certainly recognized the importance of it. It was sort of a separation, after all. You shove off for the rest of your life.

Q: That was the beginning of your career and you left her.

Admiral Miller: I'll never forget the night before I shoved off. She came in the room, and I was ostensibly asleep. I was just lying there thinking, I suppose. She came in silently and cried and cried. It made me realize then that this was just about the end of the family. So I just climbed on the train, and away I went.

Q: You went back east by yourself?

Admiral Miller: Yes. I had never been east of the Mississippi River.

Q: That was quite an adventure in itself, wasn't it?

Admiral Miller: Oh, yes. Let me see, I had just turned 17. A fellow named Crutchfield and I bumped into each other, and to kids of that age geography is very important.[*] He was from San Bernardino, California, and I was from Los Angeles, so obviously we had a close

---

[*] Crutchfield Adair, who graduated in the class of 1924 and eventually retired as a captain in 1954.

rapport immediately. We spent the night just outside the gate; that was a rooming house in those days. Of course, the next day we all went in. You will recall that at that time you had a great choice of the curriculum; French or Spanish was the choice.

Q: Yes, two languages.

Admiral Miller: Everything else was identical, which, of course, meant that you really had to march to your class. It's changed considerably since then. But Crutch and I agreed that we were going to room together, and we were both taking Spanish. We did so for four years. He died only four weeks ago, pour soul.* It was a great friendship that we developed. So there I became a midshipman. Those were the days when you didn't get out of the yard at all for the first few months.

Q: Christmas holiday.

Admiral Miller: Four big days and Christmas holiday.

Q: How did you take to the regimen?

Admiral Miller: Oh, I didn't mind it in the slightest. I just loved every bit of it. I had to study. I mean, I had had good tutoring, but basically I didn't have four years of high school by a long shot, and I had to work all the way along the line. Crutch and I were the same type. For instance, the Christmas holiday, he had a cousin who was a civil servant up in Washington, and he very kindly invited us. If we would come up, he would show us

---

* Captain Adair died 10 March 1981.

around. Well, you know what you do in Washington. You go to all the museums, and we climbed up the Washington Monument and down again. Well, the whole world was beginning to open up; it was absolutely glorious.

Q: Exciting.

Admiral Miller: Oh, exciting, I tell you. And then you began to look forward to a European cruise, and your horizon began to spread out more and more and more. Oh, that Naval Academy was absolutely the greatest.

Q: How did you take to plebe summer?

Admiral Miller: Oh, plebe summer. I was a naive little guy, and I think we had a rather large class for the time, around 1,000 or 900 and something.[*] Of course, you always had a few sophisticates, and you had a few of your college lads in there. I remember old Crutch and I were just two naive little guys hiding around behind bushes and things like that. But finally we began to find out that well, hell, they're all just about the same, after all. It worked out. Plebe summer was no problem at all.

You mentioned Dan Gallery earlier.[†] Some of those midshipmen, the class of '21, were training for the Olympics in Antwerp at that period, so they had a lot of athletes and their crews there. We walked down the middle of the passageway, and we didn't look to

---

[*] The class of 1924 started with 757 midshipmen.
[†] Midshipman Daniel V. Gallery, Jr., USN, graduated in 1920 as a member of the class of 1921, He was a wrestler in the 1920 Olympics and went on to achieve the rank of rear admiral during his active career. His oral history is in the Naval Institute collection.

the right or to the left and did just what we were told to do. It was no fun hazing somebody who didn't react to it, so it didn't present any real problems to us at all.

I'll never forget, though, the first night. We had gone down to dry our uniforms. My God, I had never heard of anybody drying out 12 pair of skivvies or 12 undershirts or anything in numbers like that. So there again, it was a whole new world opening up. And each man had a shower in his own room; my God, I found I was taking three showers a day. It was a glorious experience; everything had opened up. When taps sounded that first night, it was the saddest, most drawn out wail I ever heard in my life. It really made you think you were someplace else. But it made great impressions all the way through.

Of course, the cruise itself went to Oslo.

Q: This was your first cruise?*

Admiral Miller: This was the youngster cruise. We had six battleships: the Florida, the North Dakota, the Delaware, and so on. You drew $10.00 spending money for a ten-day stop, and you got along very well with that, because all you did was walk around the museums and things of that sort. Well, $10.00 bought the ice cream you needed once in a while.

Q: You didn't have much to draw on, anyway, did you?

Admiral Miller: I don't remember. As plebes, we drew a dollar a month, plus a one-dollar candy ticket. I had forgotten about that. You spent that candy ticket about 20 times, and

---

* This cruise was in the summer of 1921.

you were out of candy for the rest of the month. First classmen were getting $4.00 a month; they were quite well off.

Q: So this is what you had to draw on when you were on a cruise?

Admiral Miller: Oh, yes. They'd issue $10.00 specifically for each port. For instance, you'd get to Lisbon, and everybody was told kid gloves were what you buy in Lisbon. Everybody was buying kid gloves. Well, that took your money pretty fast.

Q: Did you buy some for your mother?

Admiral Miller: Oh, sure, sure. I bought the usual kid gloves and all the tidbits and things like that. I remember we got into Glasgow--or Greenock, really, is what the port was. Several of our well-heeled classmates took four or five days off and went to London. Poor old Crutch and I--the impoverished Crutch and I--when we got to Glasgow (and I think we may have even gotten to Edinburgh), we just thought of the great possibilities and what you could do if you had a little cash on hand. But that was no problem at all. Everything was a great democracy; there were no jealousies or anything.

Q: Wasn't there a certain amount of entertaining, too, of midshipmen by the native people?

Admiral Miller: Oh, to some extent, but basically we walked. We spent our time just walking. I think we stood a watch in four; every fourth day you stayed aboard ship. Of course, the minute you arrived in a port, a collier came alongside, and you started coaling ship.

Q: That was one of your luxuries, wasn't it?

Admiral Miller: Oh, yes.

Q: How did you take to that?

Admiral Miller: That was fun. Like everything else, it was real fun. I always say that I crossed the Atlantic four times on ships and every time in a fireroom; that's the way it was. I never crossed as a passenger on deck or anything of that sort. But the cruise was great: Gibraltar; Cadiz, Spain; Lisbon; Scotland. It just opened up, again, a whole world.

Q: How much preparation did you have for these various ports? Did they do anything on board ship to prepare you?

Admiral Miller: Not really. Today, of course, they mimeograph the whole poop sheet, and everybody would know what was going on. But there really wasn't anything of that sort. I don't know whether perhaps we didn't know what was going on. But the standard things were always there, parks and things like that. And I did quite a lot of reading.

In Oslo, the Vikings would be the subject they would be researching at the moment, and there were old Viking ships there. Frequently you made friends, and somebody would invite you out to his house. But the beauty of it was that it was something foreign. I mean, to this old Iowa farm boy, I tell you, that was just like a new world you were living in. Of course, on our way back we had been practicing. Down in Guantánamo we had a target practice down there. Then, finally, as you recall, on those cruises they'd take half of the enlisted crew off and fill that up with half midshipmen.

Q: And you were the equivalent of an enlisted man.

Admiral Miller: That's right, and we were using hammocks, of course, in those days. We had to learn how to use a hammock. It's sort of pathetic the first nights out. They wouldn't stretch a hammock enough, so that they were just hanging out in an absolute catenary, their fannies just about on the deck and their feet and head up as high as they could go. You learned to stretch the hammock; otherwise you couldn't get in the damn hammock, it would be so narrow. Of course, it was always a good deal for the jimmy legs, the master-at-arms, getting you out in the morning. He'd come along with a night stick and crack you on the fanny to get you out of there in a hurry.

Q: You had some of the faculty on board, too, didn't you?

Admiral Miller: Yes, the officers were picking up a little sea duty on that.

Q: Did you have any kind of classes?

Admiral Miller: Classes were not really official. Usually, the first class were the faculty that worked. The faculty proper basically were shipboard officers at that point; they could take a job on board ship or something like that. But the first class would sort of hold class. You kept a notebook, though, of the engine room and the firerooms and the navigation, and everybody had to do star sights. In general, you were getting a pretty good summer's worth of work. Of course, you were always scrubbing down decks and shining brass work in between all of these.

Q: And coaling in port.

Admiral Miller: You had a bucket, and it wasn't a very large bucket either. But that bucket of fresh water in the morning was your fresh water for the day. You'd shave and scrub your teeth and your clothes, and that's all you had of fresh water. I remember, on one of the ships I was on, we suspected there were rats in the scuttlebutts.[*] I mean, it just became horrible and impossible for drinking water. You went through all those cycles, learned to bathe with salt water and scrub your clothes with soap. Salt water and soap will just take your skin off.

As you got closer to the tropics, and as you became more senior--a second classman or first classman--you'd sort of sneak out of your billet and go up under a turret or something out there in the fresh air. You could have some idea of sleeping out there, but, of course, you had to run fast when the scrubdown started about 6:00 o'clock in the morning.

But it was great. I remember down off Cuba there one time, flying fish came aboard during the night. You'd wake up, and there would be a couple of flying fish in front of you. You'd see the phosphorescence of the water and you'd dream, and you'd go up and study stars. I guess it was just about like the astronauts today. That's what the world was to me at that particular point.

Somewhere along the line, as you were getting close to September leave, agents came aboard, and you'd buy your ticket to your 30 days' leave to California or wherever you

---

[*] Scuttlebutts were drinking fountains.

were going. In that first September leave I went out to California and visited my mother. When you were packing your bags, you were told to be careful about your shoes. The bluejackets knew you were going to shove off the following day, and the first thing you know, everything you've got is going to disappear, particularly shoes. You'd sleep with the shoes at your pillow. You didn't want to lose them. Then, of course, over the side to the motor launches and to the academy there and get your railroad ticket and repack and get out of there.

Q: The battleships came right up?

Admiral Miller: Right out to the roads there outside, which would be out quite a ways, but still they were all visible from the academy. That's about the way those cruises went.

The second cruise was up and down the Atlantic. I remember Halifax was the northernmost port, and southbound we went to Panama. I'll never forget that, because I was becoming interested in flying at that point. I don't know how we got out to Coco Solo air station there, but somehow old Crutch and I got there and begged a ride in an old H-boat; it was the first time I'd ever flown. I'd often go back. Later on, I had a PBY squadron down there, and I often thought, "Oh, boy, that first flight was an exciting time."* It was a great flight.

Q: Did your roommate also?

Admiral Miller: He went to aviation too.

---

* PBY was the designation of the Catalina flying boat introduced to the fleet in the 1930s.

Q: So it was a joint effort again.

Admiral Miller: We always worked together. We never had a cross word or anything else. The academy also gave you a great chance for physical fitness. I used to do a lot of boxing, even when I was a kid. I remember on first class cruise I came away with a letter from Admiral Scales.* He was our fleet commander. It was a 175-pound championship--all very interesting.

Q: Was Weems around?

Admiral Miller: Oh, yes. Daddy Weems was all over the place.† Not as much as later on, of course.

Q: Then he was an athlete, wasn't he? Wasn't he in boxing and wrestling?

Admiral Miller: He was in all of that. I went in for lacrosse, and I played Navy lacrosse there for three years.

Q: That was totally unknown in California, wasn't it?

Admiral Miller: At that time, until we went out in the fleet, what we found out of Santa Monica was a lot of Canadians who played lacrosse, and we made up a fleet team. We played every weekend out there in Santa Monica. Of course, today it's spread all over the

---

* Rear Admiral Archibald H. Scales, USN, Commander Battleship Division Five, Scouting Fleet.
† Lieutenant Commander Philip V. H. Weems, USN, was a noted expert on navigation.

country. Just ahead of our time it was a wild game. The class of '16--particularly Cal Durgin was the one I have in mind--they were just real mean midshipmen.[*] They'd take on the Carlisle Indians or anybody and lick them.[†] It's a tough game. Oh, gosh.

Q: It was an Indian game, wasn't it?

Admiral Miller: Yes, originally it was, indeed. Crutch went out for track.

You know, you spoke about hazing earlier. They couldn't haze Crutch. He just somehow would crawl into a humorous shell and was absolutely impervious to hazing.

Q: You mean he didn't react to it?

Admiral Miller: He didn't react. He'd give them answers and so on; they couldn't get him excited; they couldn't do anything. They absolutely couldn't handle him. So they sort of gave up on both of us. Of course, it never bothered me in the slightest. We were the class, you know, about halfway through when some midshipmen went to Congress on this thing. In must have been the last half of 1920 in which segregation was set up.[‡] You remember?

Q: Your class was segregated.

---

[*] Midshipman Calvin T. Durgin, USN. Durgin later became an aviator and was a noted flag officer during World War II.

[†] Carlisle Indian School in Carlisle, Pennsylvania, was operated by the U.S. Government to educate American Indians. The school's most noted athlete was James Thorpe, who gained fame in the 1912 Olympic Games and later played professional baseball and football.

[‡] A midshipman wrote in a letter home that he had been paddled, and that led to a congressional investigation of hazing. In October 1920, the superintendent of the academy, Rear Admiral Scales, asked the first classmen to sign a pledge that they would not do any hazing that year. When they refused, Scales set up barriers to segregate the plebes in the dormitory, Bancroft Hall, and in the mess.

Admiral Miller: Yes, you run into that. They sort of moved us in one spot and were going to protect us, by golly, or else.

Q: Wasn't that due to the fact that one member of the class was injured?

Admiral Miller: There was some such thing. I don't really recall as much about it as I should, I suppose. But we felt very abashed and a little bit ashamed of it.

Of course, the thing was sports. One thing the plebes had to do was go to all the games, no matter whether it was football or baseball or swimming or any sports.

Q: You mean this was obligatory?

Admiral Miller: The stands had to be filled by plebes, if by nobody else. The plebes were always there.

Q: And if you didn't go, what happened?

Admiral Miller: Well, you would be told about it. I don't know that anybody really didn't go. Just about all went. I went because I had never seen a football game until I went there. This was part of this whole new world that opened up. Swimming meets--had I ever seen a swimming meet? Of course not.

Q: There was a swimming hole in Iowa, wasn't there?

Admiral Miller: Oh, no. All of these were things that you wanted to see and wanted to do.

Then, of course, the plebes couldn't go to the hops; the plebes couldn't drag.* So they had afternoon tea dances, and they had the balls at night. They had quite a nice social life there, the girls coming up from Baltimore and Washington. A lot of them, of course, married in the Navy and were a part of the Navy. They danced at Dahlgren Hall, which was the armory, with wooden decks. Before a dance they'd go in with sanders trying to take some of the slivers out of the floor. They still have the old rifles on the walls along the armory there.

Q: It must have been a cold place in the wintertime, though.

Admiral Miller: Yes, I guess it was.

Q: I find it one of the draftiest places even today.

Admiral Miller: It was interesting. It would be decorated, and you would have these signal flags around, and they'd have hop cards. You'd go around and swap with midshipmen, swap dances with your drag under X-ray, or whatever flag it might be. Then the game was to decorate your hop card with colored flags and all that. It was really a delight. It was good fun all the way through.

Then, of course, you came to the point where there was the second class cruise, which was a coastal cruise, and the first class cruise became another European cruise, almost the same.

---

* In the Naval Academy vernacular of the day, to drag meant to have a date with a girl.

Q: So you had three cruises, actually. You didn't have what they now have--aviation.

Admiral Miller: No, that didn't come into the picture at all. Well, aviation hadn't really gotten into the Navy. This was way back in 1923, 1924, and so on. There was very little aviation at all. That cruise was great, and, of course, at that point you became a great big first classman. It never gave me any particular thrill to try to haze anybody or anything else like that. I was just busy, and I thought it was sort of childish too. So that never became a factor. Then your year there began to be turned towards the fleet. The first thing you knew, you were going to be out of the Naval Academy. Then the big question was: What did you put in for? What kind of a ship should you go to, what station, and so on? It was a real quandary as to how to do that.

I'll never forget Dale Quarton of the class of '22 had spooned on me. That expression "spoon" means to come through and shake hands. It's somebody you can rely on and ask to help you and things like that. Dale had been a spoon of mine. He came through and had been out in the fleet, I guess, two years then. I said, "Dale, how do you select a ship? What's the secret to all this sort of thing?"

He said, "Well, I'll tell you. Get on the biggest ship with the most gold on it and get that fear of gold out of your mind early in life so you'll never have to worry about it again." Well, I thought that was pretty damn good advice. There was only one ship that could possibly be. It would have to be the fleet flagship in the Pacific, and that was the USS California.*

---

* USS California (BB-44) was commissioned 10 August 1921. She had a standard displacement of 32,300 tons, was 624 feet long, and 97 feet in the beam. She had a top speed of 21 knots and a main battery of 12 14-inch guns. She was the flagship for Commander in Chief Battle Fleet. The Battle Fleet was a component of the United States Fleet.

Q: The California, yes.

Admiral Miller: So we organized. Red Ballinger went with me, and Crutch went on another road.* I think it just happened that 24 out of '24 went to the California as JOs.† It turned out to be the best advice we ever had, because Nimitz was a commander on there, walking up and down the quarterdeck and all these names and gold.‡ The first thing you know, gold's gold.

Q: It's just pretty ordinary.

Admiral Miller: It was absolutely the most superb advice. But even more so, we had two little UOs, little biplanes, cute little things, beautiful.§

Q: With catapults?

---

* Ensign Herbert R. Ballinger, USN, reported to the USS California with Miller. Ensign Crutchfield Adair, USN, became part of the crew of the USS Arizona (BB-39).
† JOs--junior officers.
‡ From 1923 to 1925, Commander Chester W. Nimitz, USN, served on the staff of Commander Battle Fleet, embarked in the California. During World War II, as a four-star admiral, Nimitz was Commander in Chief Pacific Fleet.
§ The Vought UO-1, a biplane with a single pontoon, received that designation in 1921 as an improved version of the VE-7/9. The UO-1 was 24 feet long, wing span of 34 feet, gross weight of 2,305 pounds, and top speed of 124 miles per hour. A version with wheels was designated FU-1.

Admiral Miller: The catapult job. One was Jim Barner.[*] He wasn't the PR type. He was a wonderful person, but he didn't indoctrinate you enough. The younger of the two, Dixie Kiefer of the class of '19, was just selling aviation right and left, right and left.[†] He put us in the rear seat of that thing and catapulted us, and, boy, he'd take us up and kick us around. He had everybody going crazy with, "Aviation is the only possible thing to do in the Navy."

Dutch Greber was on the Oklahoma, with the same type of airplane, and these two monkeys would dogfight all around the fleet there, all at anchor at San Pedro.[‡] They would fly about the height of the masts, chasing each other around like a couple of dogs. Why they weren't killed, God knows.

Later on it showed up as a real tragedy, because this kind of play went on and on and on. Well, the fleet was in the Panama Canal Zone later on, and how they happened to know that each other was there, I don't know. But Dutch was in his UO, the seaplane with wing-tip pontoons, and Dixie was standing on the dock. I suppose he waved at Dutch, but each knew who each other was, and Dutch dove on him. Old Dix, the way he was made up, by God, they weren't going to chase him off of that dock, and I suppose Dixie gave him the old signal. Dutch came back again, and the wing-tip pontoon did hit Dixie this time and broke his shoulder. It really disabled him for the rest of his career, but the point was that it destroyed the friendship of the two. Here they were like a couple of kids all their lives, and then this happened. But at any rate, that was sometime afterwards.

Dixie was ordered to Pensacola as an instructor, and this would have been the fall of 1925. We made the cruise to Australia in 1925, and he had aroused so much interest that almost the whole JO mess of our class were going to Pensacola. So we arranged, whenever

---

[*] Lieutenant James D. Barner, USN.
[†] Lieutenant Dixie Kiefer, USN. As a captain, Kiefer served as commanding officer of the aircraft carrier Ticonderoga (CV-14) during World War II. He died in a plane crash in November 1945, before he had a chance to make rear admiral.
[‡] Lieutenant (junior grade) Charles F. Greber, USN.

the fleet would anchor, to go to the ship that had an aviation medical officer aboard to get a physical exam. I think mine was at Pearl or Auckland or someplace. It ended up that 20 JOs out of this mess all put in for Pensacola, and all got it.

Q: They all passed?

Admiral Miller: They got it. We had a whole Pensacola crowd down there, thanks to Dixie Kiefer. It was the most amazing bit of proselytizing I have ever seen.

Q: Tell me about the JO mess. You were all bachelors, and it was home for you, wasn't it?

Admiral Miller: Oh, it was home. I lived aboard ship. My mother was in Los Angeles, and on the weekends I'd go up to see her. But we would need people to take watches, and a few were getting married. I wouldn't mind taking a watch; I was going to be aboard anyway, so why not? Besides, you didn't have any money. You'd draw $125.00 a month, and one or two liberties would take care of that. But there was no point in going ashore. If you were a reasonably presentable young man and, say, a lieutenant's wife had a little baby sister coming in from Omaha or someplace and was in need of an escort, you'd be invited out to their place to dinner or a dance.

Of course, also we were well indoctrinated in the dropping of calling cards. Our JO job was to go and call on all the senior officers. So we got acquainted with them to that extent. Remember, those were the days of Prohibition too. You had those sort of problems. But it was a nice life. I always felt sort of sorry for the married people who at 5:00 o'clock every afternoon were out at the gangway ready to go ashore and back again at 8:00 o'clock in the morning. I had my own home aboard, and it was great.

I played the piano in those days, and we had a piano. We had fun all the way through. Our JO mess had the class of '23 and class of '24 on. One was old Zeke Soucek and Ding-Dong Bell out of '23.*

Q: Was he Zeus? Which one was he? There were several of them.

Admiral Miller: Yes, this was Zeus. Apollo was the aviator; he was class of '21, as I recall. Then there was a third one, too, I never knew.

But we were always having fun. For example, you go to the Navy yard and hook up the phone. The way I got the name Min is one of the silly stories. I asked my mother why she named me Harold, and she said, "Well, that's easy. You couldn't give it a nickname." So I was Harold all the way through the Naval Academy. But on the JO mess there, we were hooked up to the Navy yard at Brooklyn by phone and the phone rang during lunch, perhaps, and one of the games was that any time anybody got a phone call, everybody stopped eating and dead silence went around while this poor devil had to talk on the phone.

Q: They ganged up.

Admiral Miller: So that was me in this case. This girl asked, "I bet you don't know who this is."

Those were the days of "Min" in the Andy Gump cartoon strip, so I said, "Oh, Min, oh, Min, oh, Min." And from that instant on, I was Min, which, incidentally, I wouldn't trade for anything. Nobody knows my initials or my name or anything else. But they know Min Miller. So it's a silly story, but that's the way things take place.

---

* Ensign Zeus Soucek, USN; Ensign Robert C. Bell, Jr., USN.

That JO mess was a fun deal all the way through. We ate quite well and had our own mess, of course. Once in a while the wardroom would invite you up maybe to the higher strata.

Q: To be with the captain.

Admiral Miller: We had marvelous captains, I must say, but I don't think I was ever invited up to a dinner with them. I don't think anybody else was. Those were the days when he was an isolated individual. He ate alone in all of his glory. It must have been hell, really.

I had wonderful skippers. Captain Cluverius was one; he was on the Maine when she went down.[*] He had been commandant of midshipmen the first two years I was at the Naval Academy. He was the sweetest, gentlest gentleman that I have ever seen. From the time I got back from Pensacola, and I was wearing wings at that point, he did a lot of talking. He would go to clubs and things like that in Los Angeles and was a well-known name. He'd always invite me to go along with him as his escort, so to speak. I always had skippers of that type who would usually take me along and introduce me around and so on. Tommy Symington from Baltimore, the Symington family, he was great too.[†] The relationship between skippers and JOs was pretty darn good all the way along the line. At any rate, we went to Pensacola and that was January of 1926.

Q: Having been two years at sea?

---

[*] Captain Wat T. Cluverius, Jr., USN, commanded the USS West Virginia (BB-48) from 5 June 1926 to 15 June 1928. The second-class battleship Maine exploded and sank in Havana, Cuba, in February 1898, sparking the Spanish-American War.
[†] Captain Thomas A. Symington, USN, commanded the USS Northampton (CA-26) in the mid-1930s when Miller was in the scouting squadron.

Admiral Miller: I guess that had been about 18 months. You had to have that. We were just sort of getting the feeling that aviation maybe was going to go someplace. In 1926, the Vinson Bill, I believe it was, came up with quite a lot of money for naval aviation.

By the time we graduated, which would have been fall of 1926, when I went out to the fleet, we had a total of only about 600 aviators. Within a year's time, you knew every damn one of them. You knew them by name, you knew where they were stationed, and knew all about them. It was a small place. They had a lot of World War I people there who had become pilots with no Navy background at all. After the war they had decided to stay in the Navy. They weren't mustangs at all.[*] They were civilians who came in and were flying in France, perhaps, or someplace. After the war they were a little shy on shipboard duty. Oh, they'd catapult and they'd do that sort of thing, but there was a feeling among the non-aviators: "Jesus, don't let that guy take the watch or take the bridge. He doesn't know what he's doing. Anyway, aviators are all crazy." There was a tremendous separation at that particular point.

I remember we had on the West Virginia Herb Rodd.[†] He had been on the NC-4.[‡] He was a very pleasant guy. Another one, Paul Carter, who had been in the command at Pensacola, had no more sense of PR than anything in the world.[§] He was just another body aboard that ship, was all he was. It did arouse a complete separation along that line. About the time my class started coming through here in 1926, these are Naval Academy boys. They had had their shipboard training, they could take a watch and fit right into the watch

---

[*] "Mustang" is Navy slang for a former enlisted man who has risen through the ranks to become an officer.
[†] Lieutenant Herbert C. Rodd, USN.
[‡] In 1919 the Navy flying boat NC-4 became the first airplane to fly across the Atlantic Ocean.
[§] Lieutenant Paul W. Carter, USN. This tour of duty in the West Virginia was later, after Miller became an aviator.

list, which was one of the ways of getting aviation accepted. You come aboard ship and you don't just go to sleep until you catapult. You take a watch and all.

Q: It was also working the other way. It was causing resentment on the part of the regular line officers that the aviators didn't do their jobs.

Admiral Miller: That's right. Actually, that World War I crowd didn't know any better. They had had no background on it. They were afraid of it and so they flew. There wasn't much flying, either, in those days. So the atmosphere began to change as we came along. I mean, hell, we could stand watch just as well as they could stand watch and things like that. We learned also that they resented flight pay too. We were getting 50% of base pay. It was a "What the hell? What's he doing that I'm not doing?" type of thing. Well, the answer to that was easy. You'd just simply finally persuade one of them to get in the back seat and catapult him and take him up and give him the works. That's the last time he had any concern about flight pay. So we had a counter to all these little isms if you had enough sense to use a counter, you know.

Q: Tell me about Pensacola.

Admiral Miller: Oh, that was great. We had the old N-9s, which was really an old Curtiss Jenny, JN-4, on floats.* They actually had extra wing span to give them more lift because of the pontoon. I think some of them had an old OX, 90 horsepower, but we also had 180 Hispano-Suizas then. It was a darn good little old airplane. Ten hours was the optimum to

---

* Jenny was the nickname drawn from the Navy designation JN for a Curtiss-built plane. The N-9H model had wingspan of 53 feet, length of 31 feet, gross weight of 2,765 pounds, and maximum speed of 80 miles per hour.

learn to fly in. This was winter, January and February. First we had a six-week ground school.

Q: This is 1926?

Admiral Miller: January and February of 1926. We had ground school to try to teach us theories of flight and things of that sort. You always had running concurrently an engine ground school and aerial navigation. We were using carrier pigeons then.

Q: For communication purposes?

Admiral Miller: You would watch with great interest what instructors you were going to draw. Some had reputations of being very able and very nice guys to work with and then you'd have the SOBs. They'd all be classified as snarling at you and, "For Christ sake, get that right wing up." But we had a pretty good crowd down there.

The chief flight instructor was Buddy Wieber, who died a few months ago.[*] Buddy was in '18. Oh, what a wonderful gentleman. He's the kind that would take a frightened student who was shaking, and he'd calm him down. The first thing you know, he would have him flying nicely and smoothly. He just had that wonderful talent. So ten hours was the optimum. Of course, the class was very competitive. I think I had about eight and a half hours, somewhere along in there. Bill Billings was a damn good pilot.[†] He turned me over to Buddy, who checked me out and we came into the beach.

What a thrill these things are, you know. We taxied up the beach, and he climbed out and looked at me. I looked at him sort of querulously, like "Now what?"

---

[*] Lieutenant Carlos W. Wieber, USN. Wieber, who retired as a rear admiral, died 29 September 1980.
[†] Lieutenant (junior grade) Arthur S. Billings, USN.

He said, "Go on, take it out." So I was the first to solo. That was a real thrill, I'll tell you.

Q: You had confidence?

Admiral Miller: Oh, I had no problems. No, that was no concern whatsoever. It was like driving a car. So that got us started in the air. Then from there we went over to land planes.

Up to this time, the Navy had always been on floats. Then suddenly, along about the middle of the 1920s, it began to shift over to wheels to the extent that on the old Texas they actually built a platform on the gun turret.* The guns extended out, and they had a little Nieuport and would fly it off of this platform, mostly proving that it could be done more than anything else. But you could call it a carrier if you choose.

So we were going to wheels. We had Corry Field, and we had Jennies at that point. Then finally, as time went on, we'd sort of get through that and then get into some fighters. We had some wonderful little VE-7s, Vought fighters built here in Long Island City, oddly enough, with 180-horsepower Hispano engines.† Oh, they were just beautiful things. Then they took us back and gave us the F-5L, a twin-engine plane that originally came from Curtiss.‡

---

* On 9 March 1919 Lieutenant Commander E. O. McDonnell, USN, made the first flight from a turret-top platform on board the battleship Texas (BB-35). The light planes, which had wheels, were used for spotting of gunnery practice.
† The VE-7, built by the Lewis and Vought Corporation, was one of the Navy's earliest carrier-based fighter planes. It had a wing span of 34 feet, length of 25 feet, gross weight of 2,100 pounds, and maximum speed of 117 miles per hour at sea level. It had a two-seat trainer version.
‡ The Curtiss F-5L was a flying boat that was first built in 1918; it was redesignated in 1921 as the PN-5. The aircraft had a wing span of 104 feet, length of 49 feet, gross weight of 13,600 pounds, and top speed of 90 mph.

You may remember that Rod Wanamaker, way back, commissioned Curtiss to build an airplane to cross the Atlantic.* This was about 1914, before the World War. Out of that, the British did buy the plane, finally. Of course, they didn't even try the flight. They took it to Felixstowe over in England and out of that was evolved a larger boat called the Felixstowe-3, mostly.† Then finally the Felixstowe with a Liberty engine became the F-5L, really the predecessor to our big boats today. So we had the big boats. That's where the pigeons came in.

They finally worked their way all the way around, and the happy day came when they gave you a certificate that said your naval aviator number. I think I was 3,322.

Q: Did you have any problems en route to the wings?

Admiral Miller: I busted one check, yes, along about 20 hours. I never did really know why. I went out and did it after that and had no trouble with my instructor at all. Later I went back to instruct, and I found out a hell of a lot about what an instructor could do, really. I was a sympathetic instructor. It was alleged that when we went through in 1926, the whole objective of the course was to bust up 50%. Not more than 50% could go through.

Q: Was this financial?

Admiral Miller: I think the idea was to prove that flying was a very tough business, and it was hard to learn to fly.

---

* Rodman Wanamaker was a department-store magnate who sponsored a Curtiss plane called <u>America</u>, intended for a hands-across-the-sea gesture to commemorate the 100th anniversary of the Peace of Ghent in 1815. World War I postponed the first transatlantic flight to 1919.
† Felixstowe was the site of a royal naval air station.

Q: It wasn't a shortage of funds?

Admiral Miller: I think not. It was just the principle to bust up 50% of the men. They probably got a good solid core there, you see. I busted that one check; the only thing I ever had trouble with. This isn't quite true. When we were over in Jennies, Paul Carter was my instructor. We spun in from about 20 feet in the damn thing; we got the nose too high and the question was who had control of it. Of course, it went down. But you had a lot of crackups in those days. Nobody paid any attention to it, except to get it off the field.

Q: Did you lose any members of your class in accidents?

Admiral Miller: Yes, we did. We lost two—Flood and Harrison, I think—as students. The rest of the boys all went out to the fleet, and we didn't seem to have any trouble. During the war we lost heavily, of course.

Q: Yes, yes. Who were some of the famous fliers in your class?

Admiral Miller: Oh, gee. I guess you might say Bill Davis might be the best known.[*] He flew in that Dole race to Hawaii in 1927 with Art Goebel.[†] I expect Bill is probably the best known of the lot. Swede Ekstrom was one, Ev Burroughs was another, Pinky Hopkins,

---

[*] Ensign William V. Davis, USN, who soon after that became a member of the Three Seahawks, the Navy's first aerobatic flight demonstration team.

[†] In August 1927 Arthur Goebel flew from Oakland, California, to Hawaii with Lieutenant W. V. Davis as navigator. Their plane finished first among 16 entrants in a contest for $35,000 in prizes offered by James B. Dole for a nonstop flight to Hawaii. Only Goebel's plane and one other made the complete flight successfully.

Adair, Sid Harvey.* I don't think we had a Lindbergh or anything, but I guess Bill would be perhaps the best known.† So we all went to the fleet, and everybody wanted a carrier. We only had one carrier, the Langley.

Q: Not much of a carrier.

Admiral Miller: Not much of a carrier. I went to the West Virginia.‡

Q: That was one reason why only 50% were given wings.

Admiral Miller: We had there on the number three turret a Loening amphibian, OL-9.§ Well, an OL-6 to start with; it had the inverted Liberty engine. Then we had two of the UOs down below on the catapult. I sort of inherited the big amphibian—big by the standards in those days—to catapult off the top turret. We just interchanged back and forth. We really had good fun.

Q: They were observation planes?

---

* Ensign Clarence E. Ekstrom, USN; Ensign Sherman E. Burroughs, Jr., USN; Ensign Howard V. Hopkins, USN; Ensign Crutchfield Adair, USN; Ensign Warren W. Harvey, USN.
† Charles A. Lindbergh made the first solo flight across the Atlantic Ocean in May 1927.
‡ The USS West Virginia (BB-48) was commissioned 1 December 1923. She had a standard displacement of 33,590 tons, was 624 feet long, and 97 feet in the beam. Her top speed was 21.2 knots. She was armed with eight 16-inch guns and 12 5-inch broadside guns. She remained in active service until decommissioned on 9 January 1947, after World War II.
§ The OL-9, built by Keystone-Loening, was a biplane amphibian. It had a wing span of 45 feet, length of 35 feet, gross weight of 5,404 pounds, and top speed of 122 miles per hour.

Admiral Miller: Yes, these were observation squadrons. Once all the ships were steaming along in formation, they'd all catapult when the flags signalled down. The idea was to be the first to get all three planes in the air. Everything was in competition. Then we'd form up into whatever our formations were until it was time to go back. Then the ships would maneuver to give us a slick to land in astern. For instance, the winds are from here and they'd be steaming here and then they'd do a turn over here.

Q: Make a quiet spot.

Admiral Miller: We'd land there and taxi like hell up there to the ship.

Q: And then how were you lifted aboard?

Admiral Miller: Well, at first they'd just lower a hook from a crane, of course. Then you'd have to fiddle with the damn thing and then pull the part trying to marry the hook into the airplane ring. We finally found out there was a better way to do that. You'd tow a raft. The raft had a lot of lines on it, and it formed a little slick. We'd put a hook on the bottom of the pontoon on the bottom of the airplane. You'd taxi over this rug until you got the plane forward onto the ropes. Then you'd cut your engines, and your plane would drift back and the hook would be like a carrier, inverted, and you would grab one of these ropes. Now the raft is pulling you, so you can adjust your plane and put the hook down so a crane could hoist you aboard.

Q: Was there every any danger of crashing against the side of the ship?

Admiral Miller: Well, you didn't have any clearance, but rarely did they do it. You'd have trouble sometimes, and this could even be in port. Say you were anchored in a river with a fast current or something. You were trying to get your airplane under the hook of the crane and you had your engine cut. Then they didn't quite hook it, or you got it hooked, but it was late and your plane drifted down. So instead of trying to pull your plane straight up, you were trying to pull it up at an angle. Of course, the damn wing would hook into the water on the pontoon, and you would have an inverted plane on your hands. That would happen quite often. That was what happened to Lindbergh's plane there in China when this British carrier was trying to take him aboard. The stream was so swift, they let the plane drift down and just put the plane in the water.

Q: What did you do about spare parts for your plane and repairs and that sort of thing? Were they available on board ship or in the fleet?

Admiral Miller: We had a very minute part of something like that. You had to use a lot of ingenuity, of course. If we really had a problem when we were on the coast, we'd fly down to San Diego and get something done to it. But rarely did that happen. It was more like equipment. For example, it was a pretty stingy Navy in those days, and maybe you lost a pair of goggles. Or your goggles were so damn tired by this time that the rubber didn't keep the air out. What you'd do was take the goggles and break them in two so you could turn in two pair of goggles and you'd get two new ones back instead of one old one. There were a lot of little tricks along that line.

One of the real problems of these planes aboard ship, of course, is fire. You get hot ashes from the stacks going over there. I had a plane burn up on the USS Northampton.[*] We had hot incandescent soot land on it, and, boy, she was gone. We found during the war in some cases where a ship would toss its planes overboard because they were great fire hazards with all that gasoline and everything else.

Q: Were these observation planes used at all for target practice or anything like that?

Admiral Miller: Oh, yes, usually in the summer or at some given period when the fleet had other things to do, we'd all fly to North Island and go on wheels.[†] We'd have our gunnery practice with sleeves; we'd do catapulting, too, for that matter, and bombing practices. Oh, yes, we had to keep up our gunnery just like anybody else. The problem was you couldn't just go out to the line with a floatplane aboard ship and say, "Well, I think I'll take a little spin" or something. You had to get the damn thing, break out the division, and get it in the water. It was a major operation to fly.

You had all kinds of troubles there. I was on the Northampton with Captain Harry Shoemaker.[‡] He was a wonderful old boy. By this time we were flying the O2Us.[§] This was the bigger edition of the UO. We had had them in service for two or three years. They reached the point where they had a ban on them for catapulting. There was just no more catapulting; the damn things would fall apart the next time you'd shoot them. So he had a

---

[*] The skin of the planes in that era was fabric, stretched tight over a framework and covered with dope to seal it. On page 94 Admiral Miller indicates this fire took place on board the cruiser Salt Lake City (CA-25). His memory was apparently uncertain concerning which ship.
[†] North Island is the site of a naval air station in Coronado, California, across the harbor from San Diego.
[‡] Captain Harry E. Shoemaker, USN.
[§] The Chance Vought O2U was a biplane with a pontoon float at the bottom; it entered the fleet in the late 1920s. It had a wing span of 34 feet, length of 24 feet, gross weight of 3,635 pounds, and top speed of 150 miles per hour.

target practice coming on and we had to spot for it. Well, we tried to work out a deal whereby we would fly into San Clemente and moor. Then our job was to be so exact on time that we could get off and reach the ship where it was, oh, 50 miles out, in time to be there when they were ready to fire.

We didn't have voice radio in those days; it was all key. Well, by the time we'd send a plane up to radio the ship, we were running ourselves out of gas, and it was just a plain nuisance. There we were and we couldn't catapult, so how were we going to observe? Well, old Miller, as usual, cooked up a brilliant scheme. I went up and said, "Captain, when we've gone through the battle with the Marines, we'll hoist all our planes overboard. Then when you see that we're astern of you, you kick her up to 18 knots. You make a wake for us, and we'll fly right on up there and get off and we'll spot for you."*

Well, it was a great idea on paper. But let me tell you, I was the first one in the water and, God, that was the roughest sea I ever thought I'd see. It looked smooth from the ship. The cruiser looked so big, and I felt so small, and I thought, "My God." Two of my pilots were relative youngsters out of Pensacola. Finally all four of us got there and we were able to taxi. The seas would hit the propellers—wham!--then the propeller was out.

I was the one closest to the ship, and the old captain did just what he was told. With the four of us in the water, he got up to 18 knots. Gee, when I really looked up after trying to get squared away, that ship was running away from me. I thought, "Oh, my God! Now what am I going to do?" Well, I gave her the soup, too, and I was still relatively close to the ship. You'd get up and you'd hit a wave and you'd bounce up. I was trying to nose down to pick up a little speed, but not too far down. Then I'd hit another one, and the first thing I knew, here was the stern right in front of me. I didn't have enough speed, and we couldn't turn. So I decided I'd skid out just a little bit, then skid out a little bit more, and I

---

* The water needed to be somewhat rough, because smooth water produced suction that made it difficult for a plane to get airborne.

passed the stern without any trouble at all. Aboard ship, I scared the hell out of them, but I disappeared from sight of the bridge and they didn't know what was going on.

Q: They thought you had been lost.

Admiral Miller: The other kids did a fabulous job, I'm telling you. By this time, they were damn near out in the ocean. They all got up and we all got our spotting and came back. We saved the old captain. He'd have been without any spots at all. So we solved the problem, but it was a little hairy.

Q: Did you take watches?

Admiral Miller: Oh, sure, we stood watches. Old Tommy Symington was great. We'd be coming in from out at sea there, and I'd have the deck. We'd be doing about 18 knots and get about ten miles from the lighthouse at San Pedro. He hadn't been on the bridge for half an hour and I'd send word down, "Ten miles." Nothing happened. At about five miles I sent word down to old Tommy Symington. I finally slowed us down. He didn't show up on the bridge until we were just turning and going around the lighthouse. I thought he was kind of crazy. He was taking a lot of chances, but he didn't seem worried.

That was part of the fun of this thing. I wasn't a naval aviator per se; I was a naval officer who flew airplanes. That was my point of view on the thing, and it worked. That's the way I indoctrinated all my boys. They all took their watches. It was great.

I went to the West Virginia. Also about that time, there was a thought about putting fighter planes on floats on catapult work too. They'd always have a fighter protection out.

Q: Had you had any experience in fighter planes?

Admiral Miller: Oh, in Pensacola. That didn't make any difference at all. It was all the same. The West Virginia was a battle flag.[*] That's why Cal Durgin was commanding officer of that Squadron One and Beauty Martin was skipper of Fighting Two.[†] They were both aboard. So now he had the fourth plane aboard the ship, which was an FU, although it was actually a single-seater UO. Beauty was the skipper. Each battleship had one of these single seaters on there, and they obviously had no purpose aboard. Somebody was having an experiment or something.

In January of 1927, I got my landings on the old Langley, and it wasn't very hairy because she made 14 knots, and these planes weren't going very fast either.[‡] Beauty Martin's squadron, Fighting Two, was ordered to the Langley. We'd take the UOs off floats, put them on wheels, and put them on the Langley.

Q: How many planes did the Langley carry?

Admiral Miller: Thirty-six, probably. The fighter squadron had 18 planes, and there was an observation squadron. I think there was also one or two amphibians on there; she didn't carry very many. The point is she couldn't get enough speed to fly them off.

In any event, Beauty said, "How would you like to go to Fighting Two with me?"

---

[*] The USS West Virginia (BB-48) was the flagship for Commander Battle Divisions, Battle Fleet.
[†] Lieutenant Commander Calvin T. Durgin, USN, commanding officer of Observaton Squadron One-B. Lieutenant Harold M. Martin, USN, commanding officer of Fighting Squadron Two-B.
[‡] The USS Langley (CV-1) had originally been the collier Jupiter. She was converted to become the Navy's first aircraft carrier, commissioned in 1922.

Of course, that was the ambition of everybody, to be in one of the fighting squadrons. So I said, "You bet your life I'd like to go." So he got me a set of orders, and I joined Fighting Two at North Island and aboard the <u>Langley</u>. I had all sorts of adventures there. Those were good little airplanes. The FU had only a 220-horsepower J-5 in there, but it had a Root supercharger on it. You could get it over 5,000 feet; that Root supercharger would take effect, and you could take on Boeings and everything else. It did just a beautiful job.

Six months or so after that, we all went to Seattle and drew out the new Boeing fighter, the F3B.[*] Later on, that was exchanged for old Curtiss Hawks, F6C-4s and so on.[†] But I was in Fighting Two for, I guess, about a year. I loved it. I was an engineering officer and it was just a great experience. Of course, it was an enlisted squadron, you know. It had 6 officers and 12 enlisted pilots on there.

Q: Where had the enlisted pilots trained?

Admiral Miller: They were in World War I, you see, and had come along and trained in the Navy places and so on. Just in the last few months before this, again we adopted this thing of training enlisted men as pilots. They were great pilots. They were experienced. But they were pilots; that's what they were.

An example of them would be Harshman. Remember, the first man at the end of the war that was adrift in a life raft for about three or four weeks? That was Harshman. He was one of our old boys. Anyway, they were flying people.

---

[*] Boeing F3B fighters first entered the fleet in 1928 in squadron VF-2B on board the <u>Langley</u> (CV-1). The F3B-1 was 25 feet long, wing span of 33 feet, gross weight of 2,945 pounds, and top speed of 157 miles per hour.
[†] The Curtiss F6C Hawk, a biplane fighter, went into service with the fleet in 1927. The F6C-4 had a wing span of 38 feet, length of 22 feet, gross weight of 3,171 pounds, and top speed of 155 miles per hour.

Q: How was the Langley used in the fleet at that point?

Admiral Miller: Well, the old Langley would always come along. The USS Saratoga and USS Lexington hadn't quite made it yet.* They were just about ready to join the fleet. The old Langley would go out and, of course, it all became a matter of when. Then she'd get her signal to launch the planes and she'd head to the wind. The wind might have been astern, so the Langley would have to turn 180 degrees and head astern. By the time she got through launching planes, the fleet had gone practically out of sight. So the Langley, trying to catch up, would have to do another 180 to head back with the fleet, doing 14 knots and barely make it the rest of the day. She was good for about one operation.

Q: She was a drag on the fleet, then?

Admiral Miller: Yes, absolutely.

Q: This didn't enhance the image of aviation, then.

Admiral Miller: No, but everybody recognized that when the Saratoga and Lexington came along and could do 33 knots, then things would change. The Langley proved that you could fly on board and off of a ship.

    I remember at Guantanamo once down there, she was moored to a dock, and they were flying on and off her from the dock with no movement at all.

---

* The Saratoga (CV-3) was commissioned in November 1927 and the Lexington (CV-2) the following month.

Q: Just like an airfield.

Admiral Miller: Yes. So she proved her value very clearly. She had no stacks and a flat deck. Oh, it was a small deck. I'll never forget old Logan Ramsey was coming aboard, and this Bill Billings, who had been my instructor in Pensacola, was the landing deck officer with his flags.* We had all kinds of signals. For example, to get your hook down, he'd hit the deck with his flags because you might forget to lower that hook in the air. I guess old Logan was in an O2U and didn't have his hook down. Old Bill would hammer on that deck and curse and send him around again and no hook down. Then he would drag his flags giving him the signal. I don't recall if Logan couldn't lower the hook or whether he just didn't get the word, but he finally landed without a hook there. As he started losing speed, of course, he'd have to use a lot of rudder. He finally developed a nice sine curve, extending it more and more and finally over the side.

Q: Into the drink?

Admiral Miller: Into the drink. He came up sputtering and spouting. Old Bill Billings was cursing. He didn't mind the airplane or Ramsey or anything, but that was the only propeller he had on his ship and now he lost his propeller.

Q: Incidentally, how much did a plane cost in those days?

---

* Lieutenant Logan C. Ramsey, USN. By this time Billings was a lieutenant.

Admiral Miller: Well, even the F2B fighter cost around $12,000 dollars.* So this old job cost about $8,500 or something like that. They were all wooden structure, of course. But that was the Langley. I think I was there about 18 months.

Then I got orders as instructor at Pensacola, which I looked forward to. I kind of liked to teach, and I imagine that's what your sequence shows at that point.

Q: Yes. You came there in January of 1930 as a flight instructor.

Admiral Miller: Right, down at the beach. I think before I got through, I put through about 56 students and lost only one. He's the one I busted myself. He was going to kill himself.

Q: So you got him out first.

Admiral Miller: I got him out ahead of that time. Robineck was his name, and he later became one of my faithful mechanics up in Akron.†

It was sort of interesting. But what I found was that a lot of instructors weren't doing their jobs properly. For instance, every five hours each kid had to go through a check with another pilot to see how he was doing. I'd spend that hour most of the time instructing them in what they should have had already. For example, spinning an airplane, I found that they couldn't even get their airplane in a spin, let alone get it out. So I'd spend this hour teaching them to do what their instructor should have taught them to do. It was real fun teaching.

---

* Boeing F2B biplane fighters first entered the fleet in 1928 on board the Saratoga (CV-3). The F2B-1 was 23 feet long, wing span of 30 feet, gross weight of 2,805 pounds, and top speed of 158 miles per hour.
† The USS Akron (ZRS-4) was a large rigid airship, commissioned in October 1931.

Half of the Pan American pilots were students of mine down there in Pensacola. Charlie Blair, the lad who did everything--the Navy, Army, Marine Corps--flew a Mustang over the North Pole, a single job, all of these wonderful things.* They wanted to fly and, hell, you wanted them to fly. It was just a great experience.

Q: Why were the instructors more or less inadequate at that point?

Admiral Miller: They weren't inadequate as much as inattentive, probably--or not dedicated, perhaps, would be another way to say it. Oh hell, they could teach but they didn't. They didn't quite pull it off. Not the majority by any means.

Q: Wasn't there any close supervision from the bureau?

Admiral Miller: Up to a point, but if it weren't for a check pilot to know what this kid needed, they'd have troubles. A tough check pilot could go out and bust them and say, "You can't do that. You can't come out." But if you could teach them to do it while you were out, maybe you could accomplish something too.

About that time, Harold Fick had the engine ground school.† He had one of these sets of orders maybe to go to the Langley. He could go if he could find a relief--one of those situations.

Q: Yes, they're always intriguing, aren't they?

---

* Charles E. Blair became a well-known Pan American pilot. He later married the actress Maureen O'Hara.
† Lieutenant Harold F. Fick, USN.

Admiral Miller: He started hammering on me, and I resisted practically right to the bitter end on this thing. I didn't want to teach ground school; I wanted to fly.

Q: That's from textbooks, is it, ground school?

Admiral Miller: Oh, no, just part of the whole curriculum. Obviously you do what you're supposed to do, so I went there. We were getting these college kids in at that time.

I remember the first week I had the college guys for one week on the ignition of an engine, and I didn't know one end of it from another. I stalled through that week, and I learned pretty fast what I was supposed to. Then I found it absolutely fascinating at that particular point, trying to teach these kids. It took a little imagination. I felt I should go see how you make engines; that was one way to do it. At that time, you had to be from the Bureau of Aeronautics to be approved for a cross-country flight over 500 miles.

So I wrote up an itinerary for an F2B. I had to go to Chicago, I had to go to Detroit, I had to go to Cleveland and Buffalo and I had to go every place. It came back approved, and I had my own airplane for one month to fly all over the damn country. I actually was working. How do you make spark plugs? How do you make valves? How do you do this and that? I was bringing back all these cut-away samples. I started a museum and started cutting away all these engines and so on, putting electric lights in for ignition and things of that sort. Gee, the engine is the most fascinating part of an airplane.

Q: How did you get excused from the ground teaching?

Admiral Miller: They had a new class every two months or something like that. There was just a phase there that I could fit into.

Q: Oh, I see. That was innovative, to get approval readily.

Admiral Miller: Oh, yes. I found in this world that if you can do a little dreaming and put in a good jolt, you can get it done. I had a classmate in the bureau at that time, and I said to him, "Look, this is one thing I really want to do." He probably got it put through more than my letter got it put through, but at any rate I got it. This was a very unusual thing.

In Chicago, I borrowed a plane from Hooks Marley, who had the Great Lakes air station, and flew out to Iowa to see my grandmother.* I had reached the end of my limit in Chicago. But by borrowing a plane I could go on. Oh, I had a ball.

Q: What companies did you visit?

Admiral Miller: Detroit General Motors, for example. See, they were making that Packard diesel, with a five-cylinder radial engine at that point. In Cleveland, I went to Val. It was fascinating. How in the hell do you make a valve and things like that? In New York I went to Brewster and Goldsmith magnetos and spark plugs. The old boy, Goldsmith, took me into his arms, he and his wife, an old couple, and said, "You must come up to the house and stay." They took me to a musical comedy, first row. Oh, gee, it was a glorious operation, I'll tell you.

But I did one stupid thing. On my way back, I came through Floyd Bennett and Philadelphia.† I learned then that anytime you land, the first thing you do is fill it up with

---

* Lieutenant Albert S. Marley, Jr., USN.
† The naval air station in Brooklyn was named for Floyd Bennett, an enlisted pilot. In May 1926, along with Lieutenant Commander Richard E. Byrd, USN, Bennett was in the first plane to fly over the North Pole.

gas. You don't say you'll get it at the next stop. But, like a damn fool, I told them, "I don't need any gas." I was going to get it at Anacostia. I wanted to fly over the Naval Academy and just see the old place. But it turned out to be a very hazy day and no problem flying over the Naval Academy, but I was having trouble with Anacostia 40 miles away. I decided I'd better get down. Camp Meade had a little strip, so I got down over there and got some gas because I was beginning to get worried at that point.* Well, I landed on the rifle range at Camp Meade just to get down.

Q: An emergency landing?

Admiral Miller: Oh, fortunately I hadn't been there more than five minutes when here came a little old Navy trainer that turned out to be from Anacostia. He circled and I signalled him what the problem was. He came back in about two hours with ten gallons of gas. But it was one of those stupid things you do.

Q: How far would ten gallons take you?

Admiral Miller: Well, for that flight all I needed to do was go about 40 miles and I'd be all right. But that was a great trip.

Q: Tell me, spinning around like that, what about the air lanes? Was there any control over them?

---

* Camp Meade, an Army post, later became Fort Meade.

Admiral Miller: See, this was 1930 or 1931. It was no problem. The biggest problem was communications with the Navy. Every time you crossed a naval district, you had to report in two directions, as well as to the Bureau of Aeronautics. You would find more Western Unions than anything else. It was the greatest waste of money known to man, but that's the way it used to be all the way through.

I was just having fun there, and then I decided that hell, I'd better get some more flying in anyway. So I then went over and talked to my classmate Bob Goldthwaite, who had the observation squadron there at Pensacola.* I made a deal with him, so I became his check pilot. So I was getting in as much flying as I had done down at the beach and I had my engine school. More than that, there was a magazine--I forget what it was called--run by old Charlie Grant. I worked out a deal with him. I was teaching anyway, so once a month I'd do my article on carburetors or something and get a check for about a $130.00 a month writing this series.† I was a busy guy.

Q: You were an entrepreneur.

Admiral Miller: At that point, I became interested in the stock market, and I remember buying ten shares of General Motors then which I still own. The other day I added up those ten shares I bought at $300.00 or something like that. They produced $8,000 worth of dividends. That's all at the engine ground school. Harold Fick is the one I should thank for that.

---

* Lieutenant (junior grade) Robert Goldthwaite, USN.
† Miller contributed monthly articles to Universal Model Airplane News, 1931-34. It was published in New York by Harold Hersey and edited by Captain H. J. Loftus-Price.

Q: You must have kept that in a safety deposit box.

Admiral Miller: I practically forgot it. But everything works out well. Just use your bean a little bit here once in a while.

Q: You must have been much more valuable as a ground school teacher because of all this knowledge gained on your tour.

Admiral Miller: Oh, yes. And ethyl fluid, you could describe that and stop at the ethyl plant and things of that sort.

Q: Did that start a practice? Did they send other men?

Admiral Miller: I don't really recall. Most things like that depended on the person himself initiating something. That was about the time I was getting interested in writing <u>Navy Wings</u>.* That's another chapter of its own. That took about five or six years of research to get that done. Thank God, I found old Captain Chambers before he died because if I hadn't, he would have been a lost soul.† No one ever even discussed him before that time. I found him in Washington and sat down with him for hours about those early days.

Q: Tell me something about your writings, including <u>Navy Wings</u>.

---

* Lieutenant Harold B. Miller, USN, <u>Navy Wings</u> (New York: Dodd, Mead & Company, 1937). The publisher put out Miller's updated version of the book in 1942.
† In 1910 Captain Washington I. Chambers, USN, was designated as the Navy's officer in charge of handling aviation matters. The following year the first U.S. naval officer took flight training, and the Navy bought its first plane.

Admiral Miller: Well, I always wanted to write. I'm one of these piggy people; I always wanted to do everything, except the Navy always persisted, and that kept me going. But I always did some writing on the side. I was married at that time to Jean Dupont, a girl who had been a Hollywood writer.

We began to do a lot of writing together. It started out in articles. Well, I guess it probably started out, as I mentioned, when I was thrust into the ground school there at Pensacola. I thought, "Well, gee, I deliver this course once a month all the way along the line. Why don't I write it?" So I worked up a deal with an aviation magazine, and once a month, I'd send an article in. It would be on ignition, it would be on cylinders, and so on. I found out that this wasn't a bad way to live, to have this money. So I just got into this writing thing, and it would pretty much follow what I was doing.

For example, when I later went up to the airships, I sat down and did a hell of a lot of research and wrote the story for the Naval Institute on the lighter-than air/heavier-than-air relationship. The same thing on the carriers. I wrote up the old USS Langley, the "Covered Wagon."* By that time, we also had the Saratoga and the Lexington. So wherever I went, I pursued this.† Well, I was very much interested in the field of naval aviation per se, and I was a great clipper. I had a suitcase full of clippings of things. I'd take 30 days' leave out of Pensacola and, come up to the Library of Congress, and just spend 30 days inside the library and get all this stuff. Then the question, of course, came of putting it together, and that took six or seven years.‡ In the meantime, I had been doing a

---

* Lieutenant (j.g.) H. B. Miller, USN, "Covered Wagons of the Sea," U.S. Naval Institute Proceedings, November 1931, pages 1453-1478.
† See also Lieutenant (j.g.) H. B. Miller, USN, "Shooting the Catapult," U.S. Naval Institute Proceedings, April 1933, pages 537-554.
‡ In 1931, Miller began writing a book, tentatively titled The Air-Goin' Navy, about the history of naval aviation. Although the book was never published, an early draft was praised by, among others, Rear Admiral William Moffett, Chief of the Bureau of Aeronautics.

lot of things. I'd write a story about the students of aviation for Aero Digest and about catapulting. And I had two signed articles in one issue of Scientific American, both on naval air. They shouldn't have done it; at least, they should have used a phony name someplace along the line.

By 1935, I had gotten to know Jack Towers.* One day I got a call from him, saying that he had been approached by Major Lester Gardner, who was a famous aviation man of the civilian world in World War I.† Gardner wanted to talk to me. So I got ahold of this Gardner. He and Jack Towers wanted a chronology of naval aviation, which they didn't have.

This was the day of the make-work deal, the WPA.‡ So they set up this deal where I'd fly back to New York, and guess I was on $6.00 a day. I think I was on my own up at the old Shelton Hotel on Lexington Avenue. Across the street was some government property, a great huge building there. A whole floor was empty except for desks and things like that. They said, "Here you are. Now what do you want? What do you need?" I had brought my suitcases along.

I said, "Well, I need a lot of typists."

"Gee, how many you want?" Well, I ended up with about 30 typists in there. The job was to keep them busy. I went to work all night long to get my stuff assembled for the next day. So what we'd do would be to type out each of my illegible odds and ends and stuff. I finally was ending up with a lot of chits, and they all had some sort of orderliness. My job was to arrange them so that they started coming out of the mill as a chronology. In six weeks we got that one done. It turned out, I think, something like 60 or 70 pages of

---

* Captain John H. Towers, USN, Assistant Chief of the Bureau of Aeronautics. Towers was naval aviator number three.
† Lester Gardner was secretary of the Institute of Aeronautical Sciences in New York.
‡ WPA--Works Progress Administration, a Depression-relief agency that sometimes created make-work projects in order to stimulate employment.

single-spaced typing of all this material. That was the first time the Navy knew what had happened in naval aviation. That was the beginning of Navy Wings.* In the meantime, we were also doing a lot of fiction.

Q: You and Jean?

Admiral Miller: Yes, doing fiction in those days. This other stuff was all mine. We established a character, "Bob Wakefield, Naval Aviator." Bob was a really terrific, heroic type of pilot. He had a mechanic, Ajax, who always went with him, wherever Bob went. Both of them would always go along wherever I had been, so they just followed me around. Those would sell to Boy's Life and developed a tremendous following. We got about 12 episodes in, and then we put them together into a collection that was published as a book. In this particular case, about Bob Wakefield, the tie-in was he'd get ordered to some other ship; he'd get a set of orders and that would move him on. So that worked out for three volumes.† We'd get a couple of hundred dollars for each one of those things. But the funniest thing happened. You know the book on the Akron and Macon?‡

Q: Yes.

---

* In late 1936, Miller prepared a draft of a book for commercial publication, based on his chronology of U.S. naval aviation. Originally titled Our Navy Flies, it was published in 1937 as Navy Wings.
† Blaine and Dupont Miller, Bob Wakefield, Naval Aviator (New York: Dodd, Mead, 1936); Bob Wakefield, Naval Inspector (New York: Dodd, Mead, 1937); Bob Wakefield's Flight Log (New York: Dodd, Mead, 1940).
‡ Richard K. Smith, The Airships Akron and Macon: Flying Aircraft Carriers of the United States Navy (Annapolis: Naval Institute, 1965).

Harold B. Miller #1 - 51

Admiral Miller: I have a copy autographed by Smith, and he says something to the effect, "To the person who helped me when I was a youth by writing Bob Wakefield, all of which I read." You know how that circle comes back.

Q: Yes.

Admiral Miller: It's really quite amazing. Well, that went on. Of course, during the war you couldn't do anything. After that, I got so busy with life that there wasn't much I could do about it. But I do a lot of writing now with a column for Shipmate.* I did bios for these things, so I'm getting back in touch. Down below I've got files which are absolutely priceless. I should just simply sit down and get the stuff organized and do something with it, except you're doing it for me.

Q: Getting back to Pensacola, we mentioned off tape Dr. De Foney who was quite a character there.† Tell me about him.

Admiral Miller: He had the unfortunate name which has led people to have a lot of fun--Phony, and so on like that. But he had a great confidence in his ability to determine whether or not a student was capable of flying. I worked with Barret Studley, who also had that idea; he was one of the senior instructors down there.‡ The Germans about that time had been trying to develop some means of determining whether people can fly or not. Studley had me working on this thing. We had stopwatch timings, we had reaction timing, and we had all kinds of stuff and gimmicks. I'd run these students through, and in the end I

---

* Shipmate is the monthly magazine of the Naval Academy Alumni Association.
† Lieutenant Clinton G. De Foney, Medical Corps, USN, was a Navy flight surgeon.
‡ Lieutenant Barret Studley, USN.

never felt I could tell one from another. Studley kept right on. He was not an oddball, but he was different.

Q: Clairvoyant?

Admiral Miller: Well, sort of. De Foney would come along, and he didn't go through any of this stuff. Just from a psychological point of view he knew whether somebody could fly. Maybe it's because he drove on the wrong side of the road once, or God knows what his reasoning was. But it was always said--and I think it's true--when somebody went out in the fleet and got killed, De Foney would break out his little book and hold it very close to his chest and say, "Yep, I had him too." No one ever saw the book. So he was 100% right.

Q: That's one way to be, yes. I mention Ralph Barnaby also as being at Pensacola at one point in the '30s, I believe, with his gliders and using them as a preliminary test on aptitude.*

Admiral Miller: Oh, that would be sort of a cheap way of instructing, I presume, to be part of that deal. You see, the Germans, having been knocked off by the Allies, had to use gliders as instructors. That was probably what he was following through. Ralph was a highly intellectual and wonderful person, Ralph S. Barnaby. His wife's name is Marge. I had a card from him only the other day. He's a great sculptor too, you know. He has all sorts of artistic talents.

---

* Lieutenant Ralph S. Barnaby, Construction Corps, USN. His oral history is in the Naval Institute collection.

Q: He lives in Philadelphia.

Admiral Miller: That's correct. He pulled together all the aviation stuff in the Franklin Museum down there in Philadelphia. He's a very brilliant person. He also, you will recall, launched a glider from Los Angeles at one time.*

Q: Yes, I do.

Admiral Miller: He was a bright one. He was a naval aviator, of course, but a naval constructor in the trade.

---

* On 31 January 1930 Lieutenant Barnaby made an air-to-ground glider flight, dropping from the airship Los Angeles (ZR-3) at an altitude of 3,000 feet over Lakehurst, New Jersey.

Interview Number 2 with Rear Admiral Harold B. Miller, U.S. Navy (Retired)

Place: Admiral Miller's home, Manhasset, New York

Date: Monday, 4 May 1981

Interviewer: Dr. John T. Mason, Jr.

Q: Today, sir, we begin an exciting episode in your career. That was when you became affiliated with lighter-than-air in 1932. You transferred to the unit of the USS Akron.*

Admiral Miller: Yes, that was perhaps one of the most exciting periods I had in my life in the Navy. The odd thing was that when I was a student at Pensacola in 1926 they brought an officer by the name of Rosendahl, who was head of the naval students, to give a talk with the view, I presume, of doing a little proselytizing.†

Q: And he was successful too.

Admiral Miller: But it was a very, very interesting discussion, of course. In 1926, he had just the year before been on the Shenandoah, which cracked up and fell apart in Ohio.‡ So

---

* The USS Akron (ZRS-4) was a rigid airship commissioned on 27 October 1931. She was 785 feet long, had a maximum diameter of 132 feet, height of 152 feet, dead weight of 221,000 pounds, and a maximum speed of 72 knots.
† Lieutenant Commander Charles E. Rosendahl, USN, who later became a flag officer, was for many years one of the Navy's leading exponents of lighter-than-air craft. He was the first commanding officer when the Akron was commissioned.
‡ On 3 September 1925 the rigid airship Shenandoah (ZR-1) broke apart in a severe storm near Ava, Ohio. Of the crew of 43 on board, 14 were killed.

he was quite a hero to naval aviators and to the country as a whole, as a matter of fact. But I didn't get to know him particularly well at that time.

I went back to Pensacola as an instructor in 1929, and at that time the Akron and the Macon has already been approved.* I believe it was in the 1926 Vinson Bill that the two airships had been approved, so that I knew they were under construction. I had always been interested in anything that was a little out of the normal course of events. I became intrigued with the thought when I heard that they were going to have a heavier-than-air unit attached to the airships, so I began writing letters at that particular point applying for this duty. I guess I became a bit of a pest too.

I'll never forget writing to Raoul Waller, a classmate of mine who was in the Bureau of Aeronautics at that time.† I asked him to hammer on everybody as they went by the door to make sure that Min Miller got that assignment. It turned out that I did. I was very excited about it. Two people had preceded me up there. One, of course, was Ward Harrigan, class of 1922, and Howard "Brig" Young from the class of 1923.‡ I guess they reported probably in 1931 before either of the ships had been built or delivered. The USS Los Angeles was still in commission at that time, and she had already had a certain amount of experimental work done on her.§

For example, Ralph Barnaby--who made two or three releases--made the point that an airship could carry a heavier than air and could release it from the trapeze. That part of the experiment was certainly successful. As a matter of fact, there was nothing new about that. There had been releases made by the British many years before. I wrote an

---

* For a detailed history of these two, see Richard K. Smith, The Airships Akron and Macon: Flying Aircraft Carriers of the United States Navy (Annapolis: Naval Institute, 1965).
† Lieutenant (junior grade) Raymond R. Waller, USN.
‡ Lieutenant Daniel W. Harrigan, USN; Lieutenant (junior grade) Howard L. Young, USN.
§ The dirigible was built in Germany for the U.S. Government under the terms of the Versailles treaty. She was commissioned the USS Los Angeles (ZR-3) in November 1924.

article for the Naval Institute that was published in 1935 which was a history of heavier-than-air and lighter-than-air, and I had researched quite a bit on that.*

About that time, of course, they were trying to bring along an airplane which would fit the specifications of the airships. The airships each would have a hangar, and there would be a trapeze gear which you flew on to and were hoisted into the ship itself, into the hangar. But the dimensions were so tight that it had to be a particular airplane. Well, in an effort to get more fighters aboard an airship, the Navy had already dealt with several companies: one was Curtiss, one was General, and one was Berliner-Joyce in Baltimore.

Q: Oh, yes.

Admiral Miller: Those three had the specs, and the idea was to get a small fighting plane for the carriers to get more planes aboard the ship itself. It didn't work out as a fighter for aircraft carriers. They were very short coupled and tended to go on their nose when they grabbed the tailhook, and that project was canceled. But they had this little fighter which would just exactly fit into an airship. It wasn't designed for the airship at all; it just happened that its dimensions permitted that. It weighed about 2,800 pounds and had a 25-foot, 6-inch wingspan. It was the F9C-2, called the Sparrowhawk.† The contract called for six of those, but there were two X jobs--one XF9C-1 and one XF9C-2, plus six production

---

* Lieutenant H. B. Miller, USN, "Navy Skyhooks," U.S. Naval Institute Proceedings, February 1935, pages 234-240.
† Curtiss built the F9C, which had a gross weight of 2,770 pounds, a maximum speed of 176 miles per hour at 4,000 feet, and was armed with two .30-caliber machine guns.

jobs of the F9C-2.* In effect, before we got through we had eight airplanes that were capable of being fitted into that.

Q: What was the intended mission of the lighter-than-air ship at that time--the enthusiasm that centered around it?

Admiral Miller: Even after the lighter-than-air came along, I went to a squadron that had the old PM.† That was the old Martin twin-engine flying boat, and if it got 500 miles at sea and got back 500 miles, it was doing pretty well on radius. Here now was an airship that had a range of 8,000 miles, and, by golly, that just sounded like the answer to any scouting operation that the Navy could ever require. There were a lot of minuses to this problem, too, which the lighter-than-air crowd often tended to overlook.

There weren't many places where you could land an airship. You had Lakehurst, you had a mast at San Diego, they were building Sunnyvale, and there was still a mast at Fort Lewis in Washington. The USS Patoka, a sort of a tanker, had a mast at the stern which took the USS Los Angeles on one or two occasions.

In Germany, of course, you had facilities. But basically, where were you going to put that ship if you were in trouble? It took a tremendous ground crew with some knowledge to operate those ships.

---

* Under the naval aviation designation system of the day, the X stood for experimental, F for fighter, C for Curtiss. This was the ninth model fighter plane Curtiss built for the Navy. The final numbers, -1 and -2, indicated variations within the model.
† The PM was built by Martin as the production verson of the Naval Aircraft Factory PN-12. The PM-2 version had a wing span of 73 feet, length of 48 feet, gross weight of 16,964 pounds, and maximum speed of 116 miles per hour.

Q: I suppose the enthusiasm was engendered somewhat by the German successes with the zeppelins, was it not?

Admiral Miller: The Germans were considered the answer to all airship operations. The fact was that simply wasn't the case. The Germans lucked out just about as much as anybody in the world, but you never knew about it. So we considered them the master builders, the master operators. For example, from part of the peace treaty we obtained rights to have this ship that became the Los Angeles, which was the ZR-3.* Part of that treaty permitted us to have two naval officers on every flight of the German airship Graf Zeppelin, going around the world or wherever. We always had two observers aboard. They told stories that would curl your hair about the problems that the Germans had which no one ever knew about.

For example, she was coming in from Brazil, going into Friedrichshafen, Germany. She went, of course, through the Strait of Gibraltar. Up the Rhone Valley she developed some sort of a problem, a vibration of her engines. They lost one engine; the crankshaft carried away. They lost the second engine and finally got into Friedrichshafen on one engine. Those things weren't known particularly.

They had another case when they were landing in Pernambuco down in South America, where it was a wild day. The Germans would parachute about four or five supervisors from the ship and then have a native ground crew there to haul the ship down and put it on the mast. This particular time, the ship was bucking like a bronco. It came down on a cabin that had a tall roof, a chimney, and a fire in the fireplace down below. Here was a hydrogen ship that actually came down on this chimney. They got away with that. Finally they got it off, and it didn't burn. That could have happened too. I merely

---

* This was the 1919 Treaty of Versailles, which came after World War I.

make the point that the Germans weren't the answer to this thing, and lighter-than-air hadn't proven itself.

You go back during World War I and find all this stuff. Back then the zeppelins scared the hell out of the British, but they did practically no damage whatsoever.

Q: Yes, when they came over and dropped a few bombs.

Admiral Miller: Yes, it frightened them but didn't work at all. But the point was that this enthusiasm we had was based on ignorance of the German problems.

Q: I remember the thrill that many of us had in seeing the Graf Zeppelin over Washington. It was a beautiful thing in the air.

Admiral Miller: Yes, an exciting thing.

Now, the ZR-2 was the British job. We had an American crew over there, and they were doing a test job on her. One of the things required was a complete full rudder turn over the Humber River. That turn just simply broke the ship up, and down she went and we lost all of our crew. I think we lost all of them on board that.*

ZR-1 was the Shenandoah. We decided we would build our own. Then the ZR-3 came along, and that was the Los Angeles, the delivery of the German ship. Then the four and the five were the Akron and the Macon, American built. So the enthusiasm was there. I must say there was no one more enthusiastic than I was. Just to see these beautiful things

---

* ZR-2, which did not have a name, was the British R38. She crashed on 24 August 1922, during a trial flight in England. Among the 44 killed were Lieutenant Commander Lewis H. Maxfield, USN, and 15 other U.S. Navy personnel.

I thought was the answer to everything going out 8,000 miles. At any rate, I went up to Lakehurst, New Jersey.

The Los Angeles was still in the hangar, and she either had just been degassed or still was floating. I think she was still floating, but she never flew again. They took the gas out of her and disassembled her finally, because they had to get her out of there and get room for the big ships then. Along about spring, just before I got there, the Akron had been delivered. I had kept in touch with Harrigan and Young. It must have been somewhere around the first of July when I got up there. What we had to work with then were these aircraft, the XF9C-1 and the XF9C-2. We also had about two or three of the N2Ys, the old Navy training planes with hooks on them.* So we had about five hook-on airplanes at the time.

Harrigan and Young were the two experts, of course, by that time. Yet it was still experimental, even as far as they were concerned. I'll never forget when the time came, Ward said, "Come on, let's go up." So I climbed up in the front seat of one of the N2Ys, and away we went. He made about ten landings. There was certainly no problem connected with that at all. We went on back down again, changed seats, and when he got out of the airplane, I went back. So I went up and played around with this. The first one, of course, is always a little touchy, but as time went on, it was just an every-day occurrence, as though you were landing on a field.

Now, on the F9C-2, first of all I should explain that in my three years with lighter-than-air, we never took off the ground in an airship. The reason for that was that the airship itself needed every pound that it could carry in fuel. Each plane weighed, as I say, about 2,800 to 3,000 pounds. If we had four planes aboard, the 12,000 pounds was better carried

---

* Altogether the Navy purchased six N2Y-1s to serve as familiarization trainers for pilots attached to the Akron and Macon. The N2Y-1 had a wing span of 28 feet, gross weight of 1,637 pounds, top speed of 108 miles per hour.

in fuel than in airplanes. But once you were in the air, she could carry us dynamically by dropping her tail and she could carry up to 4,000 pounds heavy. So we would always fly aboard after she had taken off.

Q: That was kind of tricky, though, wasn't it?

Admiral Miller: Well, you mean flying with the tail down?

Q: Yes, flying aboard after.

Admiral Miller: Four thousand pounds heavy, if they lost all their power, she would no longer be a lighter-than-air machine. You would have to balance out by dropping ballast in order to become zero, to have a buoyancy there.

Q: I see.

Admiral Miller: People seem to think that you just go up and fly an airship. That isn't so; it's a very technical job that you fly with a slipstick.* It's a matter of pounds and weight and air pressure. For example, if you go up there with your bags pretty well inflated, say, 80%, as you go higher that 80% becomes 85% and 90% as the gas expands. The first thing you know, you have a full bag. In this case, I think there were 13 balloonets in these ships. At that point, then a pressure valve up there would open and, if you go any higher, the gas would be lost. Then when you came down again, if what you had in there was compressed,

---

* Slipstick is a term used for a slide rule, used for mathematical calculations before pocket calculators became commonplace.

you didn't have 80% to work with. You had perhaps only 70% to work with, and now you had landing problems. So they were very tricky things.

Q: And add to that the weather, which was such an influence on this.

Admiral Miller: Oh, the weather controlled everything you did. I should explain that there was a slight feeling among heavier-than-air people. We kind of thought, "My God, all they do is wait for good weather." If they got the ship out and got it back, that was a great successful flight. The only thing that was accomplished was that, and it didn't seem to make that much difference. But the fact was that the lighter-than-air people were still, after all, learning how to fly the airships.

I must say, we were probably very harsh in our judgment on that score, because we were used to working off of carriers. We became very good friends with all of these people. They, of course, looked at us somewhat askance too. They thought, "Are these guys going to come and pull a boo-boo and fly into the ship, or how are they going to make out? Are they any good at all?" Well, we had to prove ourselves, which was no particular problem because the whole thing about flying the airplane on and off was so simple. It was the easiest thing in the world. I suppose you'd say that anything you can do well is easy.

Q: Yes, once it is mastered.

Admiral Miller: But I certainly found out the trick. As we'd fly alongside the airship, the ship would lower a red flag or a green flag. The green flag told us to come aboard when we were ready. The point of that was for the ship to be up to speed. In those earlier days, we thought we were landing pretty fast; we had a landing speed of 68 or 70, somewhere along in there. Well, if the ship wasn't up to that speed, theoretically we would stall before we could get aboard and spin out of it. Frequently, we'd get a flag to come aboard, and she hadn't gotten up to speed. You'd get up there and you'd nibble and you just couldn't make it. You'd just lose your speed and fall away, which then determined how high you should be to hook on.

Where was the danger on that? Well, we reached the point where we were hooking on at 800 feet with no problem at all on the thing. If the ship was up to speed, we got the green flag, and by this time we all knew each other and our capabilities and what we could do and they knew us too. You'd fly alongside that number one engine, which was about where the trapeze was, about 25 feet below the ship and maybe 25 feet aside from there. Then with your rudder, you would just skid under the ship slowly. We got so that we really got under there.

Now, you're under the ship and you're behind the trapeze about 25 or 50 feet. At this point, the pilot has to change from normal horizon flight by looking up, so you're now flying on something that's up above you. You get in some queer situations there because occasionally the ship would turn and you're looking at the ship. You didn't know what she was doing; all you knew was you had to hold your relative position on this thing. You'd find yourself skidding on one side or the other. It was very annoying.

Q: It called for close communication, didn't it?

Admiral Miller: Of course, we had voice radio, but by this time you were pretty busy and you didn't have time to talk. It didn't make any difference. It wasn't even a problem; it was just one of the annoying things of going aboard.

So now you were underneath it and you were behind it. Here's why it was so simple: you had only one task to do, and that was to decrease the distance between the trapeze and your hook. All you had to do was to pull it up there. You didn't care about anything else. I had gone on many times with the throttle completely closed and the ship coming down. It made no difference; the relative speed was all I was interested in and closing the distance. If the ship wanted to come to me, that was perfectly all right. Or sometimes, if the ship hadn't gotten up its speed, you'd get up there and you just had your throttle wide open. You were just pulling all you could pull in order to climb up to this thing. Maybe you made it and maybe you didn't. Maybe you would stall at that point and fall off. You'd come back and try it again.

Q: Were there any particular air drafts engendered by these?

Admiral Miller: Not of any consequence. However, there was a relative air current in that farther aft, two-thirds the way back on the ship, we had what we called a perch. It was a trapeze about six feet from the ship. It was right up against the skin of the ship, where we could transfer pilots if we had to or we could refuel the airplane back there. We couldn't take it aboard. The idea of that was that if you thought you had some problems and you wanted both planes in action fast you would have one on each hook and get up and go. That was the point of the perch. It had no other value.

The point I make is the perch at that area was a much smoother approach than farther forward because the forward trapeze was astern of the control car so you did develop some bumps that didn't amount to a damn thing. Yes, the perch was much smoother.

Q: When you talk about the possibility of refueling from the perch, was there fuel carried there?

Admiral Miller: Yes. I don't think we ever did refuel there, though. It was just an emergency sort of thing. Let me finish about hooking on. So you were back there and you were closing the distance; that's all you were doing. The ship was not up to speed, and sometimes you could just with sheer power drag yourself up there and hook on. It was a spring-loaded hook, so at that point you'd hit it reasonably hard and that would lock you on. The idea was to get on the center of the trapeze. But if the ship really turned, as often happened, you'd end up way out on the side of the trapeze. There was no problem getting back to center; you'd just kick your rudder and it would slide back down again. The reason for being in the center was that you only had about a 4-inch clearance on each wing tip as you went through the hangar door. Now you were locked on.

You may recall the tripod carrying the hook had an extension part out over the propeller. Nobody knew quite how easy it would be to hook on, so they put that out there so that you weren't trying to knock the propeller off on the trapeze. They also thought you could put that bar on the trapeze and then slide your plane in through the hook. But after we got reasonably familiar, we never did anything but put the hook around the trapeze. We never used that sliding technique at all because you had no need for it. You'd just simply hook on. At that point, you were locked on and you knew you're locked on, although there were a couple of times when I thought I was locked on and I'd sit back fat, dumb and happy and just fall off.

Q: That would be a shock.

Admiral Miller: That was no problem either; all you had to do was drop the nose a little bit and pick up a little flying speed and come back and go on again. But we learned to insure that you were on by giving a little burst of power of your prop.

Q: By testing.

Admiral Miller: Just make sure you are on that. Now, the hangar door, which would slide open at this point, now looked like a T. But you'd better have that tail just exactly straight or the wings were going to hit the hangar. So we devised what we called a saddle which at one time had a very elaborate arm that would come back and you'd hook on so the plane would have no lateral motion. That took a lot of time and was a nuisance. The Trapnell device was nothing but a saddle you'd lower down on the fuselage and that would keep it from wiggling too. So they'd just lower that down on a pivot from the ship, and you were, in effect, locked into place and they'd hoist you aboard. Of course, you cut your engine at that point.

We had the most marvelous lighter-than-air crew working with us. In three years working with them we never had a forced landing of those airplanes. We were out over water constantly all the time and never had a forced landing. It was absolutely great.

Q: Trapnell was with lighter-than-air too?*

Admiral Miller: Oh, yes. He came up with me. Four of us came up at that point: Trapnell of '23, Bob "Swede" Larson from my class, myself, and Knappy Kivette of '25.†

Let's get back to the sequence of that. We had a year then with Brig Young and we had six people up there. I remember Young and Harrigan.

---

* Lieutenant (junior grade) Frederick M. Trapnell, USN. In later years he was noted for his work in running the Navy's test pilot operation.
† Lieutenant (junior grade) Robert W. Larson; Lieutenant (junior grade) Frederick N. Kivette, USN.

Q: Four of you came up together and the two others.

Admiral Miller: It was a year on the Akron, which didn't do very much. She'd go up and down the coast, and we took her down to Miami once and worked with the fleet down there. But she pretty well stayed close to home, which was the attitude of those lighter-than-air boys at that time: get her out and get her back and have a very successful flight on the thing. At this point, Harrigan decided that he'd had enough. He and Swede Larson were detached. Swede Larson went on a cruiser, and he dove the wings off of a cruiser plane and killed himself.* Ward Harrigan retired later on and he's living down in Florida now. Brig Young committed suicide later on for some reason.†

Then the Akron went down.‡ That was one of the twists of fate that takes place. First of all, the airship never took us aboard before takeoff. That was one thing. Also, it was a foggy night, but it wasn't very high fog. The big ship took off with no problem at all, and it just went on up through the stuff. It was a little too much for those of us in the airplanes that night, so we thought we'd join them in the morning. That was a Godsend to us because that storm came up and the Akron went down. So we missed that little episode.

Q: That must have been a blow to the prospects of lighter-than-air.

Admiral Miller: Oh, it was terrible. Yet we had the Macon coming along very fast at this point. She was about ready for delivery.

---

* Larson died in a plane crash at Guantanamo Bay, Cuba, in June 1936 while attached to the USS Memphis (CL-13).
† Young died 4 April 1954 at San Diego.
‡ On 4 April 1933 the dirigible Akron (ZRS-4) crashed into the sea in a storm off Barnegat Light, New Jersey. Of the 76 men on board, 73 were killed, including Rear Admiral William A. Moffett, Chief of the Bureau of Aeronautics.

Q: Who produced them?

Admiral Miller: Goodyear in Akron, Ohio. They still have that big hangar out there. It was basically almost a German company that did it. They brought all their German talent over there into that thing.

Q: You were without a mother ship then.

Admiral Miller: We were ordered very soon to the USS Macon.

Q: With the same amount of enthusiasm?

Admiral Miller: Oh, yes. It didn't bother me. The Macon was scheduled to go to the West Coast. We sort of fiddled around there for a little while until the Macon came through. I guess that must have been the summer of 1933 when we took delivery of her.*

Q: There must have been, as a result of that accident with the Akron, more concern about the vulnerability of these ships.

Admiral Miller: I suppose there was, certainly among the people like Admiral King who wanted to prove these things.† The whole point was that if lighter-than-air was as good as people thought it was, we needed to go out and serve with the fleet and see what it could

---

* The USS Macon (ZRS-5) was a rigid airship commissioned on 23 June 1933. She was 785 feet long, had a maximum diameter of 133 feet, height of 146 feet, dead weight of 242,356 pounds, and a maximum speed of 76 knots.
† Rear Admiral Ernest J. King, USN, became Chief of the Bureau of Aeronautics following Admiral Moffett's death.

do. But the old-timers there in lighter-than-air were very loath to get out there and kick around with the fleet.

Q: They were sort of protecting their . . .

Admiral Miller: Yes. For example, the Akron was down there in the Caribbean. We were down there at that time, and there was a matter of fuel. She could find a reason to get the hell back fast even before the exercises were over. It always annoyed us, the air group that we had there. We always felt they ought to stretch us somewhat and show what could be done.

But we had all kinds of episodes at that time. While the Akron was at Lakehurst, I had a lot of classmates around. Lakehurst had the Navy parachute school too. That's where they'd train these young packers from the fleet. Their graduation exercises would be a jump with a chute that they themselves had packed. That kind of proved that they could pack a chute.

Q: And do it well.

Admiral Miller: They would take them up in a blimp with an open cockpit that had handrails along the side. One of those days they had a graduation exercise coming on, and I asked Charlie, a classmate, "How about going out with you? I'd like to see the graduation." Incidentally, we had taken sort of a lighter-than-air course while we were there. We had lots of time on our hands, and we went through most of it. We had more than a smattering of what it was all about. We certainly didn't qualify for lighter-than-air wings or anything, but Charlie said, "Sure, come on up." So I went as his number-two pilot and we went up. I had an old chief, sort of a jump master, and we were over the field.

Q: At what altitude?

Admiral Miller: I think it must have been 1,500 feet or something of that sort. One of these kids would climb out facing the interior of the ship, standing on the handrail. He was holding on, and the chief would come pat him on the back and he would fall off spread-eagle on his back and pull his chute and have no problem. We got to the last chap, a little runt, 18 years old perhaps, and he got out and the chief tapped him and he let go and grabbed back again. That guy got him by the pants and pulled him aboard.

Q: He failed, I suppose?

Admiral Miller: Yes, he wasn't keen on jumping at all. My classmate who was flying the ship just ate him up. I was ashamed of him as an officer talking to a little scared-rabbit boy the way he did. It was just terrible. I've never seen such an exhibition of temper. He said, "We went to all the trouble of flying up here, and you haven't got the guts to jump," and all this kind of stuff. It was awful. I was sore by that time.

This was the period when lighter-than-air and heavier-than-air weren't entirely simpatico. I told the gang down below--there were six of us--"By God, we ought to show these guys a thing or two." At that time, you could make a parachute jump with the authority of the commanding officer. Well, we were all attached to the Akron and were all infected by this time about it, so in our anger we said, "By God, we'll show them a thing or two." We typed out a little letter saying, "I hereby request permission to make a parachute jump, blah, blah, blah." So I carried them all in to Doc Wiley, the skipper, and asked him to sign them. He looked at them and looked at me and signed all of them.*

---

* Lieutenant Commander Herbert V. Wiley, USN.

Now we were locked up. We had to make a parachute jump just to show them up. Well, we got an old Ford airplane up from Anacostia one day and took the door off, and all of us went up and made our jump just to prove something. I don't know what we proved.

Q: To vent your anger.

Admiral Miller: We had a lot of little episodes of that sort which were always a lot of fun, really. By the time we lost the Akron, Ward was gone, and Swede was gone. There wasn't much point in trying to expand the unit. We didn't have an airship at that point in time or anything else.

Q: Did the enthusiasm hold or was it waning?

Admiral Miller: The enthusiasm was there. It didn't stop us at all; we just went right on about our business, except we had to do gunnery and things of that sort. We had no airship to work with at all. We'd fly back and forth to Akron quite often just to see how things were coming along out there. Then the Macon did come out. Commander Al Dresel brought her over from Akron to Lakehurst and the first thing you know, the time had come to go west.*

Brig Young hadn't left yet, and he ended up in Sunnyvale with us for a few months. He left after that. Trap followed him shortly. Ward had gone earlier. Ward Harrigan was a fascinating person, and very ingenious. While he was there, he designed this

---

* Commander Alger H. Dresel, USN, was the first commanding officer when the Macon was commissioned 23 June 1933. After going into service, the Macon was based at the naval air station at Sunnyvale, California.

parachute raft business that saved so many lives in the Pacific during the war. He blended together a parachute and a raft. He was always working on the theory of things.

One of the big arguments at that point--and you brought it up--was, "What is an airship for? What's it supposed to do?" Finally, there was only one thing that you could conclude--that there had to be a long-range scout. You can also conclude that those things sure needed a lot of defense mechanisms built around to keep them from getting shot down.

Q: Yes, the antiair was being improved vastly, wasn't it? Guns could shoot and the blimp was quite vulnerable.

Admiral Miller: They couldn't very well miss. So what were these planes for then? Well, they were designed as fighters. But could four planes--even if you had four aboard--do anything to defend themselves against a squadron? And, of course, this was long before the kamikaze. What a kamikaze would do is break the back of a ship one on one and would bring her down so fast it wouldn't be funny.

So the theory became that the airship had to be used as a scout and had to be kept back; it couldn't go forward. Out of that then evolved a job for the planes. We were going to be the scouts. We were going to be the base sitting back here 300 or 400 hundred miles, and we would go up and tell what we saw. That is really what finally evolved as the mission for these airplanes. As a fighter, its performance was obviously noncompetitive with any carrier fighter that was being worked on in those days. So that became the accepted mission of the airplane--to go on out and find out what was going on and keep the ship out of trouble.

In maneuvers, every time the ship started moseying around and nosing into problems, boy, she got shot down so goddamn fast that it wasn't even funny. It became intolerable. Al Dresel was a real gentleman, but he was not an aggressive commander of an airship. Later on, when Doc Wiley came along, as we'll discuss, he took a very aggressive attitude on the whole thing. So let's see, where are we now?

Q: You're about to go out to the West Coast.

Admiral Miller: My sons never understand why no matter where we are in this country I'd say, "I flew over here, and I landed over there for gas." The reason is that the airship was going back and forth constantly, and we never flew with the ship; we'd just fly independently. I covered the whole country. It was a lot of flying. We got out to the West Coast and things began to perk up. Doc Wiley had gone to sea as a navigator of some ship or other. Finally he came along and relieved Al Dresel. Doc now had been pretty well indoctrinated with the fleet itself.

An interesting thing about lighter-than-air people, they had to have alleged sea duty on a blimp or on the Los Angeles, and they'd have shore duty at Lakehurst and then have sea duty also at Lakehurst, so they never left. They never really had a feel or a touch of what the hell the fleet was doing.

Q: It was sort of a closed corporation.

Admiral Miller: Absolutely.

Q: Not very promising for advancement.

Admiral Miller: No, no. It developed to get the ship out and get it back and so on, because if we didn't have the ship, we didn't have anything to work with. Doc Wiley came along. Then we were transferred to the Macon. Trap and Brig Young didn't stay there for more than a couple of months after we got to Sunnyvale, California, and then I got the unit. So I had Knappy Kivette and picked up two new pilots. One was Simpler, who's down in Florida now, and Gerry Huff, who has died since.* So the four of us were the unit at that particular time.

I started writing memos to Doc Wiley about things that ought to be done and things we were going to do and make. I was trying to promote the airship through the airplanes. I was an avid lighter-than-air man. I thought that these things had the answers to so much, despite knowing their weaknesses.

Before Trap left, I should point out that we also, never knowing where we might have to land at sea, went down and did some landings on the carrier Lexington. We had a tailhook on it and everything else, so we'd check out our little fighters on the carriers as well. We were pretty well rounded out, as we could do most anything.

One thing had been talked about somewhat, but it never had been done. That was in a memo to Doc Wiley of all the things we should be doing. There were two primary ones: pull the landing gear and to fly singly.

Remember, there was no place else to land. We'd go out 200 or 300 miles from the ship, and I might say that when you saw the ship coming back at the end of a four-hour flight, it was a damn welcome sight--to see that blob up in the sky and have a place to go to. We always went out in pairs. Well, what were we doing? We were burning all the gas the ship carried, and we were tiring our pilots going out. Really, what could the second plane do if the first one went down, anyway? It couldn't do anything except come back and say, "You have a plane down." He could do that, although we had radio. We couldn't afford to fly twin operations out there.

---

* Lieutenant (junior grade) Leroy C. Simpler, USN; Lieutenant (junior grade) Gerald L. Huff, USN.

Old Doc Wiley was for everything. He was just an old go-getter; he was great. He approved of everything I wanted. So the next time out, I had my plane up there, and I said to take the landing gear off of the thing. We'd practiced that in the hangar and could do it all right. So we did. Now I had a plane with no landing gear. I couldn't land on the beach. It would be better to land in the water anyway. After all, the wheels would probably be butchering you in the back and you'd drown. So I got hoisted out. I had an extra 30 gallons of fuel in the back. Well, that was an hour and a half of flight time, which I'd rather have than landing gear. We were so far at sea that we couldn't go back anyway. So I had the engine going, and I pulled and dropped off and she performed just like a dream. You wouldn't know the difference except for an hour and a half extra gas.

So now we had about four and a half hours of fuel, which was great. The next thing, as the problem developed that day, okay, one plane on each side of the ship, not two on each side of the ship. The planes would come back and be relieved by other pilots going out. So we did that, and a lot of it was sort of confidence in ourselves, being alone out there. It was a hell of a lonely feeling.

The first thing you know, the tactical officer on the <u>Macon</u> developed a plan. The ship would hold whatever the course was at a speed of 60. We would double the speed on a 60-degree angle and go up so that the three of us were progressing on the line at all times. We always had a straight line. Any time we wanted to go back to the ship, no matter what side you were on, you'd turn 90 degrees and hold the compass and you'd intersect. That was the theory of it, and it worked pretty well. We'd go out, and after only about four hours it was a really good feeling to see that airship up ahead when you finally came back. You could see her compass course anyway. We had about a 400-mile front there, a tremendous scouting front.

Q: Were you operating in conjunction with the fleet at that point?

Admiral Miller: Primarily we were doing this stuff all on the side.

Q: Oh, I see. It was independent of the fleet.

Admiral Miller: Yes. Now, the weaknesses they had were very apparent. The next step came from Don Mackey, who was a great guy.* The idea then was to have the ship control the airplanes, because the plane obviously couldn't have enough communications to figure out where to do this or do that. He then would direct us. If the ship was going to hold a course and we were going to just stand there, we were locked up. We just couldn't move. If the ship were to turn and go 180 degrees, we might lose her and have no idea where she was. So while theoretically it was nice to have a 400-mile front move in ahead, it failed if the ship turned at all--60 degrees, 20 degrees, or whatever it was. Because we'd be out of position, and we wouldn't know where the hell we were.

Q: That would be fatal for you too.

Admiral Miller: That's right. So then the next step in that was to have Don tell us what to do, and he would plot us all the way through relative to the airship. That began to work very well. That's really where we were headed but of course ran out of airships. We were headed for a real good scouting operation at that point and, of course, the fleet was screaming bloody murder--Admiral King and so on--"For Christ's sake, show us what you can do." Old Doc Wiley was headed right in that direction, I'll tell you.

---

* Lieutenant Donald M. Mackey, USN.

Q: But you hadn't been given that period of grace to work out your techniques before joining the fleet.

Admiral Miller: That's right, but they had great confidence in us and, we had great confidence in the ship.

About that time, we read in the paper that President Roosevelt was going to go through the Panama Canal on the USS Houston to Pearl.* He had a second cruiser with him, the New Orleans, that had all the reporters aboard. Well, from the press accounts, we knew that they were going to come close to Clipperton Island. I was a promoter type, so I got together with Doc Wiley and said, "Gee, this is our chance. Let's go out and intercept the President. We'll drop all this new stuff on him, the newspaper published the morning before, and we'll just really let the world know he met an airship around here." He thought that was great.

By this time we always operated without wheels and never thought to keep our wheels on. That was just routine stuff. So Knappy Kivette and I went out, and each of us practiced. We had a line about 200 feet long with a waterproof rubber bag on the end. This was there at Sunnyvale. We could drop it just about where we wanted it. So we shoved off the ship, and Doc did not report to anybody; we were just going to sea for local exercises. He didn't tell anybody what we were going to do. About 18 hours later, the Macon was on the line somewhere between Pearl and Clipperton, and Knappy and I were launched in our planes. The weather was pretty stinky at that point, cloudy with squalls. So we went ahead to about where we thought we might find something and sure as hell, out of that mess were two cruisers steaming along at about 15 or 18 knots. I tell you, the reporters

---

* Franklin D. Roosevelt was President of the United States from March 1933 to April 1945.

hadn't had anything to write about at all, as you can imagine. When these two little planes dove down on them from these cloudy skies, they should have shot us down. They had the President aboard.*

Q: Yes, I would think there was a danger there. Did you identify yourselves?

Admiral Miller: Their aviators knew what we were when they saw us.

Q: What was in the bag?

Admiral Miller: Well, in the bag was a San Francisco Chronicle of the day we had left; there was the latest issue of Time; and I guess the Newsweek. I knew the President was a stamp collector, so in the bag there were also about 20 letters addressed to people: one to Min Miller, one to the President, one to Eleanor, and one to Wiley.† We both shoved off, and now we were trailing this bag. We hadn't planned it very well because we planned just a light little bag. But by this time, the bag had gotten rather bulky. I had it wrapped around my hand on the throttle, trying to keep the throttle open, and the load was just about to tear me out of that airplane. It was awful.

At this time, the Macon had asked permission to drop something, so I made a pass over the Houston's forecastle and overshot. Knappy came along behind me and he overshot. Well, both cruisers stopped dead in the water and put whaleboats over the side and rescued these things. At that point, of course, the radios were going back and forth and the President said, "Well done, Macon." Oh, he gave a great big boost, which is what we were looking for.

Q: Your ship was visible too?

---

* This incident took place on 19 July 1934. For another account, see Smith's The Airships Akron and Macon, pages 128-131.
† Eleanor was President Roosevelt's wife.

Admiral Miller: She hadn't been yet, but she finally came up in another half hour. She caught up with us. We went back to the ship and got out the lines.

Within 15 minutes of our drop, the sky was filled with messages: CNO, Commander in Chief U.S. Fleet, saying, "What the hell are you doing out there? What was in the bags?"* That's what they wanted to know.

Old Doc Wiley thought, "Oh, Christ," that he was fired from the Navy now. Knappy and I went back aboard the Macon, of course, and headed back for Sunnyvale. It was not a very happy trip back. We had accomplished what we had started to do, but it wasn't really very successful after all.

Believe it or not, about ten days or two weeks later, these letters started coming back in the U.S. mail. I don't know who opened the bags; I suppose it was the captain of the ship or the exec or maybe Roosevelt. At any rate, the mail clerk of the Houston--or whoever he was--was a very ingenious young man. He cut out aluminum airship figures and pasted them on each of the letters. The President signed each of the letters, and they came back through the U.S. mail. I got Doc Wiley to sign these and I signed them, and they turned out to be quite a plus.

The follow-up of that story is that about two years ago I got a phone call from Chicago. Even ahead of that, about a year before that, an old friend of mine in New York said, "Say, you were in aviation. I saw a letter in some stamp shop in New York City that had your name on it. Could that be you?" He described it, and I said that was one of my letters. I didn't pursue it by going up there, but about a year later, I had a phone call from Chicago. It was from a lad by the name of Bill Boss, and he said, "Are you Admiral Miller? Did you fly off the Macon?" I said yes, and he asked," Could I describe an envelope to you?" It turned out it was the same letter that had been in the window in New York City. It was the same letter and he said, "Would you mind identifying it?" I went down and got mine out. So this is now listed in all of the stamp books. There are only something like 20 of them.

---

* CNO--Chief of Naval Operations.

Q: Then they're quite valuable.

Admiral Miller: We became good pen pals, and I finally said, "Would you mind telling me what you paid for this?"

He said, "No, I paid $2,400 dollars for it." I called Mrs. Kivette, since Knappy had died in the meantime, and asked if Knappy had one of those letters in his file. She looked and said yes, he had one. I told her this story. So that was something.

I was trying to explain that Doc Wiley was all for everything and had pushed this job and he had nerve and courage. He was just great.

Q: But he might have known even before he undertook this that there would be repercussions from the Navy proper.

Admiral Miller: Oh, of course. We were trying to sell the airships. Well, we went back, and then we did all kinds of experiments. We always wondered what would happen if we did have a plane down at sea. We carried aboard the airship a 4,000-foot reel of quarter-inch cable. Its function was to carry the spy basket. During World War I, the Germans eventually used spy baskets to great effect. They'd theoretically lower somebody below the cloud level, and he would tell the airship's crew where they were and how to bomb and navigate.

Q: He was an observer, then?

Admiral Miller: Yes. He was an observer and would be lowered down in this basket below the ship. As a matter of fact, it didn't work out that well. The Germans weren't very successful at it. But we had a spy basket and played around with this thing. It was a small airplane fuselage, really, with no wings. It had an empennage, and you could use a half an inch of rudder and that's all. It had kind of a tripod wire connection to the fuselage. We couldn't make a one-wire telephone system work. We wanted a telephone from the observer to the ship. They never could make it work, so we put in a little key radio set.

Jess Kenworthy, I think, made the first flight in this thing.* In early experiments, this thing was really hazardous when it started oscillating. We finally got it stabilized in some way. Jess did this first one, and I don't know whether any more lighter-than-air people did. I said I wanted to do that. Of course, it was felt that the spy basket would be heavier-than-air's job if they couldn't fly the airplane.

So I went down in this thing, and let me tell you, it was really weird. As you lowered away, of course, it would begin to trail the ship and develop a kind of a catenary back there. You'd be a quarter of a mile behind the ship and a quarter of a mile below the ship with no sound at all. Absolutely no sound. It was just quiet and you were sitting there--just you and nobody else. But you had a parachute. What the hell you'd do with a parachute, I don't know. They'd never know if you were below a cloud and they lost you. At any rate, that experiment didn't last very long either, but it was sort of interesting to try.

Q: What were you able to observe under those circumstances?

Admiral Miller: Well, theoretically you would be under the cloud, and you would spot the enemy or get the wind drift and tell them how to navigate and things like that. The whole thing was a little cockeyed.

Q: It sounds a little primitive.

Admiral Miller: The point was you had 4,000 feet of cable. Now, what were you going to do if an airplane was down in the water? So we then rigged up a circular insulated life raft with the webbing inside the safety belt. The idea then was to lower that on the water with this 4,000-foot cable, and a downed pilot would get in the raft and get hoisted aboard.

---

* Lieutenant Commander Jesse L. Kenworthy, Jr., USN, was executive officer of the Macon.

Doc Wiley would lower that thing in the San Francisco Bay, and he would tow it from this big airship and tow it down there alongside of a buoy and you could do any damn thing you wanted with this thing.

The only regret that I have in that three-year experience was that I missed out on one thing I wanted to do. We didn't quite get to it before we lost the airships. I wanted to climb into the raft and then get hoisted aboard, just to show it could be done. But that's how we were going to tow a pilot out of the drink if we lost one. Fortunately, we never had to do that.

During all this time, we practiced gunnery. We had our own heavier-than-air problems for exercises to do. We'd fly over the San Francisco Peninsula there and fire machine guns out over the Pacific. We did a lot of work on the side and kept up with all the heavier-than-air requirements.

By this time, we also had picked up a couple of XJW-1s.* That was the old commercial Waco with two seats forward and the pilot aft. It was a biplane. We put hooks on those so that now we had a taxi airplane that could carry people back and forth to the airship. When the ship would come back from an 80-hour flight or something like that, she would have burned maybe 60,000 pounds of fuel. Now you couldn't get her on the ground because she was too light. Somehow, you have to compensate for the 60,000 pounds.

The Navy did it by water recovery gear. You'll notice in the photographs, above each of the eight engines is an apparatus about six feet in width that climbs halfway up the ship. That was water recovery gear in which the exhaust gas from the engine would be allowed to filter around through there. The cool air would condense the moisture out of the gases, and that water would then run down into our ballast tanks so that we were recovering weight. Theoretically, because of the oxygen in the air, we could get back about 115 pounds of water for every hundred pounds of fuel we'd burn. You never did because

---

* The XJW-1 was equipped with a trapeze hook on top, just as the Sparrowhawk was. The Waco planes used by the <u>Macon</u> each had a wingspan of 35 feet, length of 26 feet, and maximum speed of 176 miles per hour.

they leaked and all that, but say you got 80% back. So now 80% of 60,000 pounds means you're only short about 12,000 pounds to get down to the ground.

So when the ship would get back to the area of San Francisco Bay, we would take one of the fighters and go down and maybe we had a pilot on the ground or something. We would get one of our little Wacos, and all the lighter-than-air boys who weren't able to make the flight for various reasons, we'd taxi them up and put them on the airship so they'd get flight time. The ship might be hanging around the bay there for six hours or eight hours. It would add weight to the ship and they'd get their flight time. So now you had a ship that was reasonably close to equilibrium but still light. When you finally decided to come down to the ground and everybody was ready down there, you'd make your approach into the wind and stick that nose down and with your eight engines, eight propellers, just drive her down to the ground at probably about a 45-degree angle.

The first object was to marry the cable of the airship to the cable of the ground so you had the ship's nose locked up. They pulled it down fast and got the nose in the cone there and put together the water line. The water line was running from the bow of the ship all the way back aft. Now you start pumping water fast to get the weight of the water back there. That brought the tail down, and the tail would rest on a car which was on a circular track. Here was the mast. The length of the ship was just the length of this, so now you had a big wind sock. You had the tail locked down on the railroad car and you had the nose locked up. Now your ship was just free to swing and, depending on how much wind you had, you swung her so that she was parallel to the hangar, and then you started just pulling her into the hangar. Then she was put to bed. You didn't have many places in the world where you could do that.

Q: No, it's a very complicated procedure.

Admiral Miller: The idea of all that mechanism was to eliminate manpower. In the old days, you had to mule-haul every one of them. Of course, you had that sad case, you remember, in San Diego when the <u>Akron</u> was in there and they did have a mast, but three of the kids didn't get the word to let go in time and the first thing you know, they were 100 feet in the air. They finally pulled one of them aboard, and I think two of them fell to their deaths.* So everything was mechanized where it could be.

We then had these two taxi ships, and we'd do all sorts of things. For instance, if the ship was going to go to Miami to work with the fleet in the Caribbean, we'd all fly independently. There were four of us now. I'd usually go by way of Iowa to visit my grandmother, and somebody was heading someplace in Tennessee he wanted to visit. We'd all leave together and arrive at the same time someplace, all travelling four different routes. We were very independent, and really it was a great duty. Doc Wiley had a great confidence in us to do most anything. As I say, no one would believe that the exercise of landing aboard was so simple.

Q: And now we're coming to that fateful day, February 12, 1935.†

Admiral Miller: This was the challenge for Doc Wiley and the Macon: to go out and show the fleet what we could do. The fleet exercises were rather extensive. They were all up and down the West Coast. We had four pilots aboard: Knappy Kivette, Simpler, Huff, and myself. By then we had reached the point--as I said, with wheels off and extra gas--where we could go out for four and a half hours. We were in pretty good shape. The Macon first went around the fleet, around the islands off of Santa Barbara. I recall we went in back of the fleet, and our airplanes moved forward and made the contact that we needed to make. As a matter of fact, the ship received excellent comments from the fleet. The job we had been doing just looked like things were going to come to fruition here--Doc Wiley's hard work and the planes' progress. Things were going along very well.

---

* This incident occurred 11 May 1932 at Camp Kearny, California. For a description and photo of the one surviving line handler, see Richard K. Smith, The Airships Akron & Macon, page 57.

† The loss of the Macon is also described in Richard K. Smith, The Airships Akron & Macon, pages 151-162. A written account by Miller appears as an appendix at the back of this volume of transcript.

I think on the second day we moved forward, and by this time, we found everything we were looking for in the enemy fleet, except for a cruiser. The Macon by now was somewhere off of San Luis Obispo. It was the cruisers we wanted, so Gerry Huff and I launched and started out trying to find them. We did find them, way up towards Monterey and well offshore. When we reported them, we were out about two and a half hours, I would say. At that time we received word that the war was over, the exercises were over. We turned the ship for everybody to go home. I wasn't with Gerry now; I was alone. Gerry was also off by himself. We both returned to the ship. I met Gerry there outside the airship, and he went aboard and I went aboard. It was a very lonely feeling being outside the ship in an airplane with no place to go if you had any problems. So I made it a point to always be the last aboard and get my guys on. So I went aboard. It was the last landing ever made on the airship; little did I know at that time.

I reported to the officer of the deck, who was George Campbell, and to Captain Wiley that there was quite a tough weather front up ahead.* It was somewhere up in the vicinity of Monterey and Carmel. But we had gone through tougher ones down in the Caribbean than this one. Well, we kept on going north, and everyone was getting ready. We'd be back in Sunnyvale in another eight hours. Finally, as we were coming up to Point Sur, we were in this weather, and suddenly the ship just sort of went through some maneuvers. The nose kicked and pulled over to the right, and it went up and it went down and so on and on and on.

Q: Were there thunderstorms?

Admiral Miller: Well, I don't know if there was any thunder or lightning connected to it or not, but there were violent air currents. To you and me, it would just mean a real cloudy turbulence. I was in the control car, I remember. After all, the heavier-than-air people had nothing to do after flying except to sit there and play acey-deucy or read a book. It was

---

* Lieutnant (junior grade) George W. Campbell, USN. Lieutenant Campbell published an account of the crash in the 15 May 1937 issue of The Saturday Evening Post.

obvious in a very short time that we had a real problem on our hands. The word then came back that the ship was beginning to break up back aft, that some of the girders had carried away. Also, an effort was made to lighten the ship because we were flying heavy at that particular time. We had to get some weight off the ship, so they dropped a lot of ballast.

By this time, it was obvious that things were really not going right. The first thing you knew, we were up around 5,000 feet instead of around 1,800 feet where we had been, or perhaps even lower. We simply went up like a free balloon at this point, and the nose of the ship was up. An effort was made to get the engine started, but we couldn't. With the angle of the ship, the fuel wasn't getting into the carburetor, so until we could get the bow down, we couldn't get the engines started. Then they called for all hands together in the nose, way up there in the cone to try to get some weight up there. Finally that was done, the nose came down, and a couple of engines got started. By this time it was obvious that the disintegration was taking place back in the tail. As one ring would collapse, the broken aluminum parts would make holes in the next bag and we'd lose all that lift. So the ship was getting awfully heavy back in the tail, and the nose was still trying to get light.

By this time it was obvious the crew wasn't going to save the ship. They simply couldn't fly the ship. The only thing to do was get down in the water. The concern was that maybe we were drifting back in over the mountains behind Point Sur. With a couple of engines going, we got the ship headed back to sea and began to let down by valving. Of course, probably we were heavy at that time anyway. We started down, and then the point was whether we would come down over land or water. Well, it turned out to be over water and about 12 or 15 miles off of Point Sur. I think at about 500 feet we could begin to see the water and realize we were coming down. We landed on the water in a horizontal position, just as gently and as softly as you please. By that time, people had broken out life rafts and dropped lines from the ship and so on. The order was given, of course, to abandon ship. Those with any sense lowered themselves into the life rafts and some didn't even get wet.

Q: How large a crew was there?

Admiral Miller: We had about 82 aboard. Out of that we lost two men, as opposed to the Akron, which saved three men and lost 73.* We were just the reverse of that. Some of us stayed aboard. I was among those, and I thought, "My God, this ship is afloat. This ship will never sink. We'll just sit this out until the fleet shows up. We won't even get wet." Well, at this point those people in the boats pulled away from the ship. Incidentally, it must have been around 4:00 o'clock, and this was February and the days were short. It was cold and beginning to rain. It was not a very encouraging picture at all.

Those in boats pulled off a quarter of a mile or half a mile away and huddled in a group out there. Here we were high and dry on the ship, thinking how stupid they were. Then, the first thing we knew, instead of being horizontal in the water, the ship suddenly assumed a very slow upward movement to a vertical position. Instead of being 50 feet from the water, we were 400 feet up in the air. We were sitting there on top of a cone in this beautiful airship, the lower part of it being in the water. That didn't look as good as it did a few moments before.

By this time, those of us in the ship had gathered in the bow and were all up there around the nose cone. You heard this rumble and you didn't know what it was. Finally there was a whoosh of some currents of air or gases or something coming up from the ship, escaping through the top of it. I had always heard that helium had the unique characteristic of making your vocal cords inactive. In other words, you lose your voice if you were surrounded by helium.

Q: If you inhaled it.

Admiral Miller: I think that is true because I practically lost my voice at that time. I realized what was happening; the gas cells were breaking down below, and here was a natural cone bringing the gas up to us. I said to come on and get outside. We all scrambled out and broke out all the lines and we had a maypole up there. Everybody outside the ship

---

* One of the three survivors from the Akron was Wiley, who also survived the loss of the Macon.

was each hanging on to a line. Of course, the ship was so big that it was still practically like a haystack up there. It wasn't sharp, and you weren't in a danger of slipping off or anything. It was raining, it was cold, and we'd hear another blast and the ship would settle deeper and deeper. Every time we heard a blast, we knew another cell had carried away, another ring. Now it was getting dark; it was about 5:00 o'clock. We knew we had gotten out an SOS to the fleet, but nothing had happened as yet.

About this time, we were now down to the size of a two-story house. I guess I was probably the senior one there and said, "Well, boys, the time has come. We have to get out of here." Most of us had on a life jacket of sorts on. I think two or three didn't have any at all. So we said, "Let's get in the water and get out of here before this whole thing goes down." So we started letting go of the line and sliding over the haystack into the water, and it was cold as hell. You didn't know quite what to do. I took off my shoes and threw them away. To get rid of weight, I attempted to get my class ring off and throw it away. All kinds of silly ideas come to your mind.

Just about the time we were going in the water, there were searchlights way in the distance. The cruisers were looking for us. We turned around and there was one little bluejacket still on this haystack. He didn't want to come in the water at all, and we shouted and screamed. Finally, he let go and got in the water. He no more had gotten in there than we pulled him up; we were all swimming by this time. We had to swim over to the boats. Obviously the navigation flares ignited the gasoline that had also blown up inside this envelope. On the outside was the red, white, and blue Navy star and inside was a flame. The silhouette of the star was the most beautiful sight I had ever seen, if you're looking for beauty. She finally just sort of, like an old dog, lay down. Away she went and disappeared. It was quite fortunate that we got off of there before this happened.

Q: Before this fire broke out.

Harold B. Miller #2 - 89

Admiral Miller: In effect, you can say she burned at the end. Well, we finally worked our way over to the boats, and people would hold on. Actually, you were warmer in the water than you were in the air. Oh, it was terrible. We were there for 45 minutes or an hour.

Q: In the boat?

Admiral Miller: Some in the boat, but we were mostly in the water. Everybody had something to cling to. Then in the darkness the motor launches began to show up.

I'll never forget, a classmate of mine had the boat that I got into and was passing around a bottle and saying, "Be careful now; that's just alcohol." Well, everybody was swigging this stuff. I never had teeth chatter so much in my life. You'd just simply think they'd shake apart.

We got over to three of the cruisers, the 10,000-tonners. I think it was the Richmond that picked me up. They wouldn't let you aboard until you had given your service number and name and everything else. Then they rushed you down to sick bay and looked you over and turned you in with blankets. The first thing you knew, you were warm. We ended up in San Francisco the next morning, so it worked out quite well.

I guess it was just another point about airships that was too much; an airplane could have gotten through, but not an airship. There had been plans for a big airship, a ten-million-cubic-foot ship to carry 18 airplanes--not hangared in the airship but slung underneath on a rail. All sorts of plans had been developed. At this particular time, I was no longer a convert. I realized that the disadvantages of the lighter-than-air were too great.

Q: I suppose at that point the Navy as a whole was no longer converted to the idea.

Admiral Miller: I think even the lighter-than-air people began to think so. It was the PBY which also helped kill the airship.* For the price of four million dollars for each of those

---

* The PBY Catalina was a twin-engine flying boat that performed extensive service before and during World War II. Built by Consolidated, it first entered fleet squadrons in 1936.

airships (of course, God knows it would be a billion dollars today), you could get 12 PBYs. You put them on a search, and they could cover twice as much as the airship could, get back, and not be shot down. I think what the Navy proved was that the airships weren't here to stay.

But several things happened. For example, if it hadn't been for our building the Shenandoah there at the Navy yard in Philadelphia, we would have been even more laggard in developing aluminum durel and so on. It was that ship that caused the American Aluminum Company to get going on that stuff. The engines that were being built for the new ships were going to be the engine that turned out in World War II to be the engine they put in the Mustang, the P-51.*

Q: So something was salvaged.

Admiral Miller: I argue that the development of any of the duralumins of this engine, and the fact that they were so good, made it worthwhile probably. I read all this news today about this great airlift and they're going to fly a hundred tons of cargo and it'll stand still while they load it and unload it. They don't understand. The first time they unload it, the airship is going to pop up higher. They just don't understand anything about airships.

Q: They did use them somewhat off the Florida coast, didn't they, during World War II to spot submarines?

Admiral Miller: We were just down there at Glynnco, the station at Brunswick. We had about 400 of them during the war.

Q: Small type blimps?

The PBY-2 model had a wing span of 104 feet, length of 65 feet, gross eight of 28,400 pounds, and top speed of 178 miles per hour. Cruising speed was 103 mph.
* The P-51 was an Army Air Forces fighter plane.

Admiral Miller: Yes. The skippers of the ships felt so secure to see these blimps going around. Hell, they couldn't have protected them from anything. The only time there was a contact with the enemy was down in the Caribbean, when this blimp caught a U-boat on the surface. The crew was out sunning themselves, getting a sun bath, and the blimp went charging over there and failed to drop the depth charge they had. They couldn't shake it loose. About 200 yards beyond there, the submarine shot the blimp down with a machine gun. That's the only contact they had. Today they would have helicopters out. They also used them across the Strait of Gibraltar, where they had a submarine wanting to get into the Mediterranean.

Q: In World War II?

Admiral Miller: Yes. They served a purpose, but it was a negative purpose. They couldn't have done anything. I think their day is over. Incidentally, one other thing is that they have used blimps for timbering out in Washington state, hoisting big logs out. Hell, that's work for the helicopters. Just the other day in Florida, you see helicopters setting those big long concrete telephone poles. That's the answer to these things now. I'm afraid it's over and it's a shame.*

Q: It was a colorful episode, anyway, wasn't it?

Admiral Miller: Yes.

Q: Well, you got something out of it yourself, personally.

---

* The one surviving F9C-2 Sparrowhawk aircraft was displayed at the Smithsonian Institution in the 1950s, then put into storage. From 1971 to 1974 it was meticulously restored by volunteers. As of 1995 it is exhibited at the National Museum of Naval Aviation in Pensacola. The story of the restoration is told in Robert C. Mikesh, "That Great Hookup in the Sky," Wings Magazine, February 1975, pages 16-29.

Admiral Miller: Yes.

Q: Then you were ordered to the naval air station in Sunnyvale, which was your headquarters.

Admiral Miller: Well, I was living in Palo Alto. The reason for that was I asked for an extension there because there was a lad by the name of Fisher, a German engineer of radio. He had been the one we were working with to develop radio direction finders built within the airplanes themselves that we could use to get back to the ship. He and I did a great deal of work on that. As a matter of fact, we got a patent for this thing.* We continued working for three or four months to try to get that thing further along, at which time I got orders to a cruiser.

Q: Did that direction finder work out then? Was it used in World War II?

Admiral Miller: I don't know what really happened to the thing. I just don't know. It would have been particularly useful from the airship point of view.

Q: Then you went to the Northampton.

Admiral Miller: Yes, the Northampton, a cruiser. That was a delightful experience, catapulting off of there. We had four airplanes, of course. My first skipper was Captain Tommy Symington from Baltimore. He was a wonderful old sea dog. He was absolutely great. We had fine experiences on there. We never had any troubles.

Q: Were you integrated into the officer contingent?

---

* The patent for a "Radio Receiver and Direction Finder" was granted to Dr. Gerhard Fisher and Lieutenant Commander H. B. Miller.

Admiral Miller: Oh, yes.

Q: Did you stand watch?

Admiral Miller: Yes, I was a watch stander. I think we discussed earlier that that was one of the problems of World War I aviators. They couldn't or wouldn't stand watches.

Q: So you didn't stay on the Northampton very long?

Admiral Miller: No, the Northampton was the flag.

There was one episode that was interesting on the Northampton. You asked did I stand watch. Yes, I stood watch constantly. The way it worked out, I was just a naval officer who flew.

I remember once we were coming out of Puget Sound, and as we rounded the final cape there, we ran into all these commercial fishermen. There were hundreds of fishing boats out there. We had three cruisers, and we were steaming around 25 knots. The flag bridge was above the ship's bridge, and we were headed right for the middle of all these boats. I was waiting for the flag to tell us to slow down or move out or do something.

Q: It would be a slaughter.

Admiral Miller: Yes, and nothing came down. The flag watch officer was up there, and I finally called up, "For God's sake, what are you going to do?" I guess he must have had a mental block or something, and so I finally said, "Well, to hell with that," and I hoisted the signal. We turned around something like 50 or 60 degrees to avoid these boats. I waited to be told about that, but nobody said a word.

Q: No reprimands?

Harold B. Miller #2 - 94

Admiral Miller: No reprimand on that one. Oh, that cruiser really was great.

Q: And what was the Salt Lake City like?

Admiral Miller: Oh, she was a fine ship. The reason why they shipped us all to the Salt Lake City was that the flag was on the Northampton. They wanted to get more senior aviators on these other ships, so the flag could handle a junior one.

The skipper was Captain Coffman, and he was a true gentleman if ever.* We got along well, even when one of the airplanes caught on fire on the catapult as the result of a stack fire. Stack embers came down, and there was nothing we could do about it.†

Q: Was that a common occurrence in those days?

Admiral Miller: No, it wasn't very common. It's the only one I'm aware of, as a matter of fact. But it sure made a mess out of the deck.

Q: I guess it did.

Admiral Miller: About that time, I was getting a little anxious. I had never had big boats, flying boats. So I put in for big boats, and I was ordered to Patrol Squadron 16, which was up in the naval air station in Seattle, on Lake Washington. I had done a lot of time around Seattle, because I had taken delivery on a lot of Boeing fighters when I was in Fighting Squadron Two down in San Diego on the Langley.

I loved that area, and so this was just great, except they had the old PM-1, the poor old twin-engine Martin airplanes. They were all right, but PBYs were beginning to

---

* Captain Richard B. Coffman, USN.
† On page 34 Admiral Miller indicates this fire took place on board the cruiser Northampton (CA-26). His memory was apparently uncertain concerning which ship.

appear about this time. The skipper was Carleton Champion, who had the world's record altitude at one time in Anacostia.* He was quite a gentleman. His wife had been the daughter of an admiral. He pretty much let you do your own business. Curtis Smiley was the exec.† I was number three in the squadron. Our job was to put the air station in Sitka in commission. This was about 1937.‡ You could see the handwriting on the wall, what was going to happen.

Q: Were we setting up a station there on Sitka?

Admiral Miller: Yes, in an old Navy coaling station on a little island just adjacent to Sitka. We'd go up there and spend three months of time, come back, go back for three months. It was just heavenly; the fishing was great, the adventure and sheer beauty were just great, and snow and ice didn't bother us at all. It was marvelous.

Q: Did it bother the planes, however?

Admiral Miller: No, as a matter of fact, with Champ in there we didn't do much flying anyway. For example, we would be in Seattle and plan that tomorrow we'd go back to Sitka. Tomorrow would come, and the weather would be a little bad and so we'd say, "We'll go tomorrow." At one time we sat there for three weeks, and every day we were going to go.

Q: He was very cautious.

---

* Lieutenant Commander Carleton C. Champion, Jr., USN. In July 1927, as a lieutenant, Champion set records for both seaplanes (37,995 feet) and land planes (38,419 feet).
† Lieutenant Curtis S. Smiley, USN.
‡ The station at Sitka, Alaska, was designated as an advance naval seaplane base in 1937 and a fleet air base in early 1938.

Admiral Miller: Yes, very cautious. He also didn't mind an afternoon cocktail. He was a very fine gentleman, but he was not a driver or pusher. At any rate, we got up there and really had a lot of fun. We did a lot of pistol shooting. I did a lot of flying up there on my own. I'd just go up and take an airplane. I got to know the federal marshal, Dan Ficken, and we would take a plane someplace and go fishing. It was a ball. You'd begin to think that my life was nothing but fun expeditions. Maybe that's right, too, because wherever I went it was fun.

Q: What kind of duties did you have in connection with establishing the base?

Admiral Miller: We did a lot of carpentry work, building ramps for the seaplanes and big boats. We made a base there that we could live with. We had a tender, probably the Gannett. I would say we developed the base, and it worked out very well.

Q: How many planes would it accommodate?

Admiral Miller: We only had a six-plane squadron. We were down to practically nothing, but later on, the PBYs worked out of there. At that point, I wrote to my old friend Raddy, who was a detail officer in the bureau; we had been friends for years.* He had a lot of Alaska duty and knew about it. I guess I was a lieutenant then, and I said, "Raddy, would you mind sending me to some squadron? I don't care where. I want to go where I can be number two and when the skipper leaves, I can get the squadron."

Well, gee whiz, I had no more than written to him than he came right back and said, "You're ordered to Patrol Squadron 33, Canal Zone, Panama."

---

* Commander Arthur W. Radford, USN.

I thought, "Oh, my God, what is this?"

Q: One extreme of weather to another.

Admiral Miller: Well, I'll tell you, when I left Sitka, I literally wept. Oh, the fishing and the fun and the frontiersmen and all that up there were just so great. Then we flew our planes down to San Diego, and I was detached. They turned the PMs in and drew out PBYs.

Patrol Squadron 33 was in Diego at that time. They were also turning in their planes and were drawing out new PBYs. So I moved into a squadron with 12 PBYs. We allegedly flew nonstop down to Panama. Actually, we got broken up and were all over the sky and ended up on Fonseca in Nicaragua, where we had a tender.* We ran into a hell of a front there, and we were spread out all over the sky.

I had been in Panama about two days, and I thought, "Where have you been all of your life? This is the greatest." Wherever I go, it doesn't make any difference; the next place is the greatest, wherever it was.

Q: You were adaptable.

Admiral Miller: It was just wonderful down there.

Q: Good fishing down there too?

Admiral Miller: Good fishing down there. I got the squadron as a lieutenant. See, that's why I say the Navy's been so good to me. I took my exams for promotion. I took them there, and my half stripe came through. I had the best squadron in the world. I'd go out

---

* The Gulf of Fonseca is a large inlet of the Pacific Ocean, located near Nicaragua and El Salvador.

and see all my enlisted families in Panama and try to take care of them. It was a miserable duty for a lot of them where they could live. It was great for the officers living on Coco Solo.

Our bombing was superlative, and I'd always do the unusual. Instead of going out and just flying, we'd fly to Cocos Island and all over the place. We'd go to the San Blas Islands, and we'd see the whole area. We flew at night half the time.

There were three squadrons down there. The other two squadron commanders, one was class of '23, one was class of '22. When I got it at '24, this runt, they had a little meeting and said, "Now, we'll all kind of play this thing out on a smooth level. Nobody is going to get out of line or anything like that," one of those kind of talks. But it didn't work, because we were out there flying at night and flying every place constantly.

Q: Rocking the boat, so to speak.

Admiral Miller: Rocking the boat. It turned out that when they wanted somebody to do something, old 33 got the job. Admiral Cook came down and he had all the big boats in the Navy, ComAirScoFor.* My squadron got the job of flying around the Caribbean. It didn't set too well at times.

Then when the neutrality patrol came along, who got it?† VP-33 got it because they were ready to go.

Q: This was in 1940?

---

* Rear Admiral Arthur B. Cook, USN, Commander Aircraft Scouting Force.
† In the period from 1939 to 1941--when the United States was not yet an active combatant in World War II--the American republics maintained what was called a Neutrality Patrol of a zone in the western Atlantic. Ostensibly neutral, it in fact aided Britain in its war against Germany.

Admiral Miller: The fall of 1940, I should think. We went up one time without knowing what the hell to do. It's the only time I've ever received sealed orders to open in the air. It was sort of a farce, because where could you go but Guantanamo? There was no place you could go. So at any rate, we went up there and set up, not knowing what to do. You may recall that President Roosevelt in those days issued his orders, but there were no details. Nobody knew what the hell neutrality patrol was. If you see a German, do you sink him? Do you trail him? What do you do with him? I tried and tried to find out and nobody told me, so I said to hell with it and carried bombs and machine guns in all of my airplanes. As far as I was concerned, if I saw one I was going to go ahead and bomb it. I knew that was the intent. It wasn't the way it was written, but I was certain that was the intent.

We got into all kinds of things. The Navy had things like so many hours carburetor time and you had to change the carburetors or some such thing. We were running over. I reached the point where I was just sending dispatches to the bureau that I needed another 100 hours or something like that. That kind of stuff worked in the Navy. If somebody was going to do something, go do it and get it done. Boy, all they do is say great, great.

Q: Except some of your colleagues may have thought that it was assuming too much?

Admiral Miller: I think that probably was so. I had planes up at Key West and all over the place. One day I decided I hadn't been at Pensacola for a long time, so maybe I ought to go inspect Key West and keep on going to Pensacola. These are some of the things we did. We flew down to San Blas Islands and came back with bushel baskets full of avocados and pears at a dollar a basket and things like that. I just loved Panama; it was marvelous.

Q: Your pilots must have liked that too.

Harold B. Miller #2 - 100

Admiral Miller: Oh, they loved it, every one of them. I gave them responsibility. They'd go off and do these things.

Then the final touch was that we won the Schiff Trophy for the most flying hours from a safety point of view, no forced landings or other mishaps.*

Q: Who awarded that?

Admiral Miller: President Roosevelt himself. I went to Washington, and the ceremony was in the Oval Office. Jack Towers, Frank Knox, Admiral Nimitz, Admiral Stark, and all these people that I had come to know well were there.† It couldn't have been a better situation.

Q: It was a good platform, wasn't it?

Admiral Miller: We did pretty well at Panama. We got the trophy. I think we were number two in bombing.

Q: And the Schiff Trophy was given for a maximum flying time with minimum accident rate.

Admiral Miller: Yes. They sent the original trophy to the museum down there at the Naval Academy. I've got a miniature. It was a funny coincidence that I had done a lot of work with Admiral Jack Towers beforehand, including the Navy Wings book. That was a

---

* The Herbert Schiff Memorial Trophy for U.S. Naval Aviation was donated in 1925 by William Schiff, in honor of his brother, a Naval Reserve officer who was killed in an aircraft accident.
† Rear Admiral John H. Towers, USN, was Chief of the Bureau of Aeronautics; Frank Knox was Secretary of the Navy; Rear Admiral Chester W. Nimitz, USN, was Chief of the Bureau of Navigation; and Admiral Harold R. Stark, USN, was Chief of Naval Operations.

Towers project and later on, when I went over to London, of course, I was working for Stark. Everything is a coincidence with me.

Q: So all that was background as you saw them in the President's Oval Office?

Admiral Miller: Yes. It's simply amazing how this coincidence seems to work out.

After Panama, my flying days were really over. I was ordered to be flag secretary on the staff of Admiral Bristol.*

Q: That was in June of 1940.

Admiral Miller: I hauled out fast to San Diego and got aboard the USS Yorktown. We went tearing out to Lahaina Roads and went aboard the USS Saratoga.† There I joined Admiral Bristol, whom I had never met. I no sooner got aboard with my suitcases, they pulled up the anchor and headed for San Diego. That was my round trip on that.

We had no more than gotten to San Diego and were there for about two months when he got orders that detached him from Carrier Division One to ComAirScoFor, which was all the big boats. That was great. I had just come from big boats. He wanted to look over this big Boeing 314; that was a great big flying boat with the stub wings that Pan Am was buying.‡ So we flew up to Seattle, and by this time he and I were hitting it off fairly well.

While we were in Seattle, he got a phone call from somebody in Washington that said, "Come back here to Washington fast." Now we're in 1941, I guess. I thought, "Oh, boy, he's going to get orders." From the conversation we had, I thought he was going to

---

* Rear Admiral Arthur L. Bristol, Jr., USN, Commander Carrier Division One.
† Lahaina Roads was an important U.S. Fleet anchorage off the island of Maui, Hawaii, in the years before World War II.
‡ Pan Am--Pan American, a prominent commerical airline of the era.

England. He had been in Washington about 24 hours when he picked up the phone and called me in Seattle. He said, "Do you want to come with me?"

Assuming he was going to go to London, I said, "You bet I do."

He said, "Fine, you'll hear from me right away."

Well, by the time I had gotten back to San Diego, I got another call from him saying, "Come on back to Norfolk." What had happened was that he became Commander Support Force. You may recall that that was the outfit that was operating the North Atlantic convoys there in the early days before the war--when the neutrality patrol entered the picture--and then, of course, after the war started.

Out of all of that, we ended up with 12 squadrons of aircraft, based primarily in Argentia and Iceland, and had about 100 destroyers. We had a good many of the Coast Guard ships, cutters. We had British destroyers and some Canadian destroyers. Eventually, we ended up in Argentia ourselves. Our flagship was the Prairie, and we worked out of there. Bristol then had gathered a staff; he had Louis Denfeld, Mick Carney, Slim Ingersoll, Slim Wooldridge.* Everybody he had there made admiral so fast it wasn't even funny.† It was just hand-picked. He was working for Admiral King, really.‡

Q: King had the Atlantic Fleet, didn't he?

Admiral Miller: Yes, as the war opened. So the war caught us in Argentia. Shortly after

---

* Captain Louis E. Denfeld, USN; Commander Robert B. Carney, USN; Lieutenant Commander Stuart H. Ingersoll, USN; Commander Edmund T. Wooldridge, USN.
† Denfeld and Carney later held the post of Chief of Naval Operations; Ingersoll became a vice admiral; Wooldridge became a four-star admiral.
‡ On 17 December 1940 Rear Admiral Ernest J. King, USN, became Commander Patrol Force U.S. Fleet in the Atlantic. On 1 February 1941, the billet was upgraded to Commander in Chief Atlantic Fleet with the rank of full admiral. King held the post until he was transferred in December 1941 to Washington to serve as Commander in Chief U.S. Fleet.

Harold B. Miller #2 - 103

that, Raddy then grabbed me.* Raddy sent for me, and I was ordered now to the Bureau of Aeronautics. They started a thing called Training Literature. I went to Raddy and said, "What is Training Literature?"

He said, "I'll be damned if I know, but there's a desk in the corner. You're in Training Literature." Well, out of that came the finest collection of talent you ever saw in your life. It became my fate now to work with reserves, and I never saw one problem between reserves and the regular Navy.

Q: This was under the duress of war in the first place.

Admiral Miller: Yes. I was trying to figure out what we were going to do. I ended up with writers. York Bradford would be an example. I had Bob Taylor and every magazine writer you ever heard of. I ended up with Edward Steichen as my chief photographer.† We had every photographer from Life magazine and Bristol, Jacobs, Jorgensen.‡ We had them all.

Q: And your objective was to turn out what?

Admiral Miller: First of all, we were fighting Navy regulations. They were battleship boys and couldn't care less about aviation. So we decided that we'd do PR for naval aviation.

---

* Radford, by this time a captain, was serving as director of training in the Bureau of Aeronautics.
† Steichen had been a colonel in the Army during World War I, also doing photographic work. When the Army rejected him in 1941, he contacted the Navy and was warmly welcomed by Captain Radford into Aviation Training. Steichen's naval aviation photographic unit remained a part of Training Literature throughout the war. See Christopher Phillips, Steichen at War (New York: Portland House, 1987).
‡ Lieutenant Commander Horace Bristol, USNR, and Lieutenant Commander Charles Fenno Jacobs, USNR, of Life and Fortune; Lieutenant Victor Jorgensen, USNR, the Portland Oregonian.

Lovette was another one; he was on the battleship side of the fence.* We had some real warm situations going on.

For example, for <u>Prop Aviation</u>, we'd write the whole issue, color photographs and every bit of script. We'd turn out the whole copy. If that wasn't aviation propaganda, I've never seen it.

Q: So then who printed this--government printing?

Admiral Miller: This was a magazine. It was one of their regular issues, but it was written by Training Literature.

Everything came along. We were trying out these "Sense" pamphlets, if you've heard about those.† About flathead sense, shark sense, everything. We used to think that only a college graduate could have enough sense to fly. We sure found out later on that if you could get a guy from behind the soda fountain to come in and fly, he'd do all right, too, except maybe he couldn't read quite as well.

So we produced a series of pamphlets about safety, illustrated with cartoons and written in words of one syllable. They were written to be funny, not so serious that it would scare the hell out of you. There were about 40 of them, and I've got them around the house here.

Steichen would do posters from enlarged photographs. There wasn't a naval air station in the world that didn't have a Steichen blow-up. They'd be nearly as big as this plaque here. One I remember distinctly showed a naval aviator standing on the wing of his airplane in heroic proportions, heroic stance and everything else. Or fighting stuff or

---

* Captain Leland P. Lovette, USN, assigned to the office of the Secretary of the Navy, was in charge of Navy public relations.
† "Sense" was the name of the series, which covered a variety of topics. For an article on the subject, see <u>Naval Aviation News</u>, September 1954, pages 19-21.

aircraft and things like that. Wherever you went, you were faced with naval aviation, naval aviation, naval aviation.

I went down to talk to Joy Hancock.* Of course there was a lighter-than-air angle there; I had known Joy for years.† I used to send material in to her newsletter and things like that. I went down at Raddy's instigation; she and Raddy were very close. Raddy's instructions were that the newsletter really should be a little bit more than that now. By that time, Joy was away or shortly thereafter. So she very gladly turned over the newsletter to Training Literature. That is Naval Aviation News today. We started that from mimeographed newsletters. I still have letters from that gang all the time.

Q: How did you evolve all these different ideas?

Admiral Miller: Listening to reserves, and I'm sort of the promoter type anyway.

Q: Did you have a lot of bull sessions or what, with all these talented writers?

Admiral Miller: They would have their own bull session and come up with an idea. The problem was to keep them busy because sweet old Roark Bradford, hell, he got them over in a corner and started telling them stories about Br'er Rabbit down in Louisiana. The problem was to get them to write because they were so busy listening to this storyteller.

Out of this came this marvelous material. The other thing, our relations were excellent. I'd give them a job to do, and I wouldn't be looking over their shoulder. I'd go out to do some flying and say to Bob Osborn, "Bob, don't you want to take a little flight

---

* Lieutenant Joy Bright Hancock, USNR, was one of the early women officers serving with the Navy in World War II. Her oral history is in the Naval Institute collection. Her memoir is the book Lady in the Navy (Annapolis: Naval Institute Press, 1972).
† Lieutenant Hancock was the widow of Lieutenant Lewis Hancock, Jr., USN, who was killed in the crash of the airship Shenandoah (ZR-1) in 1925.

today?"* I'd put him in the rear seat, and we'd go to Atlanta and back for lunch--things like that.

Q: What kind of feeling did you have from Radford and people like that?

Admiral Miller: Radford said, "Keep it up." Artie Doyle was kind of number two in there.† Artie was the one who conceived Dilbert, really. You know Bob Osborn's cartoons?

Q: Oh, yes.

Admiral Miller: We got Bob Osborn in there, and he was doing all these cartoons. We had a whole series of cartoons on Dilbert.‡ They have become collector's pieces now. We had so many balls in the air out there, all promoting naval aviation.

Q: And how did you work with Tom Hamilton?§

Admiral Miller: Well, Tom was on the physical side of the training program, the V-5s.** He was out recruiting and getting all these coaches and famous people. He would plant these people all over the place. He built up a wonderful organization in places where all of

---

* Lieutenant Robert Osborn, USNR.
† Commander Austin K. Doyle, USN.
‡ Osborn's whimsical drawings, which he continued to do for many years afterward for Naval Aviation News, centered on an accident-prone character named Dilbert. The idea was to promote safety by illustrating what not to do. For more on Osborn, see Naval Aviation News, June 1974, January 1983, and March-April 1995. Also "Naval Aviation's 'Gramps,'" Proceedings, September 1991, pages 109-111.
§ Commander Thomas J. Hamilton, USN, whose oral history is in the Naval Institute collection.
** V-5 was a naval aviation cadet program that procured and trained officer pilots. At the end of the six-stage program, individuals were commissioned as Naval Reserve ensigns or Marine Corps Reserve second lieutenants.

these young cadets would be, like the four schools at Iowa, at Georgia, at St. Mary's in California and so on.

Then we had Luis de Florez, of course.* He was doing all the work on the synthetic trainers.† Hell, these guys could shoot down a German or a Jap on a screen without any trouble at all. He was wonderful. Oh, what a marvelous man Luis de Florez was. He was everything. He would go around to manufacturers who were sending out synthetic trainers to the fleet and would say, "Stop packing them in all that manila paper and burlap and stuff. Pack them with funny papers." He'd get them to run millions of copies of comics and use it as packing, because the kids out in the fleet would go crazy over these comics. Little things like that. It was morale, it was imagination, it was everything.

I'll tell you that training complex was the greatest sort of an outfit you ever saw.

Q: And it all began with one desk over in the corner.

Admiral Miller: Luis and Tom, of course, were just part of the whole training group. Training Literature started with a desk in the corner. We didn't know what the hell we were. But there were people like Raddy and Artie Doyle, and you got all these widespread thinking guys and reserves in there to think for you, too, and then produce. It was wonderful. That's why it was a very interesting thing.

Sam Meek was a senior vice president of J. Walter Thompson and Raddy and Sam Meek knew each other from someplace--I don't know where.‡ Meek was a great World War I Marine, and he was a great advocate of naval aviation through Raddy. So I met him. I met all these people through Raddy.

---

* Commander Luis de Florez, USNR, was an engineer and inventor who did much to advance naval aviation. For examples of his work see Theodore Taylor, The Magnificent Mitscher (Annapolis: Naval Institute Press, 1991).
† These trainers are now generally referred to as simulators.
‡ J. Walter Thompson was the name of a prominent advertising agency.

Many of these people later joined the Time-Life organization. One of our other publications was the identification journal.* What do German tanks look like now? What are the Jap airplanes doing? We started this journal.

Q: You were in competition with Jane's, weren't you?†

Admiral Miller: We were ahead of them, that was all. We were running over three million copies of that thing. Every two months there would be a fresh one out with all the latest information sent all over the world, to all the services--the Army, Navy, Air Force. That was one of our angles. Anything that had a lot of fun in it and ingenuity was what we were doing.

I assume the relationship with Time-Life was a patriotic thing. For example, the chairman of the board who just retired was a youngster there, and we worked all this stuff out.‡ Steichen was a Time-Life man, and he brought all the photographers in. The writers we just sort of got. They'd come in and apply, so to speak, and we got them that way. The word got around.

Q: And were they in uniform then?

Admiral Miller: No, they'd be in civilian clothes. Some would be in uniform. The word got around that this was a fun place where you do things. We had all the Navy artists too.

Q: Combat art.

---

* In size and design the recognition journal was very similar to the Life magazines of the period.
† The warship compendium Jane's Fighting Ships has been published since 1898.
‡ Hedley W. Donovan, who served as editorial director for Time-Life until becoming an adviser to President Carter in 1979, was a Naval Reserve officer during World War II.

Admiral Miller: Combat art. We'd take anything no one else would take.

Q: Did Al Murray do anything for you?*

Admiral Miller: Yes, Al Murray was one of the boys. Reeves Lewenthal really had that project in his hands. He tried to sell it to the Air Force and they turned him down. He brought it to me, which was a blessing.

Steichen's outfit branched into motion pictures and documentaries. He had stills and the documentary. Out of that came Fighting Lady, for example.† We'd write orders for these photographers and writers, and they could go anyplace. They'd go to Europe, to Africa.

Q: You didn't have to be concerned about a budget, I take it.

Admiral Miller: We didn't have a budget. The things we were doing were being well done and everyone said, "God bless, go ahead." No one ever put a restriction on us in anything.

Q: How long were you with Training Literature?

Admiral Miller: About two years.

Did I tell you the episode about Steichen and the Navy poster? Steichen came to see me one day--I guess it was in 1942. He was over 60 as the war broke out.‡ He had

---

* Lieutenant Albert K. Murray, USNR, was one of the Navy combat artists in World War II. His oral history is in the Naval Institute collection.
† Fighting Lady was an excellent color documentary about aircraft carrier operations in the Pacific.
‡ Steichen was born in 1879.

gray hair and was sweet, oh, what a gentleman he was. I've never known anything like him. He would do things like teach me how to make a good photograph, for example. The secret was to take about 100 pictures, pick out the best, and crop it. Then you have the picture you've been waiting for.

He always called me "Skipper." One day he came to me and said, "Skipper, do you know what they're doing?"

I said, "No. Who are 'they,' and what are 'they' doing?"

"Well, that damn public relations crowd down there [Leland Lovette and people like that; this must have been around July, because Navy Day in those days was October 27] have got a poster contest. Do you know what it is? It's a battleship. Now, what are we going to do about it?"*

I said, "Well, what are you going to do about it?"

He said, "I'll tell you what. I'll go up to New York." The Saturday Evening Post had a marvelous cover artist, John Falter, whose work I had followed. Steichen said, "You know what? He is in the Navy. He's a chief of the recruiting bureau in White Plains. I'll go see John." So I told him to let me know what he was doing.

About a week later he called me and said, "Skipper, he's done it!"

I said, "Who's done what?"

He said," John Falter's got the greatest poster you ever saw." I asked if it was ready for exhibition, and he said no, it was still wet and was drying at the recruiting office.

I said, "I'll tell you. I'll get an airplane and come up to Floyd Bennett Field this evening, and we'll get the poster and bring it to Washington, because now we're running out of time on the contest."

At Anacostia they knew I was crazy. I'd come up there and fly out at 10:00 at night and go in all directions. I preferred flying at night. They had a plane for me, and I

---

* Navy Day was celebrated for many years on 27 October because that was the birthday of turn-of-the-century President Theodore Roosevelt, who championed a big Navy.

flew up to New York. Falter had an apartment at Grammercy Square, and at Floyd Bennett Field they gave me a car and sent me in. Steichen was waiting for me. Falter had shoved off to go get the painting, and it was still wet; we had to be awfully careful. He had left a pitcher of martinis, and we spent half an hour having a good time there. Finally Falter came in with this gorgeous thing about so big.

Q: Was it in oils?

Admiral Miller: It was in oil, yes. It was the stern of a carrier with two destroyers following along behind and a squadron of aircraft up in the air. Well, we took this precious thing out to Floyd Bennett and put it in the little Benny Howard, which just had room for it. We shoved off for Anacostia and it was about 1:00 o'clock in the morning now. We got over Baltimore, and all my lights went out--my running lights, cockpit lights, no radio, nothing. We just lost all of our electrical power. Of all the times, this was not the time. But at any rate, we went on down and finally circled around and made the field, and fortunately the Anacostia field was sort of a common runway.

Q: Did you lose your power of communication too?

Admiral Miller: Yes, I had nothing. But it was late at night, and there was not going to be much traffic around there. The lights were on, fortunately. So I went in and I made a nice long landing and had no problems at all. I got over to Anacostia, and I phoned and said our plane just landed and we were over here with no problems. He said, "They haven't had a plane in there for 12 hours." So they didn't even know we had come in.

Q: The enemy could have done something too.

Harold B. Miller #2 - 112

Admiral Miller: The next day we took the poster down, and no question about it, this was the artwork that the Navy should have for Navy Day. And that's what we got.

Q: So you supplanted the battleship poster?

Admiral Miller: Yes. We did things like that to make people aware of naval aviation.

Q: I'd think you'd be loath to leave that job.

Admiral Miller: I was, but there was a war going on, you know, and I was anxious to get over to England. I wanted to see what was going on with the bombing and the war. Besides, everything was moving along, and everything was going great and you couldn't slow down. So then I went over to London and had the greatest year I've ever had.

Interview Number 3 with Rear Admiral Harold B. Miller, U.S. Navy (Retired)

Place: Admiral Miller's home, Manhasset, New York

Date: Monday, 11 May 1981

Interviewer: Dr. John T. Mason, Jr.

Q: Last time, you told me that very interesting story about Training Literature in the Bureau of Aeronautics during the war, a very exciting time, indeed, and one that drew on all your talents for imagination. Now you began another very interesting assignment in late 1943, when you were sent to London as naval attaché for air and assistant naval attaché at the American embassy in London. Also, you were on the staff of the Commander U.S. Naval Forces in Europe, Admiral Stark.* Tell me the scope of all this activity.

Admiral Miller: Well, also, I was aide to Ambassador Winant.† I was sort of his Navy man. So I had three jobs, really.

Q: It sounds like that--three hats.

Admiral Miller: All of them were interesting and challenging. I did not see too much of Mr. Winant, although I'd go with him to official functions and talk with him a great deal. I'd go around with Admiral Stark a great deal, but he had the ability to let you alone, turn you loose to go ahead and do your job. The prime object of the assignment was to find out

---

* After being relieved as Chief of Naval Operations, Admiral Harold R. Stark, USN, served as Commander U.S. Naval Forces Europe from April 1942 to August 1945.
† Ambassador John G. Winant.

what was going on overseas that would be helpful for the Navy to know. For example, we were interested in British developments in radar, gunnery, fuels, and all the new things.

I had rather a large staff there; they were all reserves who were talented in their particular line. I, in turn, pretty well turned them loose. They had all their contacts with the Royal Air Force and the Royal Navy, and they'd come in with their reports. I'd go over them and sign them and get them out. But then my contacts were also with the RAF and the Royal Navy.* The naval air attaché was assigned two airplanes. One was an SNJ, the Harvard or the Texan--call it what you will, that wonderful North American trainer. Then I had a Lockheed 10, a little twin-engine job, works a great deal like the Beechcraft. It was a nice little airplane.

Q: This was to expedite you getting around to various bases in the U.K.?

Admiral Miller: That's right. Very often, I'd fly up to Londonderry, for example, where the Navy had a big destroyer base, which would frequently receive the U.S. destroyers that had to overrun Iceland. In other words, theoretically, the job I did on the Support Force--our destroyers would accompany the convoys to a point about 500 miles south of Iceland, where they'd be turned over to British destroyers. But the British were running out of ships and had problems with storms and various things, so often our little old four-stackers would have to just keep on going and take the convoy on in to the Western Approaches, which basically means Liverpool and Cardiff.

So we had a big operation in Londonderry, where the ships could be repaired, and they'd be refueled and so on and sent out on the following convoy.

---

* RAF--Royal Air Force.

Q: Did this also include the PQ convoys to Murmansk?*

Admiral Miller: Oh, yes, all of them. The route, of course, basically was far to the north, south of Iceland, then the Great Circle Course on into the Western Approaches there north of Ireland into the Irish Sea. So I had plenty of reason to get over to Londonderry, and then I'd fly up to Scapa Flow, for example, because I was anxious to see what was going on in British carriers.†

I knew the Fifth Sea Lord. Our Navy's Chief of the Bureau of Aeronautics would be about the equivalent. He was a wonderful old boy. We were very good friends. We lived about three doors from each other in London, and we got along great.

Now, the angle of all this was that he, like everyone else, wanted American aircraft. The British wanted more Grumman fighters, they wanted the Grumman torpedo plane, the TBF. My objective was to help them get what they needed, but not to give them any more than that, because Admiral King was having a terrific fight trying to get similar equipment for the Pacific.‡ King was asking for only about 15% of our output, and he was having trouble getting that, because President Roosevelt had committed himself to taking care of Europe. That was the prime objective of the war. So I'll never forget just before D-Day, I thought it was time to get the scene back in Washington, and I came back.§

Before I left, I had called on the British admiral and told him I was coming home

---

* PQ was the designation for convoys from the East Coast of North America to North Russia, providing war materials to the Soviet Union as part of the Lend-Lease program.
† Scapa Flow was the site of a British naval anchorage in the Orkney Islands, north of Scotland.
‡ Admiral Ernest J. King, USN, Commander in Chief U.S. Fleet and Chief of Naval Operations.
§ D-Day, the Allied invasion of Normandy in German-occupied France, was on 6 June 1944.

for a couple of days. All Millers are "Dusty" over there, so he said, "Now, Dusty, here's my [how did he say it?] grocery list." He had a couple of hundred of this and 300 or 400 of that. He said, "How about getting these for me?"

So I came back, and Herb Riley was on the distribution end of these things.* I had been to every air station they had and knew exactly what they needed. But I was working for Admiral King, too, for the Americans. So I said, "Let's just cut this in half."

He said, "That's fine." So when I came back and told the Fifth Sea Lord, he was happy as he could be. Half was really all he wanted anyway, but you always ask for more than you get. So we had very, very friendly relations.

In July 1944, I flew up to Scapa Flow, went aboard a British carrier, and went to sea with it. Of course, in those days they were looking for the battleship Tirpitz, which was in one of the anchorages there on the Norwegian Coast. They were flying the old Barracudas, which weren't much good for anything, and they had some of our Grumman F4Fs.† But they just really didn't know how to operate aboard their carriers.

Q: What carriers did they have up there?

Admiral Miller: Well, HMS Formidable was one that comes to mind.‡ They also had carriers down in the Mediterranean. They had real problems in the quantities of ships by that time. The British, of course, are a dogged group. We had always said that the skipper of a carrier must be an aviator. The British didn't have such a thing. The skipper of the Formidable was an old submariner, a very fine person. He was making his first cruise on a

---

* Commander Herbert D. Riley, USN. The oral history of Riley, who retired as a vice admiral, is in the Naval Institute collection.
† Martlet was the Royal Navy's designation for the Grumman F4F fighter.
‡ The other carriers in the theater were HMS Indefatigable and HMS Furious.

carrier and doing his best to make it work. He just didn't have the background, although he was most eager to learn. The executive officer was a regular line officer, not an aviator, on his first carrier cruise also. It didn't seem to make sense to us. The point was I was trying to be helpful, to teach them how we did it. It was an eye-opening experience, and I was able to bring back voluminous reports as to what their capabilities were.

It was very interesting looking around for the Germans up there. We got fairly close, and the squadrons went in and dropped their bombs on the Tirpitz. It didn't accomplish anything, really, because she was pretty well protected. The British spirit was to fly and "go get 'em," but somehow or other, the reason the U.S. aviators were good is because they would keep practicing and go out over and over again. The British would make two or three flight operations or exercises but not work at it continuously. They never worked as hard as we worked.

Q: Is that explained, perhaps, because the Fleet Air Arm was more or less absorbed, wasn't it, by the RAF?

Admiral Miller: That is correct, right during World War I. The RAF held off to some extent, but the Fleet Air Arm couldn't get its own airplanes. After all, the aeronautical organization of Britain was building Spitfires and Hurricanes and things like that, rather than naval aircraft.

Q: That was where the great emphasis was, rather than a naval plane?

Admiral Miller: That is quite right. And that's why the British wanted to use these American aircraft; that's the only place they had to turn, really. I can understand that. But when it came to the operations, they just plain didn't work as hard, that's all. For example, in these Barracudas the squadron commander would be an observer. He wouldn't even be a pilot; he'd be a second rear seat man, and that was not unusual.

Before a scheduled operation, they didn't warm up their engines or anything until just before they were going to take off. For instance, if they were going to have an afternoon exercise, they wouldn't turn up their engines in the morning to make sure everything was all right. I would ask, "Why?"

The skipper, who was not an aviator, said, "Well, it wears the engines out." He didn't want that. I mean, it was a simple thing of that sort.

I must say that in the event that they wore the engine out, which, of course, is a little farfetched, we'd have another engine without any trouble, whereas the British would not.

Q: Yes, we were somewhat extravagant, weren't we?

Admiral Miller: Oh, yes. I can understand to some extent, but nevertheless, that was part of the picture we had. I remember I came back and I wrote a long report on the general carrier operations and submitted it to Di Gates, who was an old friend of mine, and Di passed it on to Admiral Towers and everybody else.* Towers noted the same impression I had had. In other words, this was verified.

The British wanted to send a squadron of carriers out to the Pacific. When I later left there, on orders back to the States, the Fifth Sea Lord said, "Now, Dusty, you don't want us out there. You want to win that Japanese war all by yourselves."

---

* Artemus L. Gates served as Assistant Secretary of the Navy for Air from 5 September 1941 to 1 July 1945. A copy of Miller's report, dated 14 September 1944, was used to supplement the oral interview in the account contained in this transcript.

I said, "Oh, what nonsense." But my report covered that type of thing. I sent a copy of the report to Admiral Nimitz.*

Nimitz commented, "We must be careful," because I had said, "The first thing you know, we're going to have to supply them all their airplanes and aircraft and everything out there in the Pacific." Then Nimitz added the logistics and all their fuel and food and everything else. There was a question of whether or not we did want them out there, because we didn't think they could contribute. First of all, the war was well over by that time. We didn't think they could contribute a great deal, but they would be a drain upon us. However, they did come out.

Q: Oh, yes, they came out. This was the political factor then. That had to be considered too.

Admiral Miller: That's exactly what it was. That's right.

At times, I got acquainted with the Eighth Air Force, and I'd go over east of London and bum rides with B-26s over France. You know, get my briefing and get my metal jacket and all that sort of stuff and get instructed what to do if I ended up in France.

Q: This was a raiding party that you were going to?

Admiral Miller: Yes, bombing, with B-26s.

Q: What were the targets when you went with them--the Ruhr?

---

* Admiral Chester W. Nimitz, USN, was Commander in Chief U.S. Pacific Fleet and Pacific Ocean Areas.

Admiral Miller: Oh, no. The B-26s couldn't get in that far. Particularly on D-day, St. Lo was the target in behind the beaches. It was interesting to see how they bombed, because only a few years before, I had been in Panama bombing with the PBYs, which required a constant level, no wing dip, no variation in speed or anything. You had to be a solid platform. But these boys had to be sure. We were being shot at; you could see all this ack-ack around. You could hear it, as a matter of fact. The Germans could never catch up with you; they were always behind you. Why, I don't know.

At any rate, you'd have about three squadrons going in, each squadron had about 18. The leader in the first squadron would, like everyone else, drop his nose a little bit and go a little faster. The first thing you knew, everybody would be going a little faster, and finally, he would drop and everybody would drop visually on him, but he was practically in a tournament. These bombs would get scattered all over the countryside. I came to the conclusion that first of all, all this pickle-barrel bombing is a lot of tripe, and secondly, the reason we didn't succeed in bombing everything is that we just dropped so many bombs, they couldn't find something they had to hit.

Q: Give me a definition of "pickle-barrel" bombing.

Admiral Miller: Oh, the Air Force used to claim that they could drop a bomb in a barrel, the accuracy, of course. Well, if you've got a nuclear bomb or something like that, of course you only have to hit within three or four miles, but a pickle-barrel, that's a lot of tripe entirely.

Q: Pin-point bombing?

Admiral Miller: So we had all of those in a great variation, and if there was ever a free-wheeler that was me. I could fly any place I wanted to fly. I'd pick up Hanson Baldwin several times and fly him around to go someplace that he needed to go--Bristol or places like that.* It was truly a great experience.

Q: Did you hand out the assignments to all these people under you?

Admiral Miller: They all had their own assignments. I knew where they were. One would be covering machine gun developments, for example. One might be covering something related to the jet engine, which was coming along about that time. We weren't spying on the British; we were just trying to get, "What are you boys doing that will be helpful to us?"

Q: There was great cooperation, wasn't there?

Admiral Miller: Free interchange, yes, all along the line. We sent in so much stuff, how could Washington have ever digested it?

Q: I know, I saw some of it as it came in.† What about ordnance? You also focused on that, to some extent.

---

* Hanson W. Baldwin, who had been a Naval Academy classmate of Miller's, was by this time the military correspondent for The New York Times.
† The interviewer, John T. Mason, worked as a civilian in the Office of Naval Intelligence during World War II.

Admiral Miller: Well, no, basically air was my province, and, of course, there were a lot of people over there for everything else. Our big Navy effort there was getting ready for D-Day, putting all the landing craft together and organizing this thing. It was a great effort.

Q: Tell me now, focus on Ambassador Winant and the several times you were with him.*

Admiral Miller: We didn't really see much of him. He was a very Lincolnesque character, as you recall. He was from Maine, I believe.

Q: He didn't communicate very well.

Admiral Miller: Yes, he didn't talk much. He was very much an intellectual man. I think he probably did a good job for the U.S. over there, but you didn't get very close to him.

Q: Can you recall any special incidents in which you were involved with him?

Admiral Miller: Not with him, no. I couldn't say that. I had more contact with people coming over. Di Gates would come over, for example.† I became acquainted with Pan Am. Pan Am was linked to the Navy at that time, and I was almost Mr. Pan Am in London during that period of time. It was one of those jobs, whatever you saw that needed to be done, go do it, and everybody would be happy.

---

* Winant detailed his 1941 experiences as ambassador in A Letter from Grosvenor Square (London: Hodder & Stoughton, 1947).
† While serving as Assistant Secretary of the Navy (Air), Gates was on leave from his position as a member of the board of directors of Pan American.

Among the jobs, I was the liaison with the Soviet military mission. The mission was primarily Navy, although it was also Army as well, but its name was the Military Mission. The number I usually rallied around would be 40 or 50. I'd take them by train up to just across from Belfast, and then we'd go up to Londonderry and look over all that stuff up there. And I'd take them down to Appledore, where we were practicing the landings. I got to know the Soviets quite well. As a matter of fact, I used to bring them home with me, a few at a time, and cook supper for them. They would reciprocate. Of course, they're great trenchermen; they eat well. They'd always bring wives along. They cover all bases.

Almost all of them had come from Siberia to San Francisco and across that way rather than the other way, which would have been a little bit difficult. So that they'd had a smattering of America. I found them very fine people. They always had musicians, piano players there, and they'd all be out dancing. They were a great deal like Americans until the commissar showed up. Then they absolutely became different persons; they became ramrod, they stopped their fun, they stopped smiling, no dancing, no music, no nothing. Nothing but a lot of stiff, stuffed shirts standing around. The political angle was incredible; they could translate themselves instantly into a figure, rather than a person. It's an amazing thing.

Q: But when he wasn't around, they were human beings?

Admiral Miller: Oh, they were just like Americans when they could be Russians rather than Soviets.

Q: They weren't secretive, then?

Admiral Miller: Oh, no, they even talked . . .

Q: Did they give you reactions to their whole system of government, however? Did they talk about that?

Admiral Miller: I usually avoided that, because they all expressed admiration for Americans. They had just a taste of it coming across the States.

Later, I corresponded with a Russian brigadier general. After I retired, I went back to one of those air shows, and I saw some of my Russian friends there. I said, "Where is the General Georgie? Where is Georgie?"

"Oh, he's back in Moscow."

I said, "Would you take a letter to him for me?" So I wrote a letter and sent it to him, and didn't hear for months. One Sunday morning down in Washington, the phone rang. They said, "Is this Admiral Miller?"

"Yes."

"Well, this is Colonel so-and-so from the Soviet Embassy. I have a letter for you." And he came and brought me a letter from Georgie.

The letter was about a half-page, and about all it said was, "I am well, hope you are the same." He couldn't write anything.

Q: He couldn't write anything. The mere fact that he was in touch with you, I suppose, endangered him.

Admiral Miller: Very, very likely. Then I began to wonder what did I say in my letter that might have gotten him into some problem.

In the job, Admiral Stark and I would frequently get invited down to what we called the Soviet bachelor quarters. They always had their meals there. They didn't associate very much on the outside. I seemed to have made inroads. Well, I had them on tour in the trains, and I had access to all the liquor in the world. They loved to drink; they were very heavy drinkers. And we'd go down there and have lunch, the admiral and I. The meal table was very long. The admiral and I would be sitting in the center, and it's that same old gag--one end saluted you, and while you were turning over there, they said, "Bottoms up." They were dry at the other end of the table, and then they reversed the process.

Q: But the guest was getting a double dose. Is that because they think it will loosen you up somewhat?

Admiral Miller: I'm sure that's what it is. Or sometimes I think it's kind of a game, too, to see if you can get somebody drunk. Of course, you learn how to control these things.

I used to take this group to the theater. In this one particular family were a general and his wife, who was a husky gal. We were really very good friends. You know, the theater was about a 5:00 P.M. deal getting in there before the bombers came over, and so the point I make is: the sky is the limit.

D-Day came along, and I'd just gotten back from a two-day trip to Washington. I would have a grandstand seat for this thing. So I called upon my Eighth Air Force boys, the B-26s, and they said, "Sure, come down. We've got a seat for you." Obviously, I wasn't flying it; I was over on the right side, and you sit on this steel and you've got a steel jacket on and all this. You could hardly walk, it was so heavy. So away we went. This was D-Day.

Q: Was this in a softening-up effort?

Admiral Miller: No, this was the invasion. This was the landing on the sixth of June at Omaha Beach. We were at 15,000 feet, and I have never seen so many ships in my life. The Bay of Biscay was just nothing but almost a bridge of ships from the south of England over to France. As I said, we were bombing St. Lo. We saw no enemy aircraft at all. Lots of antiaircraft guns, and, of course, you could see the activity down below. You couldn't identify anything really, but you knew things were going on, smoke and things. That was a real, real exciting day to see all of that.

In August, I took my little Lockheed 10 and flew over there empty, because I knew we had a lot of naval officers there from staffs that had done their jobs and were trying to get back.

Q: And you were flying it?

Admiral Miller: Yes. I flew over there and landed on these Army mats, and, boy, I no more than landed than I was surrounded by my old Navy friends from London, wanting to get back to London. The landings were over now, so I loaded up and brought them back.

Q: How many could you take?

Admiral Miller: I carried about eight back there. Boy, they were anxious to get back. The landings where the Navy was involved were practically over.

Then, of course, the V-1s started coming over, the old buzz bombs. They were very frightening, of course. You remember their method was when the fuel ran out, they tipped the elevator down so that you now had a powerless missile on its way down. Everything is all right as long as you hear them. When the noise stops, then you'd better get someplace safe.

Harold B. Miller #3 - 127

Q: You know they're coming?

Admiral Miller: Hanson Baldwin, I'll never forget. He and I were out in a couple of the raids, and he still talks about it. He really didn't have enough sense to get scared of it. But I used to go see where those bombs landed, and oh, God, they were dreadful.

Q: The devastation was pretty great, too, wasn't it?

Admiral Miller: Oh, yes, they'd hit one of those old brick buildings and set fires. All the British people were wonderful, I tell you. I didn't see any of the V-2s. I had left when they started coming over. They were even more frightening, because we didn't know they were coming. I mean, they had no warning on them at all.

Q: They were missiles, weren't they?

Admiral Miller: Yes, in the early days.

Q: Did you get involved with the Air Force when they tried to bomb their launching pads?

Admiral Miller: We were very much involved in that. We had a B-24 squadron at Dunkeswell, which is just above Exeter.* Those poor devils lived in cement blockhouses--

---

* This was a Navy operation, flying the PB4Y, which was the Navy's version of the Army Air Forces B-24. For the recollections of one of the squadron commanding officers, see Rear Admiral James R. Reedy, "Submarines and Buzz-Bomb Launchers," in Assault on Normandy (Annapolis: Naval Institute Press, 1994), pages 210-216.

no windows and just freezing cold. They were real pioneers. Well, their job was primarily over the Bay of Biscay with the B-24s.

Q: Down off Spain?

Admiral Miller: Yes, in that general area. They were antisubmarine planes; U-boats were their objective, their target. And they did a damn good job.

One of the pilots down there in Dunkeswell was Joe Kennedy.* I never knew him. They say he was a very fine person; he was the white hope of the Kennedy family, so they thought. Now, in telling about him I have to go back two or three years. When I was still in Training Literature, we had an operation out in Oklahoma which was basically an effort to fly airplanes by radio control, no personnel aboard. We took a lot of old fighters and a lot of current aircraft. The engineering group involved down there included Ralph Barnaby, Del Fahrney, and others.† They reached the point where they could just have this little black box down on the ground and fly this airplane.

Q: A pilotless plane?

Admiral Miller: Oh, yes, nobody in it, circle it around and do what they want, bring it back in and land it.

---

* Lieutenant Joseph P. Kennedy, Jr., USNR, older brother of future President John F. Kennedy.
† Part of the program involved attack drones configured to deliver weapons by remote control, a distant forerunner of the guided missile concept. See Rear Admiral Delmar S. Fahrney, USN (Ret.), "The Birth of Guided Missiles," U.S. Naval Institute Proceedings, December 1980, pages 54-60.

Q: And what was the objective?

Admiral Miller: The objective was almost sort of a pre-kamikaze without the pilots, although no one imagined kamikazes at that point. They had big dreams of forming squadrons and squadrons of these, build a lot of cheap aircraft carrying a bomb. It was a very exciting project. I actually flew out there two or three times just to look at the operation. I was very much impressed with it.

Well, that then became translated when the buzz-bombs started coming over, because the German launching tracks were quite long, a couple hundred feet long. These were all under concrete blocks and in caves and all that kind of stuff, in France, and therefore they couldn't do a damn thing about them. They'd bomb and bomb, and I guess if they hit, they didn't do any damage. They couldn't destroy the launchers. So what could you do next? Well, maybe you could fly an airplane into the tunnel and put it out of commission. So, "All right, let's try it."

Joe Kennedy had been ordered to come home, but he was so enamored with this idea that he begged for permission to stay on and make this flight. So he took a B-24 and brought all this gear and equipment over for automatic control. Whether or not they flew it without any load or not, I don't know. They probably did. In any event, they reached the point where they loaded this plane up with everything they had in the way of TNT and explosives. It was a real flying disaster, is what it was. Well, there's a heavily populated area down there, and you certainly didn't want to just fly that off with just radio control, so they decided to fly off with a command pilot. Then the crew would bail out. So now you had an airplane loaded in the air, all cocked, ready to go.

Q: And then the black box would take over after the crew bailed out?

Admiral Miller: The so-called black box was in a Lockheed Vega that was going to fly it over to France.

Q: Accompany it?

Admiral Miller: Yes, at a visual distance, sort of a formation. Joe was the pilot and a lieutenant was the second pilot, just the two of them in this airplane.* So they took off. The plane was in the air now, and they started flying to the south. They were over to the east, heading to whatever target had been selected, one of these launching platforms. They were still over England, down near Essex, I think it was. Their job now was to arm the explosives and then to get the hell out of the airplane. So they set everything and turned the control over to the Lockheed, which was a half or quarter of a mile away. The Lockheed finally said, "Yeah, we've got control. We've got the B-24 now." So all Joe and his copilot had to do was to leave their cockpit and walk aft and bail out through the bomb bay, which they started to do.

Now, at that point it's conjecture, of course, but as they were going down the passageway and closing the switches behind them, they still had open circuits all the way there. As they got closer and closer to the bomb bay, they'd close another circuit. Somewhere along the line there was a short, and the whole damn thing blew up in the air. It never accomplished anything except destroy poor Joe Kennedy.† And they dropped the project at that point.

---

* The other man in the plane was Lieutenant Wilford Willy, USN.
† This failed mission was on 12 August 1944. For a detailed account, see Hank Searls, The Lost Prince: Young Joe, the Forgotten Kennedy; the Story of the Oldest Brother (New York: World Publishing Company, 1969).

Q: They didn't go on with that?

Admiral Miller: They never followed through on the thing.

Q: And yet it had been promising.

Admiral Miller: Oh, I thought it'd have been great. Have this Lockheed just fly this damn thing right down their throat. It would have been marvelous. But that experiment died at that particular point.

There was another point too. By that time, the time we got that thing going, it was after the landings, and the Germans began to get pushed back and back. The buzz bombs had a range of about 425 or 450 miles, and as the Germans got pushed back farther and farther, we realized that we were making progress on the ground, so we might as well let it alone. That's how poor old Joe died--all the dreams and hopes and everything else. He was apparently a wonderful boy. It was just a shame. Joe's father had been the ambassador to England before the war. I mean, there just seemed to be tragedy really after him.

Q: There must be more that you can tell me about this period. Tell me about Stark's reactions to the landings and that sort of thing.

Admiral Miller: I don't know that I could even comment on that. King became boss, of course. Stark was the CNO when Pearl Harbor was attacked, of course, and King became

CNO soon afterward.* King was kind of pushing him back into a corner during that whole period.

Q: But Stark had a real job in London, didn't he?

Admiral Miller: Oh, he had a tremendous job.

Q: Say a little about how he performed.

Admiral Miller: Well, to the best of my knowledge, he performed very well. His job really was a buildup of American forces from nothing and laying the groundwork for all the tremendous number of personnel and ships to come. He wasn't really an operative man, himself. I mean, his job was almost one of, "Come along, now. We'll build up and first thing you know, we'll have a big ground force, have a big organization here," is basically what he was doing. The operations were still pretty much controlled by King as CNO; in the Mediterranean were some landings down in Italy and North Africa. That was all the operational control. Stark wasn't involved in that type of thing at all. He was much more than a housekeeper, but wasn't operational in any sense of the word.

Q: CominCh was in charge, of course.†

Admiral Miller: Oh, yes, there's no question about that.

---

* Admiral Ernest J. King, USN, served as Chief of Naval Operations from 26 March 1942 to 15 December 1945; he was promoted to the rank of fleet admiral in December 1944.
† CominCh was the abbreviation for Admiral King's title of Commander in Chief U.S. Fleet.

Harold B. Miller #3 -133

Q: Did you have anything to do with Alan Kirk?*

Admiral Miller: I knew him casually. I had no working problems with him. Of course, he was operational too. He had been a naval attaché over there at one time. He knew those people well and was well-liked. Kirk was a Scotsman anyway, to start with. No, I didn't have any operational duties. I was pretty much on my own, scouting around and getting the dope, all I could get and getting acquainted with everybody.

Q: I wonder if perhaps you'd say something about any contacts we had with the governments in exile, de Gaulle in particular?†

Admiral Miller: We had quite a lot of them. Each government in exile had somebody assigned to it. I don't think I can add anything on that line at all.

Q: Did you see a lot of de Gaulle?

Admiral Miller: No, not de Gaulle. There wasn't anybody who ever saw de Gaulle over there. Of course, every morning in the briefings in the map room we'd have all the Air Force bombings and the British bombings.

General Patton was always there with his two pearl-handled pistols.‡ He thought he was a real cowboy, and, of course, he impressed everybody. They didn't know what the hell to make of him, as it turned out.

---

* Rear Admiral Alan G. Kirk, USN, was Commander Western Naval Task Force for the invasion of Normandy in 1944.
† General Charles de Gaulle headed the forces of the Free French, which were based in London.
‡ Lieutenant General George S. Patton, USA, commanding general of the U.S. Third Army during its race through western Europe following the invasion.

It was very interesting because we always had a rundown on the Pacific situation too. This is now Guam and Saipan, and we were all following the Pacific with a great deal of interest.* We kept up on the bombings in Europe, the B-17s and so on; the so-called mass bombing produced disastrous losses. It was frightening, the number of the airplanes the Air Force would lose on those raids.

Q: When they went over the Ruhr area?

Admiral Miller: Oh, yes.

Q: Because they were well protected with antiaircraft.

Admiral Miller: You know, again, I have to say, "Bomb them often enough, and you'll put them out of commission." It took a lot of repeats on those.

Q: You mean you're an advocate of the Douhet theory?†

Admiral Miller: Well, I'm an advocate of training our people to go ahead and get hits on the first go-around. If you don't do that, you're going to have to go back. Oh, no, I don't believe in this mass destruction at all. I'm merely saying that if you don't get them the first go-around, you're going to have to go a second time and maybe a third time, if that's the kind of bombing you're going to do. If you're going to do accurate bombing, it's not involved, of course.

---

* U.S. forces invaded Saipan on 15 June 1944, a week after the invasion of France.
† Between the World Wars, Giulio Douhet was Italian Under Secretary for Air and one of the leading thinkers on the strategic use of air power.

Q: Well, those losses after a raid of that sort must have been demoralizing on the personnel?

Admiral Miller: Well, they were, but we weren't up in the briefing room. We weren't seeing much of the flying personnel; we were seeing the guys who would send them. I know the losses couldn't be replaced. Oh, yes, it could and was very serious.

Of course, the other thing that was important and that we followed so closely--this goes back two years to the Support Force and its convoy work--was the loss of cargo ships. First it's the curve of the loss of German submarines. That was a factor we followed with considerable interest. Of course, we had learned that up in Newfoundland early. The cargo ship loss was so tremendous, and the submarine losses slight. Obviously the curves couldn't even out, but they began to parallel each other to a point where the German submarine skippers were beginning to have morale problems too. They didn't know whether they were going to get back or not. Finally, by the construction of more ships, we began to get on top of that.

The problem was whether there going to be enough food even in England, to say nothing of ammunition or emergency stuff. Practically all of Pan Am's pilots were in war service at that point. Up in the north island, Loch Neigh, there was a seaplane base, and we were going to land these planes in there. But by the time you crossed the Atlantic, your payload wasn't too great. You might come in there with, say, 5,000 or 6,000 pounds of some emergency war material. This made a bridge across there going into Loch Neigh. We had Navy pilots and Naval Reserve pilots there and so on.

There was some island that we had to have that related to submarines. I don't remember exactly what it was, but all freight work was stopped in order to get this emergency material over there. They just had to have it. And the airplane did a fabulous cargo job by sheer numbers. It wasn't the load each individual airplane could carry; it was

Harold B. Miller #3 -136

the load a total number of airplanes could carry. And they were absolutely priceless. They were using bombers too. Sometimes they'd strip a B-17, put two bucket seats in there, and that would be a passenger job.

Q: What about your job of seeing what the British needed and then forwarding those requests to Washington or taking them, and the relationship you had with Lend-Lease?

Admiral Miller: Well, Lend-Lease, to me, meant an interchange of a lot of material, not necessarily aircraft. And that was not my province; airplanes themselves were my particular province, as I explained coming back with the orders from the Fifth Sea Lord. So I wasn't involved in that. Of course by that time, the British could have had just about anything they wanted and anything we could get to them, even with Admiral King screaming bloody murder.

Q: He couldn't scream as loud as Winnie could.*

Admiral Miller: Well, King would come over there. I sat in on a couple of meetings in which it was quite clear what he wanted, but he was just plain overruled. After all, Roosevelt and Churchill were like that.

Q: Well, that's what I say. King couldn't shout as loudly as Churchill could.

Admiral Miller: No, no.
    As you can easily see, I was witnessing a glorious series of events over in England. I was just having a great time. The war was coming to an end over there when I suddenly

---

* Winston S. Churchill was the British Prime Minister.

received a very strange set of orders that August. The dispatch was from CNO, passed on from CinCPac.* What it said was, "If practical, request Captain H. B. Miller be detached on order of CinCPac for duty organizing press relations for upcoming operation." That was the net of it.

Q: Was this addressed to Stark, or to whom?

Admiral Miller: Well, I guess it was to Stark. I've forgotten that angle, but it was delivered to me for comment, of course, and action. Well, I didn't know what that was all about, really, but it gave me only about four days to get the hell out of there. So I went hurrying back to Washington.

Q: How did you go back? By what route?

Admiral Miller: I went up to Prestwick and flew out of there via Iceland, down through Stephenville, Newfoundland, and then on down via an Air Force ferry plane.

Admiral Radford was then in Washington, so I went to see him.† He was an old friend of mine and popped up all through my life. I said, "Raddy, what are these orders all about? I have no idea what it's about."

He smiled and said, "Go see the Secretary. He'll tell you what they're about."

Q: That was Forrestal?

---

* CinCPac--Commander in Chief Pacific.
† By this time Radford was a rear admiral, serving as Assistant Chief of Naval Operations (Air).

Admiral Miller: That was Forrestal.* I had met him when he used to come over to England. I was with him in two or three cases. Once I drove him down to Southampton, for example, and sort of got acquainted. He was a strange little Irishman, a wonderful person, you would think a dour person, but really a fast and quick mind.† Well, having gotten to know him just a little bit, I had no hesitancy about going to his office. I knew his aides, so I went in there and said, "I'd like to see the Secretary."

They announced me, and he said, "Come in, come in." There I was, standing before the Secretary, and we exchanged about two words of cordiality.

I said, "Mr. Secretary, I'm here because of the orders I have. Raddy tells me that you will be happy to explain them to me."

He said, "That's easy. We've got problems out in the Pacific." Now I cornered him. He and I were alone in the office. He said, "We see the end of the war. We know when we're going to close this war out. And MacArthur's winning the war.‡ When this war is over, no one will ever know the Navy was in it. It's been a Navy war the whole time; no one will ever know it. If we don't get something done about our public relations job in the Pacific, I can't go to Congress. We'll get no funding, no allocations, or anything. We've got to change the whole atmosphere."

Then he went on, "Nimitz [he didn't say Admiral Nimitz]--Nimitz has got a PR out there who is a disaster. I want you to go out there and get rid of him." That's exactly what he said.

Q: I guess he's referring to Waldo?

---

* James V. Forrestal served as Secretary of the Navy from 19 May 1944 to 17 September 1947. Before that he was Under Secretary of the Navy.
† For more on Forrestal, see Townsend Hoopes and Douglas Brinkley, Driven Patriot (New York: Alfred A. Knopf, 1992).
‡ General Douglas MacArthur, USA, was Commander Southwest Pacific Force and Southwest Pacific Area.

Admiral Miller: Waldo Drake.* Strange thing about it was that I had known Waldo when I was an ensign aboard the USS California. Waldo was a waterfront reporter for the L.A. Times, and I knew him in those days. So back in he comes again; he's captain in the USNR at that point.

So I said, "Well, Mr. Secretary, why don't you just order him out?"

He said, "Nimitz likes him. He'd like to keep him out there, but something's got to be done. Raddy says you can do it, and it will take you about four minutes to get him out of there." He said, "Then I'll give you a big carrier."† I guess that was bait, probably.

Well, what do you do? You say, "Aye, aye, sir." So I went back, and Raddy laughed at me. I'm sure he's the one who put Forrestal up to it because of Training Literature. It all goes back to that sort of stuff.

Q: Let me divert you with a question and ask does Forrestal's attitude reflect a different point of view about publicity and the Navy from what Nimitz and King and others held?

Admiral Miller: I think that's probably a proper question. The answer would be yes, because Forrestal was catching hell from all the publishers. I mean, The Baltimore Sun, I guess The New York Times, everybody. What happened was that Forrestal would protest, "You don't tell about this battle. You don't write our story."

They said, "We can't write it. You've got a guy out there who won't let us write it." They hung it all on Waldo Drake. Did he represent Nimitz? I don't know, because

---

* Captain William Waldo Drake, USNR, was Pacific Fleet public information officer during much of World War II. The Naval Institute's oral history collection contains Drake's memories of serving in that capacity.
† Carrier command at that point would have been a real plum for Captain Miller, who was in the Naval Academy's class of 1924. In the 1944-45 period, the skippers of the large aircraft carriers were from the classes of 1919 to 1921.

Harold B. Miller #3 -140

when I got out there, I had no problem with Nimitz whatsoever. I suspect it was Drake. I came to the conclusion, also, that under no condition should you have a press man in charge of other press men, because you've got a competitive, jealous angle involved, and I'm sure that was part of the picture. Waldo Drake saw these skilled people coming along, and by golly, they weren't going to tell him what to do. So he'd tell them what to do. I'm sure that that was one of the angles on the thing.

In any event, Raddy said, "Go on out there now. Go do your job." So I went tearing out there.

Q: What were your feelings at that point about approaching this job?

Admiral Miller: Well, also, there developed during this period that Nimitz wasn't going to be told about this plan. I was on my own on this whole deal. Forrestal had an aide who was a publisher of Scientific American, an old friend of mine. He was my pal inside the Forrestal office. Well, I felt like a nincompoop. I didn't know what the hell I was. I went out there, and I didn't really know who to check in with; I didn't know anything. It happened that Drake was out at Peleliu when I got out there. His little cubbyhole office was empty, except it had a sign on it: "Keep Out."

It turned out that the reporters out there hated Drake. They literally hated Drake. Hanson Baldwin tells me that Drake kept a black book on them: So-and-so was nobody to be trusted; So-and-so was this and that and so on. I never saw the black book. I did go in the safe and found that he was censoring their mail. I found a few clips and things like that in there, nothing that was really hazardous or any problem or anything.

I was there, say, about three weeks. It turned out to be a coincidence that all the reporters that were out there--old Bob McCormick, Frank Kelley of the Trib--all were people I had known in Washington in Training Literature. It was just as if they'd practically moved that crowd out there. So I was not without friends at that particular point, and I could go out and have dinner with them. I'd hear all these outlandish stories about their inability to do any work, just wasting their time out there. They couldn't accomplish anything.

Q: Were you attached to Nimitz's staff?

Admiral Miller: I was attached to Nimitz's staff with no title. I was just a captain out there.

Q: And with whom did you deal on his staff?

Admiral Miller: Practically nobody. I wasn't doing anything; I was just sitting around. I called on Admiral Nimitz, and he was real nice. He had been present when that Schiff Trophy came through from Panama. I wasn't unknown to him.

There was a classmate of mine, Count Austin, who worked for Nimitz.* He was an aide of some kind, and he and I were very friendly. Well, after sitting there for a while, I finally said, "Something's got to be done. I've got orders from the boss man here, and I'd better do something." The first thing I did was walk in there one day. I took the "Keep Out" sign, pulled it off and threw it in the wastebasket, and walked on in. I thought, "I might as well make this my office." Somebody saw that, and cheers started ringing through the building. This "Keep Out" from the PR; they thought, "Gee, this must be something."

I still didn't know how to handle this thing, because they told me that Nimitz didn't know that my job was to get Drake out of there. Well, it was solved by Frank Kelley of the Trib. Frank came to me one day and said, "Min, we want to see the admiral." I had popped

---

* Captain Bernard L. Austin, USN, was assistant chief of staff for administration on the Pacific Fleet staff. Austin's Naval Institute oral history has his recollections of the process by which Miller replaced Drake.

in on the admiral once or twice. He knew I was around. As far as I knew, he had no knowledge of what the hell I was supposed to be doing.

I said, "Well, fine." I went to see the admiral.

He said, "Fine, bring the boys in." He was such a salt of the earth. He was so wonderful. So I led about 20 of them in like the Judas goat and said, "Gentlemen, sit down." I sat down, and I didn't know what the hell they wanted to talk about. I thought it was something about an on-coming exercise or something. The admiral said, "Well, gentlemen, what can I do for you?"

Frank Kelley looked around and stood up and said, "Well, Admiral, I am the spokesman for this group, and we're here to tell you that we want Min Miller to be your public relations man." I thought I was going to die.

I literally thought, "My God, if they'd just dig a hole in this deck here, that's where I'd go." The admiral, in his jovial way, laughed it off, and blah, blah, blah. Finally, everybody went away happily, I among them.

As soon as I dumped them, I came running back and said, "Admiral, all I can say is I had no idea what they were up to. I knew nothing about it."

He said, "Oh, forget about it. No harm done."

Well, Waldo came back in about two days, and about two days later, he was gone. He had orders to Elmer Davis's organization in Washington.*

Q: Did you gather that Nimitz must have known something about it?

Admiral Miller: He must have had some feeling, and I'm sure Forrestal said, "Geez, I'm glad they got rid of that dope," or something to that effect.

---

* Elmer Davis, an experienced journalist, was director of the Office of War Information from 1942 to 1945.

Q: How did Drake react to you?

Admiral Miller: Well, the reporters made no bones about their attitude towards him. He was probably happy to be getting out. As far as I was concerned, he had no particular feeling. I never saw Waldo again until years later when I was president of Radio Free Europe. I was in a hotel in Berlin, and a stranger walked up to me and said, "I bet you don't know who I am."

I said, "No, I don't."

"I'm Waldo Drake." So I saw him there in Berlin, and that was the last time I ever saw him. In the meantime, he's deceased.

Q: Yes, in recent years.*

Admiral Miller: At that point, I knew what my job was, so I went to work. This was in Pearl, before Admiral Nimitz and part of the staff moved to Guam.

I quickly sent to London for my number two, Paul Scheetz.† He could get anything done on demand. I had a wonderful radio group there, and we started out to do something. And it was so easy. I never found Admiral Nimitz was reluctant for PR, absolutely not. He was the kindest man. The sky was the limit. I could go to him and do anything I wanted as long as I was just doing it, that was all.

---

* Drake died in 1977.
† Lieutenant Commander J. Paul Scheetz, USNR, served as Miller's right-hand man in Training Literature; in London, where he was an intelligence officer; and on the CinCPac staff. He later had a distinguished career in industry and was a civic leader in Pittsburgh. Scheetz was portrayed fictionally as one of the main characters in William Brinkley's comic novel Don't Go Near the Water (New York: Random House, 1956).

Well, we had Iwo Jima coming up.* So that was what our planning was for. The first thing we did involved the hometown news center at Great Lakes, Illinois, near Chicago. The idea, you recall, was for the Navy to send in a four-liner on Johnny Jones from Aurora, Illinois. The story would say that he was doing a great job aboard the USS Mississippi, and it might be accompanied by a picture of him. If you could just get that story told to all the folks at home about little Johnny, you'd be in business.

Q: It was a great morale builder, I'm sure.

Admiral Miller: So I told the Bureau of Personnel, "I want 100 enlisted journalists out here in the fleet." By this time, the war was about three years along. All the editors of these wonderful little hometown papers like the Manhasset Press wanted to kill Japs. So they were all in other jobs, not in journalistic jobs. But they were tired, by this time, of killing Japs. BuPers had a record of them all, so they screened through there fast and sent out 100 of these enlisted guys. Then my job was to sell the idea to the captains of these ships, "I want to put one of these men on each ship to do a bio on every one of the crew and send it in to Chicago for redistribution to the hometown newspaper."

On one ship--I forget which ship it was, maybe the Pennsylvania--the skipper was adamant. I finally said, "Let's try it once. Let's just put somebody aboard and get this thing done."

"All right, we'll have an experiment, but it won't work." In about three weeks, by God, letters started coming back to that ship. The captain was getting letters from the parents of these kids: "Oh, gee, Johnny's so proud of his ship and of you," and so on like that. Well, the first thing you know, they really had this thing going. I put one of those

---

* The U.S. Marine Corps invasion of the island of Iwo Jima was on 19 February 1945.

Harold B. Miller #3 -145

journalists on every major ship. Their job was to do the bios on these kids. Little things like that began to work well.

Q: And what about the flow of information on the various engagements? Was that freer now? Did you get to the reporters?

Admiral Miller: Oh, hell, we knew what the operation coming up was. We'd get these guys who wanted to go, and pretty soon we had people covering everything. Now, the censors didn't belong in the PR; they were a separate organization. They always felt they would be incestuous or something of that sort. But we put a censor out there, and the censors finally got the word, "Stop knocking this stuff off now. Let's get the word back." So, hell, they were doing the copy and getting it off. We set up channels to the coast on the radio. Once we got to Guam, we had four channels there.* We put one on the voice radio, we had one on TV, we had one on phonographs, and we had one on telegraphic copy. The reporting just began to flood out.

When we got up to Iwo, I had 120 cameras on the island. We had some on airplanes, some on landing craft, and some hand held. You name it, and there were cameras. But that wasn't enough. What do you do with all this film? We had two flying boats sitting there in the water at Iwo. All the camera gear, all the film and everything was brought down to them. I forget what the count was on stills and motion picture film. We separated the motion and the still film into bags, and these two planes flew this stuff down to Guam, which was about 750 miles. Well, at night there was no provisions for landing these craft, so I set up a deal where I had a DC-4 standing by on the field. They came along and parachuted this material to the ground, and we kept the still pictures there, because we

---

* In early 1945 a portion of the Pacific Fleet staff, along with Admiral Nimitz, moved its headquarters from Pearl Harbor to Guam in order to be nearer the action.

had a pretty good lab on Guam. The other stuff started for Hollywood. In about four days, I'd have a set of colored film with the landing back on Guam. One set would go to Forrestal, one set would come back to Guam, and I'd show it.

Admiral Nimitz had a meeting every morning. Admiral Fraser and the British were there by that time.* Geez, they were all waiting for a morning show. "Where is the film for today?" And it was bloody; it was untouched film--just horrible stuff. But God, it was effective. I got letters from Forrestal saying, "Send me all you've got. I want to show it to the Congress."

The first thing you know, the thing was beginning to roll. Forrestal was starting to get letters from the editors saying, "At last the Navy's known." I've got photographs down below showing you all the press and Nimitz and Forrestal and everybody there. Everybody was happy with the changes. Reporters were getting everything they wanted, and Nimitz by this time was getting letters from Forrestal saying, "Hey, things are great. You're doing great out there."

Later, we had to cover Okinawa.† That was a long way off. To start off, how were we going to cover the landings on Okinawa? So I said, "All right. I want four people now. I want a still man, I want a motion man, I want a TV, and a radio man." So they sent up a B-24 from Guam. We flew to Clark Field in Manila, which we had captured by that time. Their job then was to be over Okinawa at the time of the landing and be able to stay there for two hours, at which time they'd break off and fly to Iwo Jima and get some fuel and come back to Guam with all this material. It worked like a dream.

We had a pool operation there. The radio man would cover for all the radio stations. The writer would cover for all the press, and so on. Then we'd have the wires all clear and geez, this stuff would just go swooping out practically--not quite instantaneous,

---

* Admiral Sir Bruce A. Fraser, Royal Navy, Commander in Chief British Pacific Fleet.
† U.S. forces invaded the island of Okinawa on 1 April 1945.

but damn close as we could get it. We put writers on every ship. We also set up to retransmit radio signals. We could bring them into Guam and pass them on to San Francisco for broadcast. When somebody would be home shaving in the morning, hell, he was getting a word-by-word account of the landing right there in front of his mirror.

Reuters had a husband-and-wife team out there, old Percy Finch and his wife Barbara, who's a Stanford graduate. I brought women writers out there too.

Q: Women writers?

Admiral Miller: They're wives, they're mothers, they're daughters and so on, and why shouldn't they be out forward too? So I got them first at Pearl, then got them at Guam, and then we'd take them on farther. But I had a point: "You gals can't go until nurses are there and Red Cross gals get there first." But even then, they were always pushing. So I had Percy Finch aboard the California. I remember at the landing at Iwo, they kind of got stalled out there for a couple of days, but we took an airstrip quite early and were putting DC-3s out there. Well, they had some nurses and Red Cross gals, and so I put Barbara Finch in the DC-3. She beat her husband ashore on Iwo Jima. Of course, he never lived that down.

But all of these things just opened up. I'd say, "What do you want? You want to write about this? Write about it. It'll get out."

Q: At this point, you were in competition with the Air Force, weren't you?

Admiral Miller: Oh, listen, let me tell you. MacArthur was sending people up from down south. When they were going through all this baloney of theirs, you know, they had a pet phrase out. They were sending copy out of the tropics down there at some fabulous speed of 10,000 words a minute or some absurd claim. The reporters would come up and tell me about it. What they'd do is they'd send it out awfully fast, but it's probably been held up for three days waiting for the static situation to clear up, and then they'd put this machine on and really let her rip. But it was already three days old by the time it got there. It was going out fast, but it was stale copy by the time it arrived. They sent a Colonel DuPuy up to look over our organization.* We just showed off, that's all, because we really had it going.

The reporters would say, "Don't let me go back down to MacArthur's." We had quonset huts for them to live in, I had all the whiskey I needed in the world for them and beer, but that wasn't the come-on. The come-on was their freedom; that was the thing.

Q: Did you have any problems with reporters violating security?

Admiral Miller: That's very interesting. Never, not once did we ever have a violation of that. Now, in Guam, I was always very proud to say we never had anything like that. But remember, I had absolute control of everything being transmitted out of there, because all you had to do really was cut the switch to control it.

Forrest Sherman was one of the great naval officers; he and I had known each other since I was a jaygee.† Just before Iwo Jima, I went to Forrest Sherman and said, "Forrest, we've got a great bunch of reporters here now who are absolutely trustworthy. Besides, I've got control. I mean, I can stop anything that goes out. Would you be willing to tell them before the fleet leaves Guam and Ulithi [where it was forming, for the most part] what the hell we're going to do?"

---

* Colonel Ernest R. Dupuy, USA.
† Rear Admiral Forrest P. Sherman, USN, was head of the war plans division on Admiral Nimitz's staff. Later he served as Chief of Naval Operations, 1949-51. Jaygee--lieutenant (junior grade).

He said, "Well, I'd be happy to do that." So we set it up about two or three days before they went aboard ship. It was very soon. I had the reporters all at Guam, then I'd fly them all down to Ulithi, and they'd take their ships. Once they were aboard ship, of course, they were locked up too.

By golly, we went in there, and Forrest Sherman had all his charts, his phase charts, everything. He told these people everything we had, everything the Japs had, where we were going to be then on the first day, the second day, and so on and on and on. He told everything that we knew. It was a remarkable demonstration of confidence. Well, those are the things that made the reporters play ball with us, boy, if we'd do that for them. They played ball with us. They just loved Sherman and Nimitz.

We did have one possible violation of security by a woman named Dickey Chapelle. She died when she stepped on a mine in Vietnam later on, poor gal.* We called her "the Voice." She had a very deep voice, and in spite of what I did to her, she was always a very dear friend of mine. Well, she wanted to go to Okinawa, so fine.

Q: Was she on Guam?

Admiral Miller: We were on Guam now, planning the Okinawa campaign. And I said, "Well, fine. I'll be happy to put you on a hospital ship or a cargo ship or something." Hospital, I think it was.

She said, "Well, I want to go ashore."

I said, "You can't go ashore until the Red Cross gals and nurses go ashore."

---

* U.S. correspondent-photographer Dickey Chapelle died on 4 November 1965 after being wounded by a Viet Cong mine that detonated while she was reporting U.S. Marine operations near Chulai, South Vietnam.

Well, what actually happened, about three days after the landings at Okinawa, a message came to me personally from Kelly Turner.* He said, "Get that woman out of here!" What happened was she talked to the skipper of the ship and said, "I'll get in the motor launch. I'll just go to the dock and be back. I just want to get a feel of the island," and so on. Well, she went to the dock and disappeared. The first thing you know, she was up there, wandering around in the front line. I ordered her out of the Pacific, the only one I ever threw out.

Q: For breaking her word?

Admiral Miller: Yes. The only one I ever banned. A year later, I was getting letters from her husband wanting to know why I had banned her. I never knew whether he was suspicious of her or me or what. But he was suspicious of something. Then I used to see her at the Overseas Press Club over here, and we were very friendly. But that was the only violation.

Q: She never offered an explanation for her action?

Admiral Miller: Oh, I knew. She was just being a good reporter. She was representing Uncle Billy's Whiz Bang out of Minneapolis. That was her authority for being a reporter.†

Q: What was Uncle Billy's Whiz Bang?

---

* Vice Admiral Richmond Kelly Turner, USN, Commander Task Force 51, the Joint Expeditionary Force, for the invasion of Okinawa.
† Chapelles' autobiography, What's a Woman Doing Here (New York: William Morrow, 1962), has a different version. She had already written extensively on aviation and recounted being sent to the Pacific by Fawcett Publications, publisher of Woman's Day and Popular Mechanics.

Harold B. Miller #3 -151

Admiral Miller: You must know that. It was a kind of a get-together joke book. It was about the size of The Reader's Digest. It was jokes and about a tenth porno.

Q: Not a very credible publication, then?

Admiral Miller: Oh, no. How they ever approved her in the first place, I never knew. She turned out to be a damn good reporter.

By the time the war was over, there were about 400 of these reporters. I kept them together in a thing called the Upchuckers. And we met every year, year in and year out, in various places, at Toots Shor's, or someplace around New York. The good part about it, of course, was not only meeting them, but I kept an accurate mailing list on each one of them and a roster. In those days, I had secretaries in the oil industry or in Pan Am or someplace.* That was no problem. So I was the focal point of keeping them all together through the roster. It would be a 30-page roster. That went on for 30 years, and finally I did my swan song and told them how much fun it had been, but the time had come. So we closed that out. But there was a going concern there for 30 years.

Q: Did you have anything to do with Fitzhugh Lee on Guam?†

Admiral Miller: Oh, I brought Fitzhugh in as my relief. That was the only way I could get out of there, but I haven't finished my story there by a long shot.

Well, what happened was Forrestal would come out, and I would always say, "Hi, how are you, Mr. Secretary?"

---

* Admiral Miller worked in public relations for Pan American World Airways following his retirement from active duty.
† Captain Fitzhugh Lee, USN. The oral history of Lee, who retired as a vice admiral, is in the Naval Institute collection.

He'd say, "Great. How are things going?"

I said, "I think all right."

He said, "Well, I can tell you. They're going well." Sometime during that period I thought maybe it was time for me to go back and to see Forrestal in Washington.

So I asked the admiral, "Do you mind if I make a little trip?"

He said, "No, go on. Go on back."

So I went back. I was only gone about three days. I went in to see Forrestal, and he said, "Look, I'm getting great letters from editors. The whole thing is changing. It's just great."

I said, "That's why I'm here, Mr. Secretary. Remember that big carrier?"

He said, "Oh, hell. I can get anybody to fight a carrier. Things are going well out there, and I've got plans for you. Now you go on back out and go to work." So I went back.

But as I stood there, I promised myself that when the war was over, I was going to retire on that 20-year deal, because I would not have pulled a trigger in anger. I was standing there and said, "Boy."

Well, I went back out there and shortly after that, Iwo was ready to go in February. Of course, I saw Mr. Forrestal, and I took him down and put him on a broadcast, and we talked in general about how things were. He said, "Just bear in mind I have plans for you."

"Whatever you say, it must be all right."

Q: A man of great faith, you are.

Admiral Miller: He was the Secretary. During all that period, I also should have pointed out that Forrestal sent publishers out to Nimitz. For example, they were from The New

York Times, The Baltimore Sun, or The Washington Post. Another was Eph White of the Oregonian. Forrestal was a great PR man. He knew a story. Nimitz was finding that it was kind of a lot of fun too. These people go around and spread the word, "This Navy is a great outfit." The first thing you knew, people were really beginning to believe this type of thing. So in that way, I got to know all these publishers. We all worked together.

In any event, I was beginning to hear rumors from reporters. They said, "Well, you're not going to be out here very long."

I'd say, "I don't know anything about it."

"Well, we hear things." About that time, Time magazine ran a piece on me, and someone else wrote a piece on me.* So I was the last to hear about these things. I finally got orders to report to Washington out of Chinfo.† Tip Merrill was due to go to sea, and Forrestal had been looking for somebody to relieve him.‡

Q: What had he been? Was he Chinfo?

Admiral Miller: He had been Chinfo, and then he came out and took over some destroyers and had a very exciting life out there. At that time, although I had these orders, also accompanying them was the need to find a relief. That's how I brought Fitzhugh Lee into the picture out there.

---

* "New Man with a Doctrine," Time, 21 May 1945, page 22. The essence of the "doctrine" reported in the article was that the Navy would cooperate with the news media. The article was published after Miller's return to Washington.
† In later years the Chief of Information for the Navy has come to be abbreviated Chinfo. In April 1945, when Miller reported, he became director of the Office of Public Relations, Navy Department. In June of that year his title was changed to Director of Public Information.
‡ Rear Admiral Aaron S. Merrill, USN.

Q: Had he had experience?

Admiral Miller: Not particularly, but he was the type who could very easily do the job. You know, he was a kindly person and could make friends easily. It was very difficult trying to find somebody. Later on, I got Judge Eller to relieve me down at Chinfo.* There's always the case of, "You can go, but find a relief," the old Navy phrase, of course. So I got my orders, and I went on back to Washington to check in. It was kind of a sad farewell. We had a wonderful bunch of people.

Well, there's one more experience I should mention, and that's the famous Joe Rosenthal photograph up there of Mount Suribachi on Iwo.†

Q: Oh, yes, indeed.

Admiral Miller: Well, who was the Marine war correspondent? I made the point that we were flying the films down from Iwo Jima to Guam and dropping them, and we were processing this as fast as we could. I guess I spent all my time in the office. I never went to bed in those days. One of the photographers brought this picture up to me. I guess it was probably Captain Steichen. You know, Captain Steichen was out there at this point again. And this is the famous picture. And there was a question of whether or not this was a phony photograph or whether it was real.

Q: Credibility of the press again?

---

* Commodore Ernest M. Eller, USN. The oral history of Eller, who retired as a rear admiral, is in the Naval Institute collection.
† For details, see Rich Pedroncelli, "It Only Took a Second," <u>Naval History</u>, February 1995, pages 8-11.

Admiral Miller: Absolutely. And the question was whether we should let it go. We knew we had a gem, no question about that. We had a beautiful thing, but should it go? This Marine <u>Time</u> correspondent said, in effect, "It must be a phony. It couldn't be true." Steichen was all for letting it go. He felt that everything was on the up-and-up there. Joe Rosenthal and I were very good friends, and we still are.

Q: He was the . . .

Admiral Miller: He was the AP photographer who struggled up the mountain there.* I think the real facts of the case are--and I know this is true--that the Marines had hoisted a flag of sorts. Joe got there a little too late, and he said, "Listen, guys, do it again so I can get a picture of it." I'm sure that's what happened. Whether the five had put the first flag up or not, or whether Joe kind of rounded somebody up, that I've never been able to find out. But it's an authentic picture; it may not be the actual first picture, but it was within a minute or two of the first picture, and it was set up. It will never bother me at all. Well, we let it go, and, as you know the story, that picture's gone all over the world. It's one of the great photographs. Joe got a five-dollar raise from AP for taking that photograph; that was his reward. And AP must have made hundreds of thousands of dollars on sales of rights on that picture. But that was an exciting little episode. We always had a few odds and ends of that sort of thing.

    Then, of course, I came back to Washington.

Q: Perhaps there's something on the kamikazes?

---

* AP--Associated Press.

Admiral Miller: Yes, that became quite an argumentative situation. The kamikazes showed up first in the Philippines and with rather disastrous results to the U.S. Navy. The question was whether or not we should announce that the Japs were kicking the hell out of us with the kamikazes. Our first reaction was a typical Navy reaction, which was to say nothing about it. We didn't want the Americans to think we were getting licked or anything of that sort. We finally came to realize that the Japs probably knew what they were doing to us, no matter what. I mean, if we were to tell the story, we weren't telling the Japs anything new. They certainly knew the score on what they were doing to us.

Q: You could tell that, couldn't you, from Tokyo Rose and other reports that they broadcast?*

Admiral Miller: Of course, we never believed a word she said, anyway.

Q: But she still reflected something, didn't she, of Japanese thinking?

Admiral Miller: Well, yes, but she reflected purely anti-American, no matter if she had to dig down to the bottom of the barrel to try to even find a fact on the thing.

But the Japanese certainly knew what the kamikazes were accomplishing. We finally said, "How will the Navy let us release the story? Let's reverse the point of view and let the Americans know how tough the fighting is out here." That became our theme.

Q: Was this something that Nimitz approved of?

---

* "Tokyo Rose" was the nickname of an English-speaking Japanese woman who made radio broadcasts during World War II. Full of Japanese war propaganda, they were aimed at U.S. servicemen in an attempt to demoralize them. For the most part, she was entertaining rather than effective.

Admiral Miller: Well, this was something I talked over with Forrest Sherman, and Nimitz went along with that, yes. So we then opened up the gate on kamikazes and said, "My God, we're fighting a desperate battle out here. Be sure and give us all the support you can." And of course, as we got up to Okinawa, it became truly a matter of desperation for the Japs. As a matter of fact, most people aren't aware of the fact that we suffered far more casualties at Okinawa than we did anyplace else in the Pacific. It was a tremendous thing. If the war hadn't ended at that point, there's no limit to what the casualties might have been.

There was kind of a sad episode for the Japs. The poor devils only had enough fuel to go one way. The pilot was untrained, he could take off and probably couldn't land an airplane. It was a real sad day for them and for us, as a matter of fact.

Q: Did your publicity concentrate on our night fighters in any way?

Admiral Miller: No, that didn't get much. It would come up in a strange way. For example, Butch O'Hare--you remember the name? He did that absolutely incredible thing when he had the string of nine Jap bombers approaching the Lexington, and strangely enough, in sort of a single-file formation. If you recall, Butch started out on the top one and knocked it off and kept working his way forward, and knocked off five in a row in just one flight and in about ten minutes.*

That's when I was in Training Literature. I made the point that we were PR-ing for naval aviation. That's when I went to Riley and said, "Look, we want that boy back here." Training Literature brought Butch O'Hare back. We needed a hero about that time. Things were tough, and Butch was a natural-born hero. His dad had been a well-known

---

* On 20 February 1942, while a member of Fighting Squadron Three, Lieutenant (junior grade) Edward H. O'Hare, USN, shot down five of nine Japanese bombers approaching the USS Lexington (CV-2), thereby saving the ship. He was awarded the Medal of Honor for his exploit.

race horse gambler up in Chicago. He owned a track and had a beautiful family, but he was questionable. He was sort of on the shady side of life. Butch was just the salt of the earth.

So I took Butch on a tour back to Chicago, to St. Louis and New York. Again, we were encroaching on Navy public relations; we just simply grabbed him and took him. It worked out quite well. Well, the point you make on night flying--Butch finally went back to the fleet and disappeared on a night fighter flight.* To that extent, the story was told, but the publicity wasn't really of any consequence. The Black Cats' story was told. They were the PBYs painted black.

Q: Did you concentrate on submarine activities?

Admiral Miller: I told you earlier that we formed these photographic teams, Steichen's group, and we gave them orders, and they could go just about anyplace they wanted. Out of all that came the picture The Fighting Lady, which was the story of the USS Yorktown, really. Well, Charlie Lockwood had all the submarines out there, and he was a great guy.† Percy Finch, the Reuters man, was also very close to Charlie Lockwood. Well, I had access to submarine people, and I tried and tried to get them to ease off, let us put some reporters aboard, let us tell their story. I couldn't get any place with them.

Q: What was their reason?

Admiral Miller: They wanted anonymity. Well, they were the old Navy, I mean, to that extent.

---

* O'Hare was killed the night of 27 November 1943. He was the pilot of an F6F Hellcat which was flying with a radar-equipped TBF. See Eugene Burns, "Butch O'Hare's Last Flight," The Saturday Evening Post, 11 March 1944, page 19.
† Vice Admiral Charles A. Lockwood, USN, Commander Submarine Force Pacific Fleet.

Q: The silent service?

Admiral Miller: The silent service. They wanted no story told, they didn't want anything until they saw The Fighting Lady. Then they were knocking on the door, saying, "We want a picture like that."

So I said, "Well, guys, you're about two years late. Let's see what we can do." So I put colored cameras, motion picture and stills, on several submarines, and we took a lot of footage, but the targets were all gone. There were no Jap cargo ships left, really, to shoot. It was just plain too late, so we never came up with anything worthy of the name at all. It's their own damn fault, I must say. It wasn't for my lack of trying to get them to come along.

Q: Were you in Guam when they had the court-martial of Elliott Loughlin on the USS Queenfish for the sinking of SS Awa Maru?*

Admiral Miller: No, I wasn't there, but later on, I got very much involved in some of those code-breaking things. My impression is that he did just what any one of them would have done. Hell, they didn't know who was aboard that ship when they sank it. I didn't even recall that there had been a court-martial.

Q: You had knowledge of Magic and Ultra and what they were doing, did you?†

---

* The submarine Queenfish (SS-393) sank the Japanese merchant ship Awa Maru in April 1945, despite the fact that she had been granted safe passage by the United States. The skipper of the Queenfish was Commander C. Elliott Loughlin, USN. The oral history of Loughlin, who retired as a rear admiral, is in the Naval Institute collection.
† Magic and Ultra were nicknames for Allied code-breaking efforts before and during World War II. For details see W. J. Holmes, Double-Edged Secrets: U.S. Naval Intelligence Operations in the Pacific during World War II (Annapolis: Naval Institute Press, 1979).

Admiral Miller: Any knowledge I had wasn't during that period. It was later on, because I had two classmates, Dyer and Huckins, very heavily involved in that thing.* I did a lot of work researching that, but at the time I wasn't aware that we were so hot, frankly.

The story was well known, of course, about shooting down Yamamoto.† We had had the code on that, and, of course, Midway is well-known today as the result of a code-breaking operation.

Q: Yes, but I was thinking as a public relations sleuth, which you were indeed, you must have been suspicious or something.

Admiral Miller: Well, we were aware, but that's about all. As a matter of fact, although I had two classmates closely involved, and they were practically next door, I made it a point of never opening up the subject to them.

Q: All right. Now we're coming back to Washington to take up the job in the Office of Public Relations.

Admiral Miller: The interesting thing about this was that Forrestal gave me two stars, a spot promotion, which was about eight years ahead of my class.

Q: This was your reward, indeed.

---

* Captain Thomas H. Dyer, USN, whose oral history on code breaking is in the Naval Institute collection; Captain Thomas A. Huckins, USN.
† Admiral Isoroku Yamamoto, IJN, Commander in Chief Combined Fleet, was shot down and killed in the Solomon Islands in 1943 as a result of itinerary information gained from decrypting a Japanese message.

Harold B. Miller #3 -161

Admiral Miller: This was my payoff on the job.

Q: And do you suppose this was what he actually had in mind, or was he just talking?

Admiral Miller: Well, I suspect that he probably felt he was. I mean, he was nobody's fool, you know. And I always took it as a payoff--as my reward for the work at CinCPac. That pleased me, but my mind was still on retiring, even though I had the two stars. I happened to be also the youngest admiral the Navy ever had. I mean, everything happened to me at that point.

The interesting thing was that everyone accepted me, with only two exceptions. These were senior officers trying to show me that I was their goddamned lowly captain and don't ever forget it. One was Chips Carpender.* He and I never got along particularly. He thought he was Chinfo. He had been at one time. He was grumpy, and I didn't find him very pleasant. And there was someone else from around the class of '22; I forget who it was. One day he sent word up he'd like to see me. Well, I'm a congenial type; I'd go down and see him. But what he was doing was trying to show me he could send for me. It never happened again, and it wouldn't have happened if I hadn't been a little too naive at that point.

Q: This was after you became a rear admiral?

Admiral Miller: Yes. But later, I had admirals come and sit outside my office and wait a turn to get inside to do whatever it was they wanted to do.

---

* Vice Admiral Arthur S. Carpender, USN.

I just take my hat off to the Navy; it was just a great demonstration of Navy loyalty to let this young pipsqueak--me--come along and take a place and not embarrass him. I thought it was great, great. So I had no problems at all.

I did a lot of flying. I had called Anacostia and maybe I had to go to Los Angeles, so I got myself a Beechcraft. I like to fly at night. Anacostia knew that I'd take anybody, so they'd fill it up with bluejackets or WAVES or somebody going someplace.* I'd drop them off where they wanted to drop off--in Atlanta or Little Rock, I didn't care--and I'd just keep on going. So it was a great experience of freedom. It was the first time in my life I was ever able to write my own orders at any time without asking anybody.

Q: Well, you had a great mentor there still as SecNav, didn't you?†

Admiral Miller: Well, the interesting thing about that was no one out there in the Pacific ever really knew my relationship with Forrestal, but they were a little afraid that maybe it was pretty good. I always felt that that was one way I was able to have access to things that work out. As a matter of fact, I used to write to his aide. The point was that he and I kept up a correspondence, which was really my correspondence with Forrestal, so we kept in touch. And in those early days--say, for the first month I was in Hawaii--I felt like a worm, because I felt that I was working behind Nimitz's back. But all's well that ends well, so there was no problem there.

So Forrestal said, "Go anyplace you want to go. Do whatever you have to do. Just go."

As a matter of fact, when I came back and took over at Chinfo, I said, "Mr. Secretary, I'd like to go to England for a week or so."

---

* WAVES--Women accepted for Voluntary Emergency Service.
† SecNav--Secretary of the Navy.

He said, "Sure, go ahead."

Q: What was your purpose in going to England?

Admiral Miller: Oh, I had a great love and affection for England, and I just wanted to go over and see what it looked like. The war was practically over. As a matter of fact, I was over there for VE Day, which was the eighth of May.* From London, I flew to Paris to get on a plane to Patuxent to get back to Washington. So I saw VE Day in three of the capitals that were involved.

Q: Was there any contrast?

Admiral Miller: No, everybody was happy. I tell you, in London, as it shows up so much today, all of these horror photographs and motion pictures of the prison camps and the holocausts were coming through there fast. Of course, everybody was horrified at that; they just couldn't believe that such a thing had taken place. To that extent, it was different.

When I came back, our problem was to beat MacArthur to Tokyo.

Q: Did you have any particular mission assigned to you as Chinfo?

Admiral Miller: No, no. Let's just keep going. I did a lot of travelling, visiting with publishers and places all over the country. I was in the air all the time. An example would

---

* VE--Victory in Europe.

be the time I went with Admiral Leahy and Jock Clark to Yankton, South Dakota.* Clark was part Indian, and he wanted to go up to the Indian country.†

Q: He was part Cherokee.

Admiral Miller: Yes. So I took an old Beechcraft and flew the three of us up to Yankton, South Dakota. They gave their speeches, and we danced for the Sioux Indians. We all made chiefs. For instance, I'm a Sioux chief named Flying Charger. It was fun.

Q: I can't imagine Admiral Leahy dancing, though.

Admiral Miller: It was the most amazing thing you've ever saw, this old boy there hopping up and down like an Indian. It was really funny.

Q: Did you all get bonnets?

Admiral Miller: Oh, yes, we had all the headdresses. I think they came from Sears-Roebuck, probably, but they reached the ground in any event. It was a very exciting thing. That's that big Corn festival up there, you know, that Corn Palace, all the ears of corn built around it. It was great, things of that sort.

Then we reached the point where we still fighting MacArthur, of course, and knew damn well . . .

---

* Fleet Admiral William D. Leahy, USN, was chief of staff to President Harry Truman in his role as commander in chief of the armed forces. The event was Midwest Farmer Day on 3 September 1945.
† Rear Admiral Joseph J. Clark, USN.

Harold B. Miller #3 -165

Q: You took this office in April of 1945, so things were still happening out in the Pacific.

Admiral Miller: Yes, we had Okinawa still going on. That had gotten started before I left, and that went on for several months. Well, that's when the Jap war ended out there, August 15.

Q: You said that we were still fighting MacArthur. Would you elaborate on that and explain it?

Admiral Miller: Well, we thought the Navy did a pretty good job out there, and so I cooked up a plan, and Forrestal was more than agreeable: "The war's over, let's get Admiral Nimitz back, but let's get him back before MacArthur comes back." I'm sure the Army was probably thinking along the same line.

Q: This had to fall, then, in August?

Admiral Miller: It would have been August or early September. We brought him back very shortly after peace had been declared. We organized parades in Washington, New York, Dallas, and San Francisco. We brought him to Washington first and put on a tremendous show. Then I took him up to New York.

Q: Was Nimitz alone?

Admiral Miller: Nimitz and his wife and Forrest Sherman, the three of them. I tagged along, and it was great. The Army was sore as a goat. Nimitz was back there getting his adulations. Then we brought him up to New York and put him on TV, the first TV he had ever seen. As a matter of fact, the first TV most of us had ever seen. And he was very close to Cardinal Spellman, who used to come out to the fleet there.* We circulated. Incidentally, one of the Nimitz daughters became a nun.

Q: Yes, Mary, whom I know.

Admiral Miller: Yes, so he had sort of a Catholic angle, but he was certainly far from that.

Q: Nimitz was not Roman Catholic, nor Mrs. Nimitz.

Admiral Miller: No. I don't think he had any particular religious feelings at all. Then the problem was to get him down to Dallas and back to Texas, his old home state. I finally went to the admiral and said, "Now, will you be honest with me? Tell me, where is your home?"

He kind of looked around and he sssshhhed with his finger and he said, "Don't tell anybody, but it's Berkeley, California."

Q: Not Fredericksburg, Texas?

Admiral Miller: That was the first time I had ever heard that from him. I said, "Well, let's make it in Texas now, anyway, temporarily. So we won't mention Berkeley."

Well, let me tell you. When Dallas, Texas, was announced, I began to get phone calls from a lieutenant commander reserve who had been out of the Navy now, by the name

---

* Father Francis J. Spellman was military vicar of the United States. He had become archbishop of New York in 1939 and a cardinal in 1945.

of Johnson, Lyndon B. Johnson.* He said, "Admiral, you know, I'm from Texas too. If the admiral's down around in my district, I sure want to go down there with him." I did everything I could to keep him out and stop him. He would call, and I would stall, and he'd call, and I'd stall. I thought I had him stopped. We had a DC-4 over in Anacostia and shoved off at 6:00 that night. Forrest Sherman and the admiral were aboard, and I was working at my typewriter writing a speech for him.

Who shows up but Lieutenant Commander Johnson, and by God, he gets on that airplane, and he's with us. He made it, which showed that his talents were developed early in life.

Q: He was a determined man not to be beaten.

Admiral Miller: Well, we went through Dallas, and, of course, there was a tremendous parade there. Then we flew down to Austin and had another big parade down there at the capital, at which point Mr. Johnson insisted that the admiral go down to a little ranch he had down around Fredericksburg, a place that the admiral knew well.

Q: Well, that's where the admiral was born.

Admiral Miller: So we went down and looked over the old Steamboat Hotel. I was down there a couple of years ago; they're sort of resurrecting that, doing something with it. The Nimitz Museum, of course, is there now. Hubbard is doing a very nice job there.

Q: Doug Hubbard, whom I know.

---

* Johnson later served as President of the United States from 1963 to 1969.

Admiral Miller: Yes. But we had to go out to the ranch. I have pictures of us, the admiral and Mrs. Nimitz and Forrest and I sitting back on a horse-drawn surrey going down Fredericksburg's main drag. But Admiral Nimitz was loving all this. It was just great. He was just a sweetheart on all these things, and his wife, of course, she was a darling, too.

I had a Beechcraft flown down to Austin, and from there the admiral was going to go to San Francisco for a parade. Forrest and I decided we wouldn't go out there. We turned him over to somebody at that point. We got in the little Beechcraft and came back to Washington. So we accomplished our purpose. We did beat MacArthur back, and we thought we did a damn good job for the Navy.

Q: Now, backtrack just a little bit and tell me if you had any role in the arrangements for the surrender ceremony on the USS Missouri.

Admiral Miller: Well, at that point, I had Paul Smith. Paul Smith was the editor of the San Francisco Chronicle.* He was a commander, well-versed and experienced and everything else. I had him out there. And of course, Fitzhugh Lee was with Nimitz.† We kept out of that; that was a fleet operation, except for sending certain people out there.

Q: There were a lot of sticky arrangements as they pertained to MacArthur, weren't there?

Admiral Miller: Well, that was a fleet operation. That didn't reach back into Washington. Oh, yes, he was a very big fellow, of course.

---

* Paul C. Smith, editor-in-chief, San Francisco Chronicle.
† Lee's Naval Institute oral history covers his handling of publicity arrangements for the surrender on board the Missouri.

Q: Well, and also the selection of the Missouri as the vehicle. That reached into Washington and the White House, didn't it?

Admiral Miller: Well, President Truman took care of that, yes.* We weren't really involved in it.

Then, of course, we had the A-bomb test in Bikini, too, coming along. Admiral Spike Blandy, what a man he was; he had that thing.† I don't know whether I brought Paul Smith back for the publicity on that or whether it was Fitzhugh Lee. We ran that out of Washington. Of course, there was a great demand for space for reporters.

Q: Yes, and there also were reporters for the Russians and others.

Admiral Miller: Oh, yes, we always had problems like that. But those are the two major events of that period. As time went by, of course . . .

Q: What about demobilization?

Admiral Miller: Well, of course, we were fighting that battle all the time. Every ship became a troop carrier, whether it was a carrier or a coal burner or no matter what it was, every ship was carrying people back. The problems were, "I want my son back," "I want my boy back." We were always handling those hand-holding operations.

---

* Harry S. Truman, from the state of Missouri, was President of the United States from 1945 to 1953.
† Vice Admiral William H. P. Blandy, USN, Commander Joint Task Force One for the atomic tests at Bikini.

Q: Yes, but the Navy had to deal with it in terms of public relations, didn't they?

Admiral Miller: Yes. Well, the decision really was do you start breaking up crews in the fleet in order to get everybody back, or do you keep some ships fully manned? Ships were being denuded; some were half-manned and in real trouble. They weren't fighting vessels at that point. They just simply steamed and carried people.

Oh, yes, we had all the problems. And "Could Johnny come home? Because Charlie, next door, is home. Where's Johnny?" But they usually didn't amount to anything.

Q: It seemed to have been so precipitous, however, after World War II.

Admiral Miller: I thought it was too damn fast. It seemed a shame to break up that organization completely. On the other hand, you couldn't have taken this half and said, "All right, we'll break you up and keep these." You couldn't have done that very easily. I guess on the whole it probably worked out all right.

Q: Do you want to talk about combat art as one of your component parts of your job?

Admiral Miller: Yes. Well, as I mentioned before, Reeves Lewenthal was one who really brought the combat art . . .

Q: He was a reservist, was he?

Admiral Miller: No, he wasn't in the service at all. He had a PR connection with a pharmaceutical company in Chicago. He tried the Air Force or the Army, one or the other, and was turned down for some reason. Later on, of course, the Air Force went heavily on to this artwork. But we jumped at the chance to take him under our wing as artist. And again, I make that point about Radford and Artie Doyle back then in Training Literature--we could do just about whatever we had to in order to get the job done. We were able to write orders for these lads, and they were just sort of free-lance and could go anyplace in the world they wanted to go and paint. Of course, Steichen was involved in all of this.

Then all that work would be pulled back together again and put into pamphlets and brochures and things of that sort. Also, we frequently did lithographs that were sent around to various stations. It was part of a morale-building operation. They were innocuous people. By that, I mean they weren't in anybody's way at all, and they generally were very good PRs. For instance, there was a series of portraits of admirals. I'm not aware of them having a plan to say, "Now, we want this list of admirals painted for historical purposes." I don't recall ever having set anything like that up. The artists just sort of went around finding their subjects and brought this in.*

Each one of them had specialties, of course. There was that bunch in New Mexico--was it Peter Scott? Seems to me that's his name. He had his own style. We had another artist who did lighter-than-air and in a very blown up fashion. They all had their peculiarities. There were so many of them. Oh, yes, Tom Lea, who wrote the King Ranch stories, he did his cowboy type of things.† Everybody under the sun--it was invaluable work for us. That Navy collection still is being circulated throughout the country, I believe, on exhibits and so on.

Q: Well, there is a great collection in Washington.

---

* In fact, there was a plan, as recounted in the Naval Institute oral history of Commander Albert K. Murray, USNR (Ret.), who painted many of the admirals' portraits in the post-World War II period.
† For more on Lea's art, see Brendan Greeley, "Paso por Aqui," Naval History, April 1995, pages 8-17.

Harold B. Miller #3 -172

Admiral Miller: Oh, yes. So with the Steichen stills and with the artists and their paintings and so on, we had a pretty darn good record of things. And the work you're doing of recording these memories is invaluable.

Q: Well, the artwork really covers so many of the operations of World War II. It's surprising that the Air Force people couldn't anticipate this.

Admiral Miller: Well, later on, the Eighth Air Force did. I've got one of their booklets around here. They've got that splashy stuff which is really very effective. But I don't know what their problem was with Reeves Lewenthal. Maybe the problem was with him. I don't know. But we were grateful to him. That, of course, led us into Salmagundi, the artists' club down on Fifth Avenue. They've always been Navy, of course. The exhibits are always available in there, and you could always get a room during the war. They were just marvelous to the Navy, just marvelous.

Q: Did you have anything to do, or did you facilitate the actions of Admiral Morison?*

Admiral Miller: Well, he was almost as controversial a character during the war I presume you may have run into. I've had several letters, oddly enough, in the last couple of years, one from a lad out in Denver, Colorado, asking particularly about the accuracy of Morison. What I had to tell him was I had read, I thought, most of his writings and had no reason to doubt him, but I do think that history really shouldn't be written on the spot. I think it should be written 15 or 20 years later, because then you know what really happened. I

---

* Rear Admiral Samuel Eliot Morison, USNR, was a noted civilian historian who received a Naval Reserve commission in order to collect material for what eventually became the 15-volume History of United States Naval Operations in World War II.

suspect strongly that many of the things he has written, published early, no doubt were accepted as facts at the time but wouldn't be accepted as facts today.

Q: I think you're probably quite accurate in that, but the thing is, this is the broad history of the naval warfare, and it hasn't been done since.

Admiral Miller: Oh, there's no question. I still don't know, really, the technique. I don't think I met him at that point. I met him later on. I got him to give a talk at the Overseas Press Club, and some correspondent there was taking him on. Morison was giving back just as good as he received relating to the accuracy of his books. I think he had a team, did he not?

Q: Oh, yes, yes. He had quite an extensive team working under him. And he carried the writ from FDR himself which gave him carte blanche where he could go wherever he wanted to.

Admiral Miller: Yes, yes. They commissioned him and gave him all those sort of things, of course. And, of course, it's what he saw at the time. That's what he wrote about. But I've got to say that that book written 20 years later--after all, hindsight's not too bad either, you know.

Q: No, and the opportunity to examine documents and gather things together. It only stands to reason that it would be more accurate.

Admiral Miller: That's right.

Q: Did Chinfo in your time engage in making movies or doing anything of that sort?

Admiral Miller: Not really. We saw a need for training films and things like that. Of course, during the war, Luis de Florez was the great incentive for training films when he was there. Also, he helped develop synthetic training, which was teaching somebody how to fly on the ground.

Q: Link trainer?

Admiral Miller: Yes, and others. That type of thing which is just so accepted today. So de Florez was making training films all over the place. As I recall, we did a little bit, but not so extensively. After all, we were so loaded up with training films at that point, and the war was practically over.

Q: No, I was wondering more in terms of promoting recruiting since the demobilization was so devastating to the Navy and the need to get more bodies in the Navy, and whether Chinfo did anything about promoting that.

Admiral Miller: I don't think we realized at the time that the fallout was so hazardous at that particular point, because the ships were going out of commission pretty fast by then. Of course, later on, you realize these things. No, I would say that we weren't really aware at what was going on to that extent. Perhaps we should have been.

Chinfo was a job that you really should be there quite a while. I don't know what the background is for these lads who become Chinfo today.* It happened that I went there because of Training Literature and doing a lot of writing. I had had a certain amount of background for the job. I don't know whether these boys today have it or not.

Q: You were saying off-tape that Forrestal had the title changed?

Admiral Miller: It was a title. It was chief of public relations, and he and I had long talks about this thing. That title sort of gave the inference that you were trying to direct or change people's line of thought forcefully and deliberately. Why not make it chief of public information so that the information is available?

Q: And getting out.

Admiral Miller: We agreed that this would be a far more accurate and probably a digestible title--public information rather than public relations. I think we were sound.

Q: One has the connotation of dispensing things, and the other of being more aggressive.

Admiral Miller: Forcing it, yes. But regardless of name, the action is what counts anyway. As a title, I think "information" is probably a more acceptable title.

Q: Did you have anything to do with the WAVES, as such?

---

* Current practice is for the Chief of Information to be a Navy public affairs specialist rather than a line officer.

Admiral Miller: Not a great deal. They started coming out to Pearl, I remember, shortly afterwards. Of course, Joy Hancock and I have known each other for years, and I always followed her career with great interest. Then Winnie Quick came out to Pearl, one of the early ones.* I follow them now purely as a matter of interest.

Q: But no publicity?

Admiral Miller: No, no.

Q: Do you want to make some comments on working with reservists?

Admiral Miller: Well, as an old-line aviator, I originally felt, like so many of us, that it took something like a college degree to enable you to fly properly. As time went on and I got into Training Literature just as the war was beginning, we realized that we just couldn't be restrictive like that. We'd take anybody that was physically sound and had two good feet. We'd take anybody that came along, really, and that's why Training Literature got started, trying to bring the educational level down to a point where anybody could understand what we were trying to say and to teach.

    Well, what that meant was that they were practically all reservists. So beginning about that period, my experience lay quite heavily with reservists. Occasionally you used to hear stories--well, it would be from both sides. The reserves would say, "Well, the regulars there are a bunch of flat-foot, sticky people, etc., etc." And the regulars might feel strange about the reservists. But I was always proud to say that never did I find any problem

---

* Lieutenant Winifred R. Quick, USNR, was one of the first officers in the WAVES. Later, she was director of the WAVES. Now Captain Winifred Quick Collins, USN (Ret.), her oral history is in the Naval Institute collection.

between the regulars and the reservists. I certainly had none, and I never observed any. Any job that I held where I had control of personnel, first of all, I wouldn't have permitted it. But secondly, it didn't happen. It just naturally didn't happen. We always had good relationships.

God knows we couldn't have moved without them, and I think, as I talk to reservists these days (that is, people who were in the war), they invariably will say that they never had any sad experiences, and primarily the experience they had was the greatest thing that ever happened to them, serving in the Navy during the war. So all this wish-wash about problems or confrontation between regulars and reserves--I never saw it. I'm inclined to think it didn't take place, but I certainly never saw it.

Q: Add something here to . . .

Admiral Miller: Well, when I was an ensign, the fleet was small. The first thing you know, you knew just about everybody in the fleet. By that, I mean you knew reputations plus or minus. Goodness, no, you didn't know them all, but practically everybody had a reputation, good or bad of some sort. I began to wonder what is there about a naval officer that makes him eligible and probably selected as Chief of Naval Operations. In looking around, I came up with three names of people whose jobs and whose background and whose reputation and what I had heard about them and knew about them would be logical candidates for Chief of Naval Operations.

Q: And in due time?

Admiral Miller: In due time. They were all lieutenants at that particular point. They were either aviators, or they were working on staffs, assigned to staffs. And it turned out, the three were Mick Carney, Arthur Radford, and Forrest Sherman. When they were lieutenants, it was obvious that these three were going to be Chief of Naval Operations in due course of time. And that's the way it worked out.

Q: Except for Radford, who didn't become CNO.*

You retired shortly thereafter. You want to tell me about that?

Admiral Miller: Well, my decision to retire, as I said earlier, was at the time of my spot promotion. I would revert back to captain, of course, and I still had not pulled the trigger in anger. Forrestal was still with us at that particular point. Incidentally, I was in demand. I had many jobs offered to me, and I was particularly anxious to go to Pan American. That didn't work out, as I'll explain later. But it seemed to me I was young. If I was going to make the break, now was the time to make the break.

Q: How old were you at that point?

Admiral Miller: Well, let's see. I'd have been still only 43. So I made that decision. I talked with Mr. Forrestal about it. He said, "Well, I wouldn't argue against it." So I turned in my suit, which was effective 1 December, 1946. I could have wept, of course, because the Navy was the greatest, certainly the greatest to me, but I left.

---

* Radford served as Chairman of the Joint Chiefs of Staff, 1953-57, a position that outranks the Chief of Naval Operations.

Interview Number 4 with Rear Admiral Harold B. Miller, U.S. Navy (Retired)

Place: Admiral Miller's home, Manhasset, New York

Date: Monday, 8 September 1981

Interviewer: Dr. John T. Mason, Jr.

Q: Now, today I'm looking forward to the account of your activities in retirement, because they were extensive. Last time, you dealt with the end of your career when you were director of public information, and you served in that capacity for about a year and a half. When you finally came to retirement, you decided to retire on the first of December, 1946.*

Admiral Miller: That's right. That was the break point there.

Q: Here you were retired at the end of 1946 with a promising career before you. Will you take up the story at that point?

Admiral Miller: Well, I had had lots of job offers of various kinds, but I was very much wedded to aviation. The airlines had treated me very well, in particular Pan Am, because Pan Am consisted almost entirely of naval personnel, naval aviators, naval mechanics. Their aircraft were flying boats, and it just seemed to be an ideal situation.

---

* Miller actually left active duty on 31 July 1946 to join TWA. His official retirement date was 1 December 1946.

Q: Yes, and their record in World War II was magnificent, wasn't it?

Admiral Miller: Oh, yes, the whole line was put at the command of the Navy, of course. And besides, many of its pilots by this time had been students of mine in Pensacola in 1929, and I'd kept in touch with them. So I sort of felt I was part of the family.

Well, I was working particularly through a man named Sam Pryor, who was the vice president and assistant to Trippe.* I told Sam what my thoughts were on this matter, and he said, "Go see Juan Trippe. Go see Juan Trippe."† Well, trying to see Juan Trippe was like trying to see the good Lord. He was always busy, and there seemed to be no point to it. I finally got fed up with this "Go see Juan Trippe" business. I was getting no place. I knew Jack Frye was president and founder of TWA.‡ He was certainly a great fellow. He and I got together and we flew around together a few times, and one thing led to another.

Well, we were having lunch, and he said, "Gee, you know, you really ought to come over here. We're not as old as Pan Am, but we're getting there," and so on. I was sore at Pan Am at that point, so I shook hands with Jack Frye and said, "Well, sure, I think that's a good idea." I think I had about a month to go on active duty then.

So now I had agreed to join TWA. I called Sam Pryor and said, "Sam, here's what's going on. I just talked to Jack Frye, and I'm going to go with TWA."

Well, he hit the roof. "Stop it! That's not the thing to do." But nothing came of this conversation.

---

* Samuel Pryor joined Pan American in 1941. At the time he was vice president of Southern Wheel Company and assistant to the president of American Brake Shoe and Foundry. He was also a Republican national committeeman from the state of Connecticut.
† Juan Trippe was the founder and chairman of Pan American. For detailed coverage of the man and airline, see Robert Daley, An American Saga: Juan Trippe and his Pan Am Empire (New York: Random House, 1980).
‡ Jack Frye was the head of Transcontinental and Western Air, which later became Trans World Airlines.

Harold B. Miller #4 -181

I then had a call from Dave Ingalls, who had been Assistant Secretary for Air for the Navy, and I had known him very well.* He was also a director of Pan Am at that time. He was a captain in the Naval Reserves, among other things. He said, "Now, Miller, this is nonsense. What is it you want?"

I told him what I had wanted. I wanted to go back to England, and I wanted to operate Pan Am in Europe. He said, "You can have anything you want." Well, by that time it was too late. I had shaken hands with Jack Frye, and in the Navy that was a commitment. The day I walked into TWA, I literally could have wept. I no more wanted to go with TWA than a man in the moon. I presume one might say that I simply outfoxed myself in my efforts to put a little pressure on Pan Am.

Q: What job were you going to hold in TWA?

Admiral Miller: Oh, vice president of public relations was the thought, and that was the job that I got. But, being a naive young naval officer, I didn't realize that Jack Frye was having personal troubles inside TWA.

Q: What was his job there?

Admiral Miller: Well, he was president and founder. TWA needed money, and his chief stockholder, whom he had to go to for money, was a guy by the name of Howard Hughes.† So Jack Frye had his problems too. When Howard Hughes would decide that he wanted an airplane, he'd just take an airplane off the line, one of the new Constellations, and that was hundreds of thousands of dollars a day going down the drain.

---

* Captain David S. Ingalls, USNR. In World War I Ingalls became the Navy's first fighter ace. From 1929 to 1932 he was Assistant Secretary of the Navy for Aeronautics.
† Howard R. Hughes (1905-1976) was an American industrialist who gained fame in the 1930s as an aviator and motion picture producer. He later gained a controlling interest for a time in Trans World Airlines.

Q: He was difficult even in those days?

Admiral Miller: He was difficult indeed. He wanted to check out on a Connie, and Jack Frye had tried to take him up and instruct him. Jack said, "Well, hell, this guy can't even fly." That, of course, wasn't entirely true, because Hughes had done a few things with the Lockheed, going around the world and all that. He could fly airplanes, but he apparently could not or was unable to check out on the Connie. Jack wouldn't check him out. He finally went to somebody in Lockheed who checked him out. At any rate, Hughes was giving him trouble. So it was obvious that my job was very tenuous, and Jack Frye's was certainly very tenuous. We went to a board meeting in New York one day, a year later, and we both got fired by Howard Hughes--fired by the Great Man.
So then what do you do, of course?

Q: Would you stop and say a little about Howard Hughes and your relation with him? He was such a colorful character.

Admiral Miller: He was just about what everybody had read and thought about. He wore his tennis sneakers to the board meeting, he was very slender, he didn't have a great deal to say, but what he said was it. I mean, there was no questioning him at all. He had a good grasp of finances, because he had something like 400 million dollars in TWA.

Q: And money does talk, doesn't it?

Admiral Miller: Oh, yes. Equitable Life, of course, was also one of Jack's financial angels at that particular point. We used to go up there and talk with them. But that was the end of that.

Q: Did you have personal dealings with Hughes?

Harold B. Miller #4 -183

Admiral Miller: Only during board meetings. No, I never had anything to do with him. I wouldn't have wanted to, as a matter of fact. Even then, he was somebody you didn't want to really mess around with. At least I didn't want to.

Q: A dictator, was he?

Admiral Miller: His reputation was not particularly savory, and he had surrounded himself with some very questionable characters too. They were emissaries that he would send out.

And so that ended that chapter. Jack Frye was very close with Supreme Court Justice Clark, a big, tall boy. He, at that point, was not yet a Supreme Court justice; he was the United States Attorney General under Truman.* Clark had the powers to dispose of German properties that we'd taken over during the war. One of them was General Aniline and Dye.

Q: Oh, yes.

Admiral Miller: He, in effect, gave that to Jack Frye, who became its president.

Q: Was it the idea of liquidating that or . . . ?

Admiral Miller: I don't recall the details on that. But it was U.S. property by that time, and it has been ever since.

Q: Oh, it's a continuing thing?

---

* Tom C. Clark served as Attorney General, 1945-49 and as an Associate Justice of the Supreme Court, 1949-67.

Harold B. Miller #4 -184

Admiral Miller: It continues, yes.* It's basically chemicals. Then they had cameras and film as well, which they later dropped. Jack carried on there for several years.

Well, about that time, Senator Brewster was in real trouble.† He was alleged to be a Pan Am flunky. That was through Sam Pryor and Trippe. Trippe, at that point, was trying to create the chosen instrument, which would have been a single international airline for the U.S. In other words, there were only two: Pan Am and TWA. The idea was to put the two together into one line. This was Trippe's thesis. It became a hell of a fight down in the halls of Congress.

Q: It was considered a monopoly, was it?

Admiral Miller: Well, that was the argument. The whole point was that Trippe would be the president of the whole outfit, of course. That would be the way he would operate.

Q: How did Hughes react to that?

Admiral Miller: He was fighting that, of course, tooth and nail. I was still with TWA. That was just before our blow-up. So I got involved in that. In any event, I got to know some of the attorneys of Pan Am, oddly enough. So I was without a job at that particular point. Jack Frye had landed safely with this nice, big chemical company.

I had a call from Brewster and his particular group at this time. By now the Pan Am-TWA fight was all over. Now, what they wanted down in the Senate and the House was an aviation policy to be set up by the Congress. And they wanted somebody to do that. So I got a call to come down to Capitol Hill, and I took on the job as director of the Congressional Air Policy Board. Out of that came a tremendous thing. I ended up with a

---

* Today known as GAF.
† Ralph O. Brewster, a Republican, represented Maine in the U.S. Senate from 1941 to 1952.

staff of about 50 people, all of whom were essential. They all had relations with aviation; they were aviation writers and analysts and all that sort of thing.

Q: Was this to be a continuing thing?

Admiral Miller: For only one shot--to come up with a policy.

Q: What kind of deadline did you have, or did you?

Admiral Miller: At the start there was no particular deadline, but it ended up taking a solid year, just exactly a year. Oh, I had the most tremendous committee, both from the House and from the Senate and then from industry. I had all the aviation names that meant anything, including Jimmy Doolittle.* I have a copy of this report down below. I'd call the meetings and bring them in, including all of these aviators. I set up the committee. One reason I was doing this was because I always wanted to know what they did down on the Hill, and I never had any experience on the political angles down there. So I thought this was a great opportunity, and it turned out to be so.

Q: Were some of the members of Congress and the Senate sitting on the committee?

Admiral Miller: Oh, yes. It was about a third Senate, a third Congress, and a third civilians. We would get together about once a month, as I recall. Out of that, I would distill the main ideas and then farm them out to my staff to develop. So the first thing you know, we had this whole thing moving with a common front. Of course, you always had certain people

---

* A long-time figure in U.S. aviaton, James H. Doolittle was probably best known for leading a flight of B-25 Army Air Forces bombers in an attack against Tokyo in April 1942. Other members included General H. H. Arnold; Ralph S. Damon, president of American Airlines; Rear Admiral Luis de Florez; J. H. Kindelberger, president of North American Aviation; and Admiral John H. Towers.

who carried weight. You could consult with them as you went along and get a pretty good idea of whether you were on the right track or not.

Q: You mean members of Congress?

Admiral Miller: Yes. Brewster was one of those. I had a congressman from California who was absolutely great, Carl Hinshaw. In any event, at the end of a year, we came up with a pamphlet of 80 or 90 pages which represented U.S. national policy on air. It was very well received, so I felt that that year was well worthwhile.

Q: Had the Air Force been set up as a separate service?

Admiral Miller: This is 1948, I guess it would have had to have been.*

Q: Symington must have been a factor.

Admiral Miller: Well, Symington was Secretary of the Air Force at that point.† Stuart Symington was a very dear friend of mine. He suggested to me one day, "You know, you're in the wrong service. Why don't you take off that blue uniform and put on a light blue uniform?" He was very serious about it.

Q: Well, of course, that was the effort in 1949, too, to win over all the naval aviators.

Admiral Miller: Yes. So at any rate, I was out of a job again after finishing this work with Congress. It was a very successful operation. But about that time, a lad from Texaco said,

---

* As part of the unification of U.S. armed services and the creation of the National Military Establishment (later the Department of Defense), the Air Force became a separate service in September 1947.
† W. Stuart Symington was first Secretary of the Air Force, holding office from 18 September 1947 to 24 April 1950.

Harold B. Miller #4 -187

"Gee whiz, they're looking for somebody at the American Petroleum Institute in New York," which, in effect, was a trade organization for all the oil companies. I had never heard of it, I must say. They were looking for some public relations talent. So I took that job, and we moved up from Washington to New York.

Q: Tell me the scope of that job.

Admiral Miller: That job had a national scope.* What was going on then was that the oil industry--as always--was in bad with the public. The public always thinks the oil companies are cheating on their prices, they're getting bad quality, they're a bunch of crooks, which, of course, isn't so. My job was to make them love the oil industry. I don't think I succeeded in that, although I tried awfully hard.

Q: No, I don't think you did, because the public still has that attitude.

Admiral Miller: But what that did was provide me with an acquaintanceship throughout the United States. I was on the go a great deal of the time. We would set up local committees of oil people, even down to jobbers or service station people, in an effort to educate the schools. We came up with all kinds of materials, drawing sketches, illustrations, pamphlets and so on in an effort to point out, from our point of view, that this was a perfectly legitimate operation, and there was no skullduggery involved at all. That was in all of the states. We'd have meetings in the Northwest and down in Los Angeles, just all over the place, so I got to know hundreds and hundreds of people all over the country.

Q: And who financed this? The separate oil companies chipped in?

---

* Miller became director of the Oil Industry Information Committee, under the auspices of the American Petroleum Institute.

Admiral Miller: They put in a percentage. We had a budget running about three and a half million dollars, and we did advertising, we made a couple of movies. But the main effort was to get to the schools and have the local oil man go to a school and say, "Here's some material that would be worth your while." What is oil? How do you drill it? And so on, with all these illustrations. It was an educational program, basically.

Q: Did you use the radio?

Admiral Miller: Yes, we did. We had one set of radio programs. Of course, as you can imagine, the oil companies are highly competitive, and trying to get them all to agree on any one subject was not the easiest thing in the world.

Q: I suppose the educational aspect was something they would agree upon.

Admiral Miller: They agreed that that was the object but how to achieve that, then there's where the disagreement would start. One would want to go one road, and one would go down another road.

Q: Standard Oil was the leading one, I suppose, in the country?

Admiral Miller: Yes. I should say Esso in those days, Exxon today, probably. Texaco was powerful, but Exxon was always gracious about things. Exxon was a great company. They weren't one of these fly-by-nights. Sun Oil was gracious.

Q: Sinclair was in.

Admiral Miller: Sinclair wasn't particularly active. Then we had all these--Conoco, of course, and Standard of California, Standard of Indiana, Standard of Ohio, we had all of them. After ten years, they finally decided that, hell, they were paying a lot of money, and they weren't getting anything, really. So they broke it up.

Q: You mean the whole effort was discontinued?

Admiral Miller: Yes, the whole effort was discontinued.

Q: But it has been taken up by individual companies now on television, hasn't it?

Admiral Miller: Oh, it probably did a lot to indoctrinate individual companies. Mobil, of course, all you have to do is look in <u>The New York Times</u> and read their ad almost every day, several times a week certainly. And PR, really, is what it amounts to. It's just great.

And Exxon is too. But working together--there is another point involved in that. One of the views that has always been held by the public is that, "They're just one big combine anyway. I don't know why they have all these different companies, because it's just one company."

Q: The gas is the same.

Admiral Miller: So if they could all get together and put money in the common pool for common effort, it would prove that they were just one company. Finally, that view also prevailed: "You'd better break this thing up and go back to the individual efforts, because it just looks bad." That was one of the arguments to break it up, and it's probably a pretty good argument too.

Q: How did the international oil companies figure in this picture?

Admiral Miller: Well, if you take the big four over there in Saudi Arabia, for example, Standard of California, Texaco, Mobil, and Standard of New Jersey, they never functioned as an international outfit at all. All those had their national companies over here, and that's what it would be. We always kept completely clear of any international angles.

Q: I was thinking of Royal Dutch, for instance.

Admiral Miller: Well, Shell has a company, but you have a Shell up in North America, too, and that was old Max Burns. He was a wonderful man. Deceased now, but he was great. Jimmy Doolittle was working for Shell, too, and you could get all sorts of cooperation. But basically, I doubt that we did anything.

But there are interesting stories about that job. When I first went up to API, we decided to run a series of ads, and obviously the logical ad you would want would be about what oil had contributed to the war effort. That would be a natural.

Q: Being so near to the . . .

Admiral Miller: That's right. Let's see, this was 1949 now. So I said, "Well, gee, I know a fellow we can get." We wanted to use a picture and have a tagline on it, so to speak. Nimitz would be the logical one. Someone--I always thought it was Nimitz--came up with that line, something about, "Beans, bullets, and oil had won the war."

Well, I talked with Nimitz about that, and he said he didn't think he'd said that. He said, "I think that was Bill Halsey."

In any event, I wrote to Admiral Nimitz out there in Berkeley. I had kept in touch with him after the war, and we were on a very friendly basis. For example, my two boys are a late family for me. Hell, I was 55 or something when they were born.* In any event, as each one was born, each would receive a handwritten letter from Admiral Nimitz. "Dear Blaine" or "Dear Barry." Of course, they are priceless. He would write, "I knew your dad, blah, blah, blah," this and that, which is just part of the proof of the great man that he was.

---

* Harold Blaine Miller, Jr., was born in 1956, when Admiral Miller was 53. Barry McGee Miller was born in 1957, when the admiral was 54.

In any event, I wrote to Admiral Nimitz and said, "Here's what we're planning to do. We think you would be the most powerful man to discuss the value of oil during the war. If you'd be willing, I'd be happy to send a writer out there. There would be no work involved at all. You can pass on the copy, you can change it, you can do anything you like."

Well, in practically the return mail, I had a letter from him in which he had written the copy. It was wonderful copy. We didn't change one word of it, and that was the ad, in his inimitable way of putting first things first, it was just absolutely a priceless ad.

Q: And it was a testimonial to what the oil companies had done?

Admiral Miller: That is right. Well, when it was all over, I said, "My God, we've got to pay him. He can't do this for nothing. He needs money like anybody else." Well, prices were not too exorbitant in those days. Everybody agreed, "Gee, $400.00 would be about a fair return on that." So I wrote him out a check for $400.00 and sent it out to him and said, "I wish it could be more," and that sort of thing.

He wrote back and said, "You know, this is the greatest thing that happened to me in a long, long time. This means I can put on another bathroom."

I remember once going out to see Kettering. We wanted Kettering to use on one of these ads too.*

Q: Now, his position at that time was . . . ?

Admiral Miller: Well, he was an emeritus type out of General Motors. He had come up with ethyl fluid, for example, and all these exotic technical things. He was one of the deans of the scientific world. I was, again I say, this naive naval officer. But my job was to go

---

* Charles F. Kettering was an electrical engineer and manufacturer. He was president of General Motors Research Corporation and vice president of the General Motors Corporation. He invented a number of systems for cars.

out there, and I went out to Yellow Springs or some kind of springs there in Ohio. We walked all around, and he said he was working on what makes the grass green.

Q: Chlorophyll.

Admiral Miller: I had asked, "Well, what are you doing these days, Doctor?" I think I called him "Doctor." He was still working on chlorophyll.

He said, "What makes everything green?"

Like a fool, I said something about, "And why do you want to do that?"

And he said, "My God, if I can do that, we could feed the whole world." He was working on a chemical to get bigger crops and things like that. Well, I didn't get him to sign. He was involved in his own science, in his own research. But those were the sort of things that were very interesting. You got to meet a lot of great people.

Well, time went on, and that was ten years right almost to a day when the OIIC broke up.* So again I was out of a job. Well, it just happened at that point that Pan Am had lost their PR. So I called up. I had kept in touch with Pryor and all my Pan Am contacts.

Q: He was still there?

Admiral Miller: He was still there.

Q: So was Juan Trippe, wasn't he?

---

* From 1952 to 1953, during a leave of absence from the Oil Industry Information Committee, Miller served as president of the National Committee for a Free Europe, the sponsor of Radio Free Europe and the Crusade for Freedom. In addition, from 1953 to 1957, Miller served as the executive director of the President's Committee for Traffic Safety. In 1961 he was the national president of the Public Relations Society of America.

Harold B. Miller #4 -193

Admiral Miller: Yes, Juan Trippe was still there. So I kept in close touch with everybody over there. I called Sam and said, "Sam, I think you need a PR over there."

He said, "We sure do. What are you doing?"

I said, "Well, this just happened."

Well, at any rate, he said, "All right. Just relax. I'll be in touch."

I had laryngitis at that point for a couple of days. I was at home one day when the phone rang. It was Juan Trippe on the phone, and we had a pleasant conversation.

He said, "Well, come in and see me." So finally, after all the years, when it was so difficult to see him, the great mountain came to the mouse. So I went with Pan Am at that point.

Working with Pan Am was always a problem. You never did quite know who was running anything. Trippe never had an organization table or anything else. He just ran it from his office. I had access to him. I'd go in and have lunch with him and discuss new engines being developed and things of that sort.

Q: What job did Pryor have at that point?

Admiral Miller: Well, Pryor never had a specific job. Pryor was kind of a loose end. Nobody knew exactly what he did, except he had access to Trippe. He was a vice president, but vice president of what? Well, just a vice president. And he was a floater. One day he would be here, the next day he'd be in Tokyo, the third day he'd be down in Buenos Aires. No one ever knew really what he was doing, as a matter of fact. Incidentally, Sam is still out in Hawaii, in Maui. He's, I guess, 85 or so, but he's not in very good shape. His wife died and that sort of broke him up. So most of that gang's gone. Trippe's gone, Harold Gray's gone.*

But at any rate, I didn't know if I was working for Trippe or for Pryor, because there was no organization. You didn't know who the hell you were working for. I would

---

* Harold Gray, formerly chief pilot of Pan American, succeeded Trippe as president of the airline in 1963 and briefly took over from Trippe as chairman and CEO in 1968.

see one or both, depending on whatever I felt should be done. I would write annual reports for Trippe, and I'd do other things for Sam Pryor, pull a lot of his irons out of the fire from time to time.

Q: What was the thrust of your efforts?

Admiral Miller: Well, Pan Am, a great deal like the oil industry, didn't particularly have a savory reputation. It had the respect of people as a worldwide institution, but people in aviation itself would always look askance at Trippe and, "What the hell is he up to now?" You never quite knew, and they'd automatically think some kind of skullduggery. They didn't know what it was going to be, but it would be something. He could outthink any of them; he was so far ahead of anything. Perhaps it was a competitive situation, but there was almost a little fear involved too.

Bear in mind that there was a group of old-timers, and Trippe obviously was the doyen of them. You had Smith of American Airlines, of course.* You got Jack Frye, who had been with TWA. You had Bob Six of Continental. You had Bill Patterson of United.† Those are really the people who made aviation. Of them all, Trippe was certainly number one. He had great vision, great courage in financing too.

Q: Talk a little about him, because he is such a colorful person.

Admiral Miller: Well, he was an absolutely remarkable person. I don't think he had a host of friends. He could be very distant. You didn't know really if he was a friend of yours or not. He was a very strange individual.

Q: What was his background? Was he Latin or what?

---

* Cyrus R. Smith.
† William Patterson, president of United Airlines.

Admiral Miller: Well, first of all, he had sort of a dark complexion. You might say he was a Latin, and the name Juan would prove that he was a Latin. Well, actually, I asked him one day. I said, "Juan, how much Spanish do you know?"

He said, "I don't know a word of Spanish."

I said, "Well, come on, give now." Well, he had an aunt by the name of Juanita, a favorite aunt of his parents. He was named Juan in respect for her. He came from an Eastern Shore family down there in Maryland, and the Trippe family had come over from England. I did a bio on him at one time. They came over in the 17th century and settled over there. The name Trippe is still down around there.

And, of course, you remember Trippe in the Navy. We've had three ships named Trippe, for example.* A young Trippe was very much involved in the Tripoli pirate deal over there in the Mediterranean.† Somehow, Juan's father got to New York and was a partner in some brokerage house. It certainly wasn't one of the big ones. It was some name that you wouldn't even know today, and I don't remember what it was.

Juan Trippe went to Yale. You will find later the results of that. One way to get into Pan Am was to be a Yale graduate. The Navy might have been the second, but Yale was by far, far the first. He was a crew man up there. He was sort of large physically, tended to get a little bit heavy as time went on, not fat, but sort of heavy. He played a little football. I don't think he was very particularly good at that. Another man in his class was Trubee Davison. It's hard to tell what his class was, because World War I interrupted his college years. Trubee Davison came along and organized the Yale aviation unit.‡ Trippe was always interested in aviation as a student at Yale, and he was quick to join up with this unit.

---

* Actually, four ships: a merchant sloop converted to a warship in 1812; torpedoboat destroyer number 33, commissioned in 1911; a destroyer, DD-403, commissioned in 1939; a destroyer escort, DE-1075, commissioned in 1970.
† Lieutenant John Trippe, USN, had considerable service in the Mediterranean during the first decade of the 19th century. He died in 1810 while commanding the USS Vixen.
‡ In 1916, F. Trubee Davison, son of a prominent Red Cross official, formed the First Yale Unit with some of his classmates. On 24 March 1917, the 29-man unit enlisted in the Naval Reserve Flying Force and left soon afterward for naval aviation training.

Trubee set up a hangar and a headquarters here on Long Island at Huntington. They had about three airplanes. They were on their own; they had no particular designation. Then Jack Towers, who later became Admiral Towers, became involved with them and brought them all into the Navy. At that point, they all were sent down to Miami for Navy training, Trippe among them, all of them on seaplanes. Trippe qualified as a naval aviator but never got overseas. He was quite a youngster even at this time. He was about 19, I should think, but he was a qualified naval aviator.

Well, with the war over, he went back to Yale. They always say to Sheffield. I mean, that was one of the schools. I don't know Yale that well, but it's one of the schools there. So when I say it's difficult to say what class he was, he kind of jumped with the war in between. So to the best of my knowledge, he was the class of '22 at Yale. After the war and before he graduated, he became involved in the Yale Graphic as an editorial type.* The business manager was also a guy from Greenwich by the name of Sam Pryor.

Sam was very energetic. He was always on the go, and they became quite close friends. Well, when he graduated, they had some Jennies up there, and he went down to air races.† He actually was flying. Later on, he didn't fly at all. But he was an active aviator during that period. The Navy offered to sell some old seaplanes. They must have been N-9s, I should think, probably, as you go back on these things. He bought six of them for some ridiculous price. He set up a ferry service between the Hamptons and New York City, and his job was going to be flying the stockbrokers back and forth. They could spend the night in the Hamptons and then work in the city during the day. That carried on for about a year, and it went busted. He just couldn't make it go. So he was always aviation-minded right from the very beginning.

I never did conclude that story about the name Juan. He's dark complexioned, and since he went south--he went toward South America--everybody assumed he was Spanish.

---

* Trippe was founder and editor of the Yale Graphic, a general-interest college magazine.
† Jenny was the nickname drawn from the Navy designation JN for a Curtiss-built plane. Following World War I many were sold as surplus to private owners and were widely used for barnstorming.

He never did straighten them out on this thing; he let them assume that. It was a good international angle.

When he had parties at his home, they'd have a Christmas party there, and they'd bring in Pan Am executives from all over the world. I mean, it was laid on very precisely. You could be invited for cocktails, or you could be invited for cocktails and dinner. The line of demarcation was very clear between those invited for dinner and those invited just for cocktails. Well, it may have been that you'd see Juan Trippe quite often during the week or during the year, for that matter, and he may have recognized you and may not have recognized you, but at the party he was very jovial. He'd say, "Oh, well, come, let's have a drink," and he was utterly gracious.

Q: Then business and social life were separated?

Admiral Miller: Absolutely. And a lot of people got in trouble staying over a little bit towards the dinner hour when they weren't supposed to be there. We had a lad from Washington, and there was a time when Mrs. Trippe said, "Bill shouldn't be here at all." He had always been for years and years. He hadn't been invited, but it was a Christmas party; he just assumed. She said, "Get him out of here." That was a very painful operation, I'll tell you. Trippe could be very charming, or he could be very distant.

He'd work alone. He wasn't a conference man, particularly. He sort of worked alone in his office.

Q: He sounds like a dictator type.

Admiral Miller: Well, he was, there's no question about it, in a very soft voice, a dictator. You knew damn well what he meant. Once we were working on an annual report, and for some reason the weather was down, and we couldn't fly. He had his own plane; it was an old B-23, one of the early bomber types. He always used it, but this time we had to get on a train at the last minute. It was a real scramble, and we worked on the annual report in a club car all the way down and had a drink or two. He liked to have a drink here and there. But he was a strange man.

As public relations director, I was very historically minded. I thought, "My God, the history of Pan Am, what they've done, the firsts they've established--the first to fly to Hong Kong, the first to fly the Pacific, and so on."

Q: He organized the company, did he?

Admiral Miller: That's right. It was his company from the very beginning. There are so many histories written about that, I don't think there's much point in my getting into all of the history. But I can tell you one story. In the old days, all the airlines were subsidized, of course. He told me once, "Well, this is the way we had to work. You got $4.00 a pound for flying mail, but you only had to buy $2.00 worth of stamps in order to put a package in the mail. So you could make two dollars on everything you could send." So he said, "We used to send telephone books or bricks back and forth. We made two dollars on every pound." They used all sorts of devices. He was really a strange man.

Q: Was Mrs. Trippe also rather odd?

Admiral Miller: No, she was a very determined person. She was a Stettinius out of Pittsburgh, of steel. She was a sister of Edward.* And I asked Trippe once, "Why do you have so much interest in Liberia? I don't see that much business down there." One of the ports of call during the war was Roberts Field down there, Fisherman's Lake. The flying boats could go in, and later on they had a field.

Q: Was it at Monrovia?

---

* Edward R. Stettinius, Jr., was U.S. Secretary of State, 1944-45.

Admiral Miller: Yes, Monrovia. That was between the hump of South America, Belem, and the locations where we were ferrying all this stuff up to Africa or up to Egypt to help us in trying to get the Germans out of North Africa. So you go all the way around the bend, and that was a very important point during the war. Of course, I didn't join them until 1957, but I said, "Why so much interest in Liberia?"

He said, "Well, the reason for it is that Ed Stettinius was very much involved in lumbering, the basic thing there in Liberia. When he died, he left things in such a mess, somebody had to straighten it out. So we just took it over to try to keep the family [he didn't say fortune]--to keep the family heirs . . .

Q: To keep them from the poor house?

Admiral Miller: Essentially that's about what it was. So Trippe was involved in a lot of things of that sort.

He didn't like to give speeches very much. I remember once trying to get him involved the first time they had a telephone with a visual on it--I mean, you could see who you were talking to on the telephone, it had a TV set up there. Many years ago they were trying that out as the new thing, and I tried to get him to make an appearance on it. I couldn't get him out of the office, even, on that. But if you could put up with the generalities, you found him a very attractive person.

Q: What do you mean put up with the generalities?

Admiral Miller: Well, once, oh, God, I was sore at him. He had a male secretary, old Bob Lord. He'd been with him for years and years. He was a faithful person and such a nice person. Besides Bob Lord, he had another secretary, a beautiful girl named Kay Clair.* Well, time came and Bob Lord died here in New York. Juan Trippe had a board meeting in Hawaii set up for the next day, and the board was gathering to shove off. Well, Trippe

---

* Kathleen Clair.

went out to the board meeting. I mean, Bob Lord had done his slave work for him, as long as the company existed, 20 or 30 years. I never forgave him for that particular thing.

Kay Clair, who was just darling, was very close-mouthed. She would never say anything that took place inside that office. I guess I was waiting to see Trippe one day, and I said, "Have you ever had any thanks or anything for this job you're doing?"

She said, "Oh, yes. One time Mr. Trippe said, 'That's a good job, Miss Clair.'" After 20 years, he called her Miss Clair. Once in that period he said, "That's a good job, Miss Clair."

Q: I trust he paid well. Did he?

Admiral Miller: Pan Am didn't pay well, no. But the funny thing about it, people still thought Pan Am was a great company, and, of course, you had all these travel privileges. Some people would take off every weekend and go to Africa or South America or someplace. They did a lot of that sort of stuff.

Well, I started to make the point that I was very historical-minded. I knew the history of Pan Am inside out. Well, there was an aviation artist in New York whom I knew, and I knew he could do these airplanes in flight beautifully. I decided that, by golly, what Pan Am needed was an art collection of its airplanes. So I set out and worked up ten firsts: the first flight to Key West, for example, the first flight to Hong Kong and so on. I researched each of the flights and wrote an eight- or ten-line history on each one. It had other things. You had to give credit to the engine manufacturer and the plane manufacturer. You had to be damned sure of what you were doing.

Q: You couldn't overlook anybody.

Admiral Miller: Absolutely. So I sat down, and I worked like a dog on that. I came up with ten legitimate firsts that I could justify. What I wanted was 12, because I wanted it for the famous Pan Am calendar. Every year they come up with a calendar, and I wanted 12. Well, I could only get ten. But at any rate, I got started anyway on this thing.

So I took on old Jack McCoy, this artist. He went to work with these histories, and he did the most beautiful work you've ever seen on these airplanes. For example, the airplane going to Buenos Aires. The research we did on that thing: what time of day was it? Where was the sun at that time? Where were the shadows? He could draw this thing and make it talk. We ended up with ten of the most beautiful original pictures you ever saw. Well, I wanted to show them to Trippe.

I sent Jack over to Bristol, England. There's a print shop over there that's absolutely--it's supposed to be the number one in the world. We decided that we would get 5,000 prints of each one of these things. I was now talking about almost $100,000. I didn't have it in the budget, but, Geez, Pan Am needed it. Always when I was in the Navy, if I thought they needed something, I'd just go do it. So I got these paintings all in order, and I wanted to show Trippe. At this point, I had never even told him about it. So I set up in the boardroom. By this time, I was getting to know Lindbergh very well. We thought a great deal alike on this type of stuff; if you need it, you've got to go get it. So I set up in the board room on tripods all these paintings. Lindbergh said, "Well, sure, I'm available."

So I went in to get Trippe. Well, Trippe was just putting on his coat to go someplace. I had to chase him down the hall, really, to get him stopped. I said, "Now, Slim's over here. You've got to come see these." So he went into the boardroom.

Q: "Slim" being Lindbergh?

Admiral Miller: Lindbergh. Trippe went in there and slowed down and took a careful look at every one. He got to the Hong Kong plane, I remember, and said, "Betty and I were in that airplane." And he was just as enthusiastic as he could be on this whole thing.

Kennedy was President at this point.* I set up a deal where the number one print would go to Trippe, obviously, and number two would go to Kennedy.

Q: What did you do about the two missing months?

Admiral Miller: We made them up since. We were never able to use them for a calendar until later, but they were used in all sorts of publicity. Well, the funniest thing happened. Trippe ordered them all locked up. He put them in the storeroom and locked the door, and that was the end of that. He didn't distribute anything at all.

Q: What was the rationale?

Admiral Miller: I could never find out. I tried to get it from him, and I could never find out. The only thing I could make out of it was that also in one of the storerooms were thousands and thousands of first flight covers that Pan Am had flown all over the world. The only thing I could imagine was that they were increasing in value, so if you sold them ten years from now, you'd get more for them than if you'd sell them now. That's the only thing I could figure out.

Q: Did he pay willingly for these at the time?

Admiral Miller: Oh, yes, there was no problem with the payment. But I never knew whether he was sore at me. He just went ahead and did it without talking to me. He loved the paintings. Later on, they broke down, and we offered them up for sale for something like $50.00 a set to Pan Am employees and $100.00 for outsiders and stuff like that. And they are moving, but for about three or four years there, they were absolutely locked up. Craziest thing.

---

* John F. Kennedy was President of the United States from January 1961 to November 1963.

Q: But they aren't now?

Admiral Miller: No, now they're moving. They're available now. So here's a sample of Trippe's eccentricities. I couldn't figure it out. I couldn't find anybody who could.

Q: Well, couldn't your friend Sam Pryor interpret him?

Admiral Miller: Now, Sam's relationship was a very odd one. The way Sam got in Pan Am, although he had been an associate of Trippe's at Yale, was that Trippe wanted to get involved in politics. I mean, after all, that had to do with flying mail, and that meant income for Pan Am. Trippe was very much involved with political campaigns. He was having a meeting down in Washington at the old Statler Hotel. It was before my time, but I've heard this, and I think it's correct. Trippe was there in a room with the Washington representative of Pan Am--Bill somebody-or-other--and about three or four other people. They were trying to figure out some political advantages one way or the other, who could get the Senator so-and-so?

Well, at that time, a little guy, Sam Pryor, knocked on the door and walked in. And they let him join in the conversation. At least he knew Trippe to that extent, and Trippe knew he wasn't a spy or anything like that. The question came up, "Who knows So-and-so."

He said, "Oh, Joe? I know Joe."

"And what about Charlie?"

"Oh, Charlie's an old friend of mine." The first thing you know, Sam had a job as vice president of Pan Am. What was the job? Was it politics or what the hell was it? It was hard to tell, because there was nothing in writing in the Pan Am building or anyplace else. Well, Sam went on working in politics.

Sam was an operator. You may remember the famous case with Wendell Willkie.* The Republican convention was in Philadelphia in 1940. I don't recall who he had to knock down to get the nomination.† Sam was alleged to--and I know he did--have printed up hundreds and hundreds and probably thousands of illegal entrance tickets to the hall, and he flooded the place with Willkie adherents. Willkie got the nomination. Sam kept up on this political thing.‡

Q: He was an operator, then?

Admiral Miller: Oh, he would do things. He was really a sweet guy, but he was always getting in trouble. He had Christmas cards the likes of which you've never seen. It was a hand-painted card with thousands of names of his friends in a spiral design. The idea was to find your name on this thing. His imagination was beyond all belief. For instance, one time he had sent his boys over to Vienna to pluck a string or two in the Vienna Boys' Choir. Well, now, this Christmas card was a recording of the Vienna Boys' Choir, assisted by young Pryor. That kind of stuff. God, he had some of the most imaginative things in the world, all promoting Pan Am, of course.

Well, you can say that Sam Pryor was spending a lot of money uselessly, or you can say that he was making a lot of friends for Pan Am. Everybody knew Sam Pryor. He was very proud of the fact that he knew the narcotic group down in the Treasury Department, and he went down there one time. They said, "Well, don't you want to qualify?" Well, of course he did. So he took the gunnery training course down there, on the pistol range, and qualified as a customs man. He actually went on a raid with them at one time. At any rate, it qualified him to carry a pistol. He would sit there with a jacket on, trying to get this thing off. Then you would see this shoulder holster that he had a pistol in.

---

* Wendell L. Willkie was a lawyer and business executive who in 1940 won the Republican Party nomination for President of the United States. In that year's general election he was defeated by the incumbent, Franklin D. Roosevelt.
† Willkie's primary opponent was Senator Robert Taft, Republican of Ohio.
‡ Pryor was eastern campaign chairman for Willkie that year.

It became the topic of conversation. Or if you rode home with him to Greenwich, he would open his briefcase. You thought, "My God, he's got a pistol in there."

As for the briefcase, you knew it was Sam Pryor's because for years he had never taken off a destination string. He took the tags off, leaving nothing but strings hanging. It looked like a thread factory or something like that, hanging on the handle of a briefcase. All talking pieces.

Q: One would almost assume that he was quite compatible with Juan Trippe.

Admiral Miller: Well, no one ever really knew. I was in his office once when Juan Trippe called him. He had brought Halaby in by this time.*

Q: Oh, yes.

Admiral Miller: And I could hear Trippe's voice. He said,

"Sam, have I made another mistake?" Oh, he regretted Halaby from the beginning.

Q: Didn't Halaby's daughter marry King Hussein?

Admiral Miller: Yes, she's Queen Hussein over there in Jordan.† And, of course, Halaby's not an Iranian; he's a Lebanese, probably.‡ I bet he's a middleman for more things than you can shake a stick at. A very interesting person.

One time Sam said to me, "Look, can't public relations pick up this tab?" And what it was, Sam considered himself a PR. He and his wife were out in Hawaii. He got

---

* Najeeb E. Halaby, formerly a Lockheed test pilot, served as administrator of the Federal Aviation Administration, 1961-65. He was senior vice president of Pan Am, 1965-68; president of Pan Am, 1968-72; chairman and CEO of the airline, 1969-72.
† Lisa Halaby married Jordan's King Hussein and became known as Queen Noor.
‡ Halaby was born in Texas in 1915.

acquainted with some little gal writer out there. I have no idea who she was. She said, "I've got to go back to New York tomorrow."

Sam said, "Well, we're going to New York tomorrow. How are you going?"

She said, "Well, going on Pan Am and going on down the coast," and so on.

Sam said, "Well, why don't you come with us? We're going the other way." So he drags her all the way around to New York by way of Africa and Asia and so on. But it was an airline rule that they couldn't give anything free. You had to somehow account for that passage. Well, Sam just foisted it off on my budget.

He had a couple of baboons that he would take around with him. Finally, United Airlines wrote him a letter and said, "Mr. Pryor, you are no longer welcome on United Airlines aircraft." The damn baboons would tear the damn seats apart on an airplane.

Q: He must have had an interesting job there.

Admiral Miller: He was a character. He was also a doll collector. You must have heard of this museum over in Greenwich.* They had an estate with an old barn. He had dolls from every country in the world. He had hundreds of mechanical banks. Take a slingshot at a penny from a bow and arrow over here and it goes in the bank, or he'd have somebody hammering it into the bank. He had collections of everything under the sun, which attracted public attention. Because of his doll collection, he got an invitation to visit the Empress of Japan. He parlayed everything based on these collections. Trippe never really knew what the hell he was doing, and he never told Trippe anything in particular. But he was a Trippe man.

Q: And he was there when Trippe wanted him.

---

* Pryor's International Doll Library grew to more than 8,000 dolls by the 1960s. Most of the collection was presented to Japan when he moved to Hawaii.

Admiral Miller: Oh, yes. So that was the kind of an operation that Trippe ran. He was the boss man, and don't ask him any questions.

Q: Were his employees relatively happy?

Admiral Miller: They would approach Trippe in sort of a military manner of, "You wanted to see me, sir?" Then they would stand there and wait to be told what the hell he wanted to see you about. They were happy to be in Pan Am. They felt all this other stuff was justified to be with Pan Am, but it wasn't necessarily a congenial thing for many people. He wasn't intimate with really anybody, as a matter of fact.

Q: Well, how long did you stay with them?

Admiral Miller: That was ten years too. Another ten-year period, at which time I reached retirement. Pan Am was very good to me; I had lots and lots of stock options given to me, all of which later became worthless. Yes, I fell in love with Pan Am. That was my problem. This great company which could never have any problems. And so I rode the stock down to the bottom. I would have been in very good shape if I had divorced myself from Pan Am. My advice to all naval officers: don't fall in love with a company. Stock is stock; if it goes up or down, handle it absolutely independently.

Q: Handle it accordingly, yes.

Admiral Miller: So we had trips. My boys have been all over the world, and we still do.

Q: You still have that right, do you?

Admiral Miller: Yes, my wife and I. The boys are too old for travel privileges now. But it's been a great experience, and we loved it. I knew so many of the pilots, and I knew all of the people around the Pan Am Building. It was a great experience.

So at that point, I was contacted by one of my old Navy boys, Cliff Lord. He and Turnbull wrote the History of Naval Aviation, which is based pretty much on my earlier book, Navy Wings.* Cliff had been a young jaygee around the Navy Department when I had Training Literature. He was very good at keeping in touch throughout the years. About this time, here I was free and easy again, even if I was in retirement.

Q: What year was that?

Admiral Miller: That would have been 1968. So I called Cliff, who was president of Hofstra University, and said, "I hear [which I had heard] that you need some PR out there."

He said, "We sure do."

I said, "Why don't you come and have lunch with me?"

There was another thing--the Sky Club in the Pan Am Building. You had a lot of perks that were very helpful in your work if you didn't abuse them, which I don't think I ever did. They were very helpful.

Cliff and I got along very well. We sort of re-established our relationship. So he said, "Well, come on out." So I went out to Hofstra University, which, after all, is a stone's throw from here and carried on there as their vice president of PR until 1973, I guess it was. The time had come to call it a day at that point, at which time I came home.

That was a great experience working with these kids. I never had any experience with a civilian university before.

Q: What was your objective there? How did you promote Hofstra?

---

* Clifford L. Lord and Archibald Douglas Turnbull, History of United States Naval Aviation (New Haven: Yale University Press, 1949).

Admiral Miller: What we wanted was students. At that time, all the schools, as they have always been, were fighting for students. We wanted the name of Hofstra to become a place in the education world and the art world and the music world. For instance, we had the Shakespeare theater, which, next to Stratford-on-Avon, has the most important Shakespeare productions in the country. Well, they had a lot to offer, except nobody knew about it. The word Hofstra alone didn't meant anything. Hofstra, what is it? Is it a dog? What is Hofstra?

Q: Yes, what is the origin of that word?

Admiral Miller: Well, there was a Dutchman by the name of Hofstra, who came over and set up a big lumberyard and made a mint of money. He had no immediate descendants, and he said he'd like to leave his fortune to start a university. He never saw the university; he just left the money. It's a darn good university. It has a law school, an enormous library-- something like 600,000 volumes, which makes a very important university out of it. A lot of it is built on the old airfield out there, Mitchel Field.* It's a great school, has about 10,000 students. The object was to let people know what Hofstra had to offer.

Q: To publicize its merits?

Admiral Miller: That's right, in order to get students and keep it going.

Q: That must have been an interesting final chapter in your career.

Admiral Miller: Yes. I didn't have to go running around to Seattle or anyplace. I learned all about SATs and all about students and all about student rebellions and uprisings, which

---

* Mitchel field was used by the Navy in the World War I era.

we had like everybody had in those days.* I got acquainted with the whole of Long Island. As you say, it really amounted to a good finish.

Q: I want to thank you for this resumé of your very interesting career. I mean, you've combined so many different elements.

Admiral Miller: Oh, life's been very good to me, I'll tell you. We've got tapes here, a tape of the boys asking questions. My gosh, one night I sat out here for three hours, and they said, "We thought we had heard everything about you. We hadn't heard any of this before."

---

* SATs--Scholastic Aptitude Tests, used by many colleges and universities to evaluate the abilities of potential students.

A13-1(350124)
W (N.C.1753)

DEPARTMENT OF THE NAVY

OFFICE OF THE JUDGE ADVOCATE GENERAL

WASHINGTON, D. C.

JUL 19 1940

From: The Judge Advocate General.
To: Lt. Comdr. Harold B. Miller, U.S.Navy,
          U.S.S. SARATOGA, c/o Postmaster, San Francisco, Cal.

Subject: Grant of patent on joint application of Harold
          B. Miller and Gerhard R. Fisher, Serial No.
          123,872, filed February 3, 1937, for Radio
          Receiver and Direction Finder.

Enclosure: (A) Original grant of Patent No. 2,207,750.

    1. This office takes pleasure in forwarding herewith the original grant of patent on the subject application which matured on July 16, 1940, into Patent No. 2,207,750.

    2. Although the original grant of the patent is forwarded to you, the co-inventor has equal right thereto. A printed copy of this patent is being forwarded to Dr. Gerhard R. Fisher.

W. B. Woodson.

Copy to: Dr. Gerhard R. Fisher, 745 Emerson St., Palo Alto, Cal.

NAVY DEPARTMENT
BUREAU OF NAVAL PERSONNEL
WASHINGTON 25, D. C.

January 4, 1945.

Dear Min:

    From all reports you are doing a grand job in Public Relations in the Pacific and I know that the Secretary wants to keep you there for some time. However, I spoke to him the other day on the matter of your getting a carrier in the summer and I feel sure he will concur. So, in the meantime, I suggest you just continue to do your good work in the Pacific public relations.

    We just sent "Slim" Wooldridge to sea all fattened up and rarin' to go. You, no doubt, have seen him by now.

    Please let me know if we can do anything for you or your gang at this end.

    With very best regards,

                    Sincerely,

                    L. E. Denfeld,
                    Rear Admiral, U.S.N.

Captain H. B. Miller, U. S.N.,
Public Relations Officer for CincPac.,
c/o Fleet Post Office,
San Francisco, California.

C O P Y

We had been engaged for two days in maneuvers with the Fleet which was in passage enroute to San Francisco from the Southern operating bases. Our mission consisted mainly of scouting and we had made every endeavor to escape detection. To this end we had sent the planes far ahead while the ship kept well out of sight inback of the Channel Islands. Strong winds were encountered as usual off Point Arguello while a bit of fog prevailed in the late afternoons.

One of the other pilots and I had made a scouting flight on the second afternoon, returning to the Macon about four o'clock. At that time the Commander-in-Chief gave us orders to return to Sunnyvale at our discretion. Doc Wiley decided to go home before our base was closed in as some rather foul weather was due to sweep in during the night. We were flying up the Coast about two miles off the beach and around thirty miles south of Monterey. We got one rather good sock from an air current, but though we had a rise of 1200 feet a minute, it really didn't amount to anything and the ship was brought back on an even keel with no difficulty. Shortly after five after we had been flying at 1200 feet in a fog for about ten minutes or so the bow suddenly gave a tremendous lurch to starboard and she nosed down violently. A tremendous amount of activity could be observed in the control car and I had the distinct feeling that the ship had got out of control.

There were about ten of us in the smoking room, just abaft the control car proper. We were told to hurry to the bow--in the very extreme portion where the ship was moored to the mast when on the field. Another ten or twelve men were sent up there shortly afterwards. It appears that part of the tail surfaces were wrenched off and that we had lost all steering control. The wrecked girders tore the after three cells apart. It is not definitely established whether a gust of wind initiated the lurch or whether a material failure caused the sudden motion with the resulting loss of the cells. The cells immediately deflated, thus making the ship extremely tail heavy and she took up an angle of about thirty degrees --tail low. Great quantities of fuel and water ballast were dropped aft and with our weight forward it was hoped to get the ship on an even keel. In the meantime, the loss of ballast resulted in the ship jumping up to about 5000 feet, still in the clouds. For a moment or two it appeared as though control could be obtained, but once more the ship went down by the tail and it was obvious that she would be lost. Helium was valved forward to assist in lowering the nose, but it could not be done and this additional loss of lift caused the ship to start down with rather a high rate of speed.

By this time we all had on life preservers and had broken out our life rafts---carbon dioxide inflated. As we descended through the clouds the word was passed that we would probably land on the water and to prepare to abandon ship. Frankly, I yet couldn't realize that we really might go into the drink. At last the water showed up as we got lower and sure enough we were settling in very rapidly. By dropping the remaining ballast the Skipper was enabled to slow up the rate of fall sufficiently to give us the gentlest of landings. Just like a feather pillow. The fog prevented us from seeing the beach and there were no vessels in sight---this was about five-thirty and the darkness was rapidly folding in.

Aft along the cat-walks the men were launching their boats as the water rose on the hull. We could hear the ship breaking up and she would groan most ferociously. For perhaps ten minutes we floated nearly horizontally, but as the breaking-up progressed forward the ship began to stand up on her tail. We had considered jumping or climbing down ropes at first, but the thought didn't appeal to me---that cold water. About eight of us stayed on while the others went down lines and into boats. Aft practically everyone had abandoned the ship immediately. Those of us left soon found ourselves about 125 feet in the air instead of the nice, conservative 40 feet we had previously been. For a while I thought that we had been crazy to stay aboard, but it turned out to be for the best. The ship kept settling nearly on the vertical. Shortly after this some of our men went down on lines we had rigged from the cone and they came down on top of the control car. In fact, one officer sat down while on the forward end of the control car---showing you how vertical the hull was standing.

It was now quite dark and the boats were not as close aboard as we should have liked. We shouted and we yelled It happened that they were attempting to get closer, but it is a tough job rowing one of those blunt-nosed things. Then I let out a shout and found I had nothing but the tiniest peep. I thought I was crazy until the others set up a yell and they, too, had nearly lost their voices. Then we realized we were being gassed with helium. We climbed outside of the hull and held our heads away from the ship. Finally, we got ourselves cleared out.

We shot off about twenty Very pistol shells from there. Then, blessed sight, we saw the beams of far-distant searchlights in answer to our radio for help. They appeared to be so close -- the searchlights -- but they were miles away. For a moment I thought we were not going to get wet, but that proved to be an illusion. By this time we had only about fifteen feet of the hull left above water-- just a bubble. I decided that I had enough and I wanted to make a boat before it was totally black. Besides, it was misting and getting more foggy. So, I threw away my shoes and started to slide down the cover. My foot slipped and the five ahead of me must have thought the ship was going down for they all leaped into the water like a bunch of wet rats. As it was the hull was breaking under our feet. Looking back I saw one lonely blue jacket remaining on the ship. I shouted for him to come on. He leaped into the water and away we went for a boat. There were already six in the boat so five of held on to the side and in the water.

Surprisingly enough the water was not at all unpleasant. Rather it was invigorating. Swimming and kicking kept me warm except as a wave would lap up over my neck. The wind, then, would nearly freeze my skin. The searchlights came on closer and closer. When clear of the hull a fire started and at last the cover burned off as she went down. Shortly afterwards a huge gasolene fire started on the water and caused us considerable worry for awhile. We worked the boat closer to the cruisers and at last had got within about 400 yards of one of them when they got boats in the water and over to us. We had been in the water about 45 minutes by that time. I casually reached out to pull myself aboard the boat and found that I couldn't move my legs. They cramped themselves into knots. Some kind soul pulled us aboard and then a most violent reaction took place. It seemed as though I would crack all the enamel from my teeth. I could not keep still and shook as though I would fall apart.

Stumbling aboard we got hot showers and were turned in. In fifteen minutes or so most of us were normal and ready to go. Three cruisers in all picked up men. Most of us knew that the Navy would keep on hunting until they found us so we didn't have much to worry about. It was quite fortunate we didn't have to go to shore and through the surf for it is a mountainous coast and the breakers were huge that night. Probably wouldn't have got away with it.

On the whole we got away with it in fairly good shape. All decisions were correct. It is unfortunate we lost the

two men--both excellent men and one of them had sent out our
calls for assistance. We lost all of our planes and most of
lost our clothes. That, of course, is nothing compared to
the possible loss of life had not the Captain handled the ship
so well. I feel that during the past year we proved the
utility of the airship type of craft. Perhaps they need some
redesigning, but they can and will do the Navy much good.

I think this accident is identical to the Akron's except we were only slightly heavy and hit the water with zero air speed.

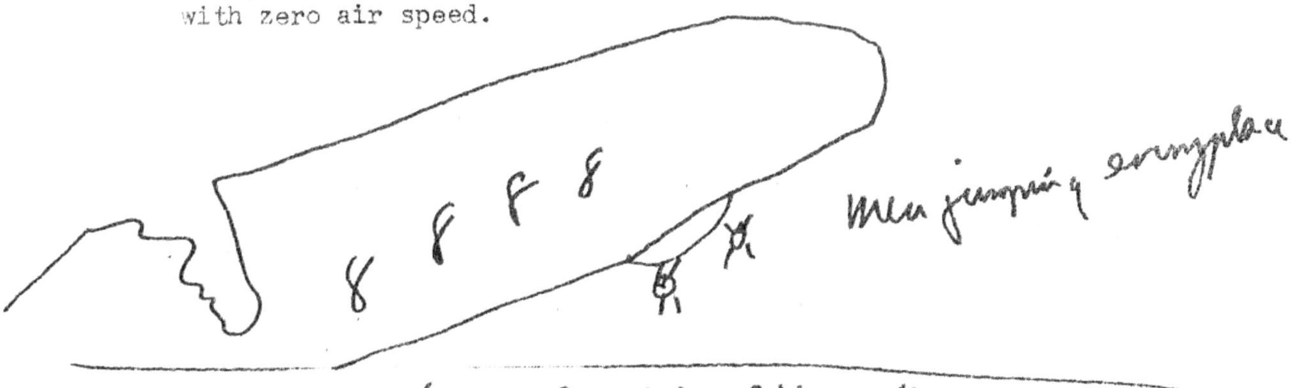
Men jumping everyplace

Ships landed like this

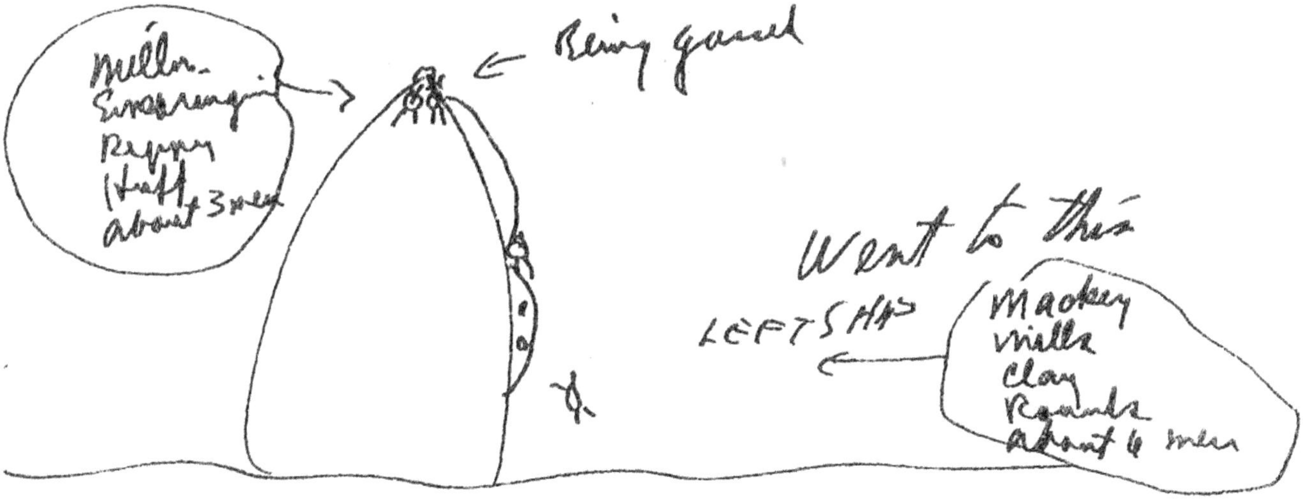
Being saved
Reppy
Huff
about 3 men
Went to this
LEFT SHIP
Mackey
Clay
about 6 men

The Cone
Where we got off!

Index To

Reminiscences of

Rear Admiral Harold B. Miller

U.S. Navy (Retired)

Accidents
Lieutenant Logan Ramsey had a landing mishap when he couldn't get his hook down while coming aboard the aircraft carrier Langley (CV-1) in the late 1920s, 40-41; the German airship Graf Zeppelin, filled with hydrogen, came down on a chimney in South America, 58; loss of the airship Macon (ZRS-5) in a storm off New Jersey in April 1933, 67; line handlers were killed while tending the Akron near San Diego in 1932, 84; the airship Macon (ZRS-5) was lost off the coast of California on 12 February 1935, 84-89; Lieutenant Joseph P. Kennedy, Jr., was killed in August 1944 in a B-24 while trying to make a bombing attack on German rocket sites in France, 128-131

Adair, Ensign Crutchfield, USN (USNA, 1924)
Entered the Naval Academy in 1920 from California, 6-7; death of in 1981, 7; as a midshipman, 7-8, 10, 14-16; reported to the battleship Arizona (BB-39) upon being commissioned in 1924, 20; took flight training in 1926, 31

Airships
Advantages that accrued from the program in the U.S. Navy, 90; ineffectiveness of blimps for antisubmarine warfare in World War II, 90-91

See also Akron, USS (ZRS-4); Graf Zeppelin, Los Angeles, USS (ZR-3); Macon, USS (ZRS-5); Shenandoah, USS (ZR-1)

Akron, USS (ZRS-4)
Range gave her a strong scouting capability, 57; operated with F9C fighter planes in the early 1930s, 60-66; weight and gas-volume considerations, 60-62; operations with the fleet in the Atlantic, 67, 69; loss of in a storm off New Jersey in April 1933, 67; pilots made a parachute jump in the early 1930s, 70-71; line handlers killed tending the ship in 1932, 84

Alaska
Establishment of a Navy seaplane base at Sitka in the late 1930s, 95-96

Alcoholic Beverages
Soviets tried to get American visitors drunk in London in 1944, 125

American Petroleum Institute
Public relations efforts on behalf of the oil industry, 1948-57, 186-192

Antisubmarine Warfare
Ineffectiveness of blimps for ASW warfare in World War II, 90-91; the PB4Y Liberator was used for Navy ASW operations out of Britain in 1944, 127-128; increasing success of Allied antisubmarine forces against German U-boats as World War II progressed, 135

Army Air Forces, U.S.
Bombing runs from England to the European continent in 1944, 119-121, 125-126, 134

Aviators
Lieutenant Dixie Kiefer was an enthusiastic recruiter for aviation while serving in the battleship California (BB-44) in the mid-1920s, 21-22; the naval aviation community was quite small in the mid-1920s, 25; World War I aviators still on active duty in the 1920s and 1930s had limited naval experience, 25-26, 93; line officers resented extra pay given to naval aviators in the late 1920s, 26; flight training in 1926 at Pensacola, Florida, 26-31; operated floatplanes from the battleship West Virginia (BB-48) in the late 1920s, 31-33; operated floatplanes from the heavy cruiser Northampton (CA-26) in the mid-1930s, 34-36, 92; in the aircraft carrier Langley (CV-1) in the late 1920s, 37-40; flight training at Pensacola in the early 1930s, 41-43, 46-48, 51-52; Miller's writings on U.S. naval aviation, 47-51, 55-56; Lieutenant Ralph S. Barnaby's experimental work with gliders in the 1920s and 1930s, 52-53, 55; operated the rigid airships Akron (ZRS-4) and Macon (ZRS-5) in the early 1930s, 55-89; the Training Literature section of the Bureau of Aeronautics was established in 1942 to assist in training aviators and to publicize naval aviation, 103-112, 176; in World War II the Royal Navy did not use aviators as skippers of aircraft carriers, 116-117; Lieutenant Joseph P. Kennedy, Jr., was killed in August 1944 in a B-24 while trying to make a bombing attack on German rocket sites in France, 128-131; Trubee Davison formed the Yale aviation unit in 1916, later joined the Navy, 195-196

B-24 Liberator
Bomber in which Lieutenant Joseph P. Kennedy, Jr., was killed in August 1944 while trying to make a bombing attack on German rocket sites in France, 128-131

See also PB4Y Liberator

B-26 Marauder
Army Air Forces bomber used for attacks on the European continent in 1944, 119-120, 125-126

Baldwin, Hanson W., (USNA, 1924)
Newspaperman who sometimes accompanied Miller on flights in England in 1944, 121; endured German rocket attacks in London in 1944, 127; observed that the Pacific Fleet public relations officer, Waldo Drake, blacklisted some reporters during World War II, 140

Barnaby, Lieutenant Ralph S., CC, USN
Experimental work with gliders in the 1920s and 1930s, 52-53, 55; worked on pilotless aircraft in the 1940s, 128

Billings, Lieutenant Arthur B., USN
Served in 1926 as a flight instructor at Pensacola, 27-28; landing signal officer in the aircraft carrier Langley (CV-1) in the late 1920s, 40

Blimps
Ineffectiveness of blimps for antisubmarine warfare in World War II, 90-91

Bombs/Bombing
Army Air Forces bombing runs from England to the European continent in 1944, 119-121, 134; Lieutenant Joseph P. Kennedy, Jr., was killed in August 1944 in a B-24 while trying to make a bombing attack on German rocket sites in France, 128-131

Brewster, Ralph O.
Maine senator who convened a group in 1947 to write U.S. aviation policy, 184, 186

Bristol, Rear Admiral Arthur L., Jr., USN (USNA, 1906)
In quick succession in 1940-41 served as commander of Carrier Division One and Aircraft Scouting Force in the Pacific, plus the Support Force in the Atlantic, 101-103

Bureau of Aeronautics
In the early 1930s approved Miller's proposed itinerary for a cross-country training trip, 43-44, 46; in the mid 1930s assistant bureau chief John Towers got Miller involved in compiling the history of U.S. naval aviation, 49-50

See also Training Literature

California, USS (BB-44)
Had the Battle Fleet staff embarked in the mid-1920s, 19-20; equipped with UO biplanes, 20-21; in 1925 almost the entire junior officer mess chose to take flight training, 21-22; life for junior officers, 22-24

Camp Meade, Maryland
Miller landed in this Army post when his airplane ran low on fuel in the early 1930s, 45

Carney, Admiral Robert B., USN (USNA, 1916)
Was one of the excellent officers on the staff of Commander Support Force in 1941, 102; even as a lieutenant, he appeared to be a future Chief of Naval Operations, 178

Carpender, Vice Admiral Arthur S., USN (USNA, 1908)
Former chief of public relations who in 1945 was unpleasant to his successor, Miller, 161

Carter, Lieutenant Paul W., USN
Aviator who had limited naval experience while serving in the battleship West Virginia (BB-48) in the late 1920s, 25; instructor in 1926 at Pensacola, 30

Champion, Lieutenant Commander Carleton C., Jr., USN (USNA, 1920)
Former aviation altitude record holder who commanded Patrol Squadron 16 in the late 1930s, 95-96

Chapelle, Dickey
Woman reporter who went ashore to cover the invasion of Okinawa in 1945, even though prohibited from doing so, 149-151

Clark, Rear Admiral Joseph J., USN (USNA, 1918)
Accompanied Miller on a trip to visit Indians in South Dakota in September 1945, 163-164

Cluverius, Captain Wat T., Jr., USN (USNA, 1896)
Gentlemanly officer who commanded the battleship West Virginia (BB-48) in the late 1920s, 24

Combat Art
Navy program for painting scenes from World War II and portraits of wartime leaders, 170-172

Communications
Cumbersome requirements for cross-country Navy fliers in the early 1930s, 46; Lieutenant Donald Mackey facilitated operation of F9C fighter planes from the airship Macon (ZRS-5) in the early 1930s by giving them radio guidance, 76

Congress
Senator Ralph O. Brewster convened a group in 1947-48 to write U.S. aviation policy, 184; work of the committee, 185-186

Convoys
The Support Force operated in the Atlantic in 1941 to protect convoys bound for Europe, 102-103; U.S. Navy destroyers operated out of Londonderry while conveying in World War II, 114-115; convoys to north Russia, 115, 123; increasing success of Allied antisubmarine forces against German U-boats as World War II progressed, 135

Davis, Ensign William V., Jr., USN (USNA, 1924)
After going through flight training in 1926, went on to become a member of the Navy's first flight demonstration team in the late 1920s, 30-31

Davison, F. Trubee
Formed the Yale aviation unit in 1916 and took it into the Navy the following year, 195-196

De Florez, Commander Luis, USNR
Had a major role in developing aviation training simulators in World War II, 107; made training films in World War II, 174

De Foney, Lieutenant Clinton G., MC, USN
Navy doctor who claimed in the early 1930s at Pensacola to be able to determine which students were capable of flying, 51-52

Demobilization
Effects of after the end of World War II in 1945, 169-170

Doyle, Commander Austin K., USN (USNA, 1920)
While serving in the Bureau of Aeronautics in World War II, provided considerable support to the Training Literature section, 106, 108, 171

Drake, Captain William Waldo, USNR
Was replaced as Pacific Fleet public relations officer in 1944 because Secretary of the Navy James Forrestal felt the service was not getting adequate publicity, 138-143

Dresel, Commander Alger H., USN (USNA, 1909)
Was not aggressive while serving as the first commanding officer of the airship Macon (ZRS-5) in the early 1930s, 71-73

Drones
Lieutenant Joseph P. Kennedy, Jr., was killed in August 1944 in an unsuccessful attempt to send a pilotless B-24 to bomb German rocket sites in France, 128-131

Durgin, Lieutenant Commander Calvin T., USN (USNA, 1916)
Was mean as a lacrosse player at the Naval Academy in the mid-1910s, 16; commanded Observation Squadron One-B in the late 1920s, 37

Education
Miller's experiences in school in Iowa and California in the 1910s, 3-5; at the Naval Academy in the early 1920s, 7-8

F2B
Boeing fighter plane that cost around $12,000 in the late 1920s, 41; Miller used for cross-country learning trip in the early 1930s, 43-46

F-5L
Curtiss-built flying boat used in 1926 for flight training at Pensacola, Florida, 28-29

F9C Sparrowhawk
Curtiss-built biplane fighter plane that wasn't suitable for aircraft carriers but did fit into the rigid airships of the early 1930s, 56-57; operations from the airship Akron (ZRS-4) in the early 1930s, 60-66; operations from the airship Macon (ZRS-5) in the early 1930s, 60-66, 73-80, 82; landing on the carrier Lexington (CV-2), 74; in July 1934, F9Cs from the Macon dropped a package near the cruiser Houston (CA-30), which had President Franklin D. Roosevelt on board, 77-80; one example in the Smithsonian, 91

FU
Vought fighter plane that was carried experimentally on board the battleship West Virginia (BB-48) in the late 1920s, 37; used by Fighting Two in the aircraft carrier Langley (CV-1) in the late 1920s, 37-38

Falter, John
Artist for The Saturday Evening Post who worked for the Navy in World War II and did a painting for a Navy Day poster in 1943, 110-112

Fick, Lieutenant Harold F., USN (USNA, 1920)
Taught ground school during naval flight training at Pensacola until Miller relieved him in 1930, 42-43, 46

Fighting Two
Fighter squadron that operated from the aircraft carrier Langley (CV-1) in the late 1920s, 37-38; made up mostly of enlisted pilots, 38

Fires
O2U floatplane caught fire in the mid-1930s from smokestack sparks on board a heavy cruiser, 34, 94

Flight Training
As conducted in 1926 at Pensacola, Florida, 26-31; Miller's perception that in 1926 the Navy had an attrition rate of 50% for flight training, 29-30; at Pensacola in the early 1930s, 41-43, 46, 51-52; ground school on engines, 43, 46-47; at Miami in World War I, 196

Forrestal, James V.
As Secretary of the Navy in 1944, arranged for Miller to be Pacific Fleet public relations officer, 137-142, 162; positive response to Miller's efforts in the Pacific, 146, 151-152; sent newspaper publishers to interview Admiral Chester Nimitz, 152-153; in 1945 gave Miller a spot promotion to rear admiral and made him head of Navy public relations, 160-161; fully supported Miller as head of Navy public relations, 162; in 1945 changed the title of the Navy's publicity office from "Public Relations" to "Public Information," 175; talked with Miller at the time of Miller's retirement from the Navy in 1946, 178

France
    Army Air Forces bombing runs from England to France in 1944, 119-121, 125-126; Lieutenant Joseph P. Kennedy, Jr., was killed in August 1944 in a B-24 while trying to make a bombing attack on German rocket sites in France, 128-131

Frye, Jack
    Founder and long-time head of Transcontinental and Western Air, 180-182; went to General Aniline and Dye after TWA, 183-184

Germany
    Airship operations in the 1920s and 1930s, 57-59, 68; in World War I, 59, 80; V-1 rocket attacks on London in 1944, 126-127; Lieutenant Joseph P. Kennedy, Jr., was killed in August 1944 in a B-24 while trying to make a bombing attack on German rocket sites in France, 128-131; Army Air Forces bombing attacks in World War II, 135; increasing success of Allied antisubmarine forces against German U-boats as World War II progressed, 135

Gliders
    Lieutenant Ralph S. Barnaby's experimental work in the 1920s and 1930s, 52-53, 55

Goldthwaite, Lieutenant (j.g.) Robert, USN (USNA, 1924)
    Was a flight instructor at Pensacola in the early 1930s, 46

Graf Zeppelin
    Operations of this German airship included provision for U.S. naval observers, 58; problems of operation, 58-59

Great Britain
    V-1 rocket attacks on London in 1944, 126-127

    See also Royal Navy

Greber, Lieutenant (j.g.) Charles F., USN (USNA, 1921)
    Injured fellow pilot Dixie Kiefer while flying a UO biplane in Panama in the mid-1920s, 21

Guam
    Site of U.S. Pacific Fleet headquarters in early 1945, 145-149

Halaby, Najeeb E.
    Served in various capacities for Pan American World Airways in the 1960s and 1970s, 205

Hancock, Lieutenant Joy Bright, USNR
    Reserve officer who was involved in the publication of a naval aviation newsletter in World War II, 105

Harrigan, Lieutenant Daniel W., USN (USNA, 1922)
Served in the airship Akron (ZRS-4) in the early 1930s, 55, 60, 66-67; designed a combination of a parachute and raft, 71-72

Hazing
At the Naval Academy in the early 1920s, 16

Hofstra University, Hempstead, New York
Public relations efforts on behalf of the school in the 1960s and 1970s, 208-210

Houston, USS (CA-30)
In July 1934, F9Cs from the airship Macon (ZRS-5) dropped a package near the Houston, which had President Franklin D. Roosevelt on board, 77-80

Huff, Lieutenant (j.g.) Gerald L., USN (USNA, 1929)
Served in the airship Macon (ZRS-5) in the early 1930s, 74, 84-85

Hughes, Howard R.
Eccentric industrialist who gained control of Transcontinental and Western Air in the late 1940s, 181, 184; flying capabilities, 182

Ingalls, Captain David S., USNR
In 1946 tried to arrange a job for Miller with Pan American World Airways, 181

Ireland
U.S. Navy destroyers operated out of Londonderry as part of the process of escorting transatlantic convoys in World War II, 114-115, 123

Iwo Jima
News media coverage of the invasion of in February 1945, 145-149; photo of the Mount Suribachi flag raising, 154-155

JW-1
The XJW-1 model was used with the airship Macon (ZRS-5) in the early 1930s, 82-83

Japan
Pacific Fleet approach in 1945 in terms of informing the American public about Japanese kamikazes, 156-157

Johnson, Lieutenant Commander Lyndon B., USNR
As a congressman in 1945, the future President managed to wangle a trip to his home state along with Fleet Admiral Chester Nimitz, 166-167

Kamikazes
Pacific Fleet approach in 1945 in terms of informing the American public about Japanese kamikazes, 156-157

Kennedy, Lieutenant Joseph P., Jr, USNR
Killed in August 1944 in a B-24 while trying to make a bombing attack on German rocket sites in France, 128-131

Kenworthy, Lieutenant Commander Jesse L., USN (USNA, 1916)
As executive officer of the airship Macon (ZRS-5) in the early 1930s, took a ride in an unstable spy basket, 81

Kettering, Charles F.
Inventor who was uncooperative when approached in the 1950s to write a testimonial on behalf of the oil industry, 191-192

Kiefer, Lieutenant Dixie, USN (USNA, 1919)
Enthusiastic recruiter for naval aviation while serving in the battleship California (BB-44) in the mid-1920s, 21-22; injured in Panama by fellow pilot, 21

King, Rear Admiral Ernest J., USN (USNA, 1901)
As Chief of the Bureau of Aeronautics in the early 1930s, was concerned about airship operations, 68, 76; as CNO in World War II wanted to get adequate resources for the Pacific, despite British requests, 115-116, 136; took control of the fleet after replacing Admiral Harold Stark in 1941, 131-132

Kirk, Rear Admiral Alan G., USN (USNA, 1909)
Operational commander for the invasion of Europe in world War II, 133

Kivette, Lieutenant (j.g.) Frederick N., USN (USNA, 1925)
Served in the airship Akron (ZRS-4) in the early 1930s, 66; served in the airship Macon (ZRS-5) in the early 1930s, 74, 84; in July 1934, was the pilot of a F9C that dropped a package near the cruiser Houston (CA-30), which had President Franklin D. Roosevelt on board, 77-80

Lacrosse
Played at the Naval Academy in the early 1920s, 15-16

Lakehurst (New Jersey) Naval Air Station
East Coast base for U.S. Navy rigid airship operations in the early 1930s, 60; site of school for parachute packers in the 1930s, 69

Langley, USS (CV-1)
Fighter plane operations in the late 1920s, 37-38; had difficulty operating with the fleet in the late 1920s, 39; characteristics, 39-40; landing accident involving pilot Logan Ramsey, 40-41

Larson, Lieutenant (j.g.) Robert W., USN (USNA, 1924)
Served in the airship Akron (ZRS-4) in the early 1930s, 66-67; death of, 67

Leahy, Fleet Admiral William D., USN (USNA, 1897)
Accompanied Miller on a trip to visit Indians in South Dakota in September 1945, 163-164

Lee, Captain Fitzhugh, USN (USNA, 1926)
Served as Pacific Fleet public relations officer in 1945, 153-154, 168-169

Lewenthal, Reeves
Played a role in the Navy's combat art program during World War II, 109, 170-172

Lexington, USS (CV-2)
F9C fighter from the airship Macon (ZRS-5) landed on board in the early 1930s, 74

Lindbergh, Charles A.
Famous aviator who had problems trying to operate with a British ship in China, 33; association with Pan American in the early 1960s, 201

London, England
V-1 rocket attacks on the city in 1944, 126-127

Londonderry, Ireland
U.S. Navy destroyers operated out of as part of the process of escorting transatlantic convoys in World War II, 114-115, 123

Los Angeles, USS (ZR-3)
Rigid airship that launched a glider in a test in 1930, 53, 55; operations with the Patoka (AO-9), 57; obtained from the Germans in the 1920s, 58-59; stored at Lakehurst, New Jersey, in the early 1930s after being degassed, 60

Lovette, Captain Leland P., USN (USNA, 1918)
As the head of Navy public relations early in World War II, gave short shrift to naval aviation, 104

MacArthur, General of the Army Douglas, USA (USMA, 1903)
Army general whose staff issued a great deal of publicity in World War II, 147-148, posed a challenge to the Navy, 163-165, 168

Mackey, Lieutenant Donald M., USN
Facilitated operation of F9C fighter planes from the airship Macon (ZRS-5) in the early 1930s by giving them radio guidance, 76

Macon, USS (ZRS-5)
Delivery to the Navy in 1933, 68, 71; operations of F9C fighters as scouts in the early 1930s, 72-80, 82; in July 1934 the F9Cs dropped a package near the cruiser Houston (CA-30), which had President Franklin D. Roosevelt on board, 77-80; use of spy basket suspended below the airship, 80-82; weight and gas-volume considerations, 82-83; the airship was lost off the coast of California on 12 February 1935, 84-89

Mail
In July 1934 Miller dropped some envelopes near the cruiser Houston (CA-30) with President Franklin D. Roosevelt on board, and in later years the envelopes became quite valuable, 79-80

Martin, Lieutenant Harold M., USN (USNA, 1919)
Invited Miller to join him in Fighting Two on board the aircraft carrier Langley (CV-1) in 1928, 37

Medical Problems
Miller had a torn leg as a boy, early in the century, 5; Lieutenant Dixie Kiefer suffered a broken shoulder in an aviation accident in Panama in the mid-1920s, 21

Miller, Rear Admiral Harold B., USN (Ret.) (USNA, 1924)
Boyhood in California and Iowa at the beginning of the 20th century, 1-3; parents of, 2-3, 6, 10, 14, 22-23; grandparents of, 2-3, 44, 84; preparations for the Naval Academy, 4-5; as a Naval Academy midshipman, 1920-24, 7-19; served in the battleship California (BB-44), 1924-26, 20-25; origin of nickname "Min" in the mid-1920s, 23-24; served as a pilot in the battleship West Virginia (BB-48), 1927-28, 24-26, 31; flight training in 1926 at Pensacola, Florida, 26-31; designated naval aviator in November 1926, 29; served as a pilot in the heavy cruiser Northampton (CA-26) in the mid-1930s, 34-36, 92-94; served in the aircraft carrier Langley (CV-1) in 1928-29, 37-38; as a flight instructor at Pensacola, 1930-32, 41-47; commercial writing career: books and magazine articles, 46-51, 55-56; first wife, Jean Dupont, 48, 50; service as an F9C pilot in the crew of the airship Akron (ZRS-4) in 1932-33, 54-67, 69; service as an F9C pilot in the crew of the airship Macon (ZRS-5) in 1933-35, 68-80; served in Patrol Squadron 16, 1937-38, 94-97; commanded Patrol Squadron 5/33 from 1938 to 1940, 97-101; service from 1940 to 1942 with Rear Admiral Arthur Bristol, 101-103; as head of the Training Literature section of the Bureau of Aeronautics, 1942-43, 103-112; served as assistant naval attaché in London, 1943-44, 113-137; as Pacific Fleet public relations officer, 1944-45, 139-160; spot promotion to rear admiral in 1945, 160-162; service as head of Navy public relations in 1945-46, 162-177; retirement from the Navy in 1946, 178-179; civilian public relations man for TWA, 180-184; work on panel that in 1947-48 worked out U.S. aviation policy, 184-186; public relations efforts on behalf of the oil industry, 1948-57, 186-192; public relations for Pan American World Airways, 1957-65, 193-208; public relations for Hofstra University, 1968-74, 208-210

Morison, Rear Admiral Samuel Eliot
Historian who wrote a multi-volume history of U.S. naval operations in World War II, 172-173

Movies
Commander Luis de Florez made Navy training films in World War II, 174

N2Y
Trainer aircraft used by the heaver-than-air pilots assigned to the airship Akron (ZRS-4) in the early 1930s, 60

N-9
Pontoon version of Curtiss Jenny used at Pensacola in 1926 for Navy flight training, 26-27

Naval Academy, Annapolis, Maryland
Academics in the early 1920s, 7-8; life in the Bancroft Hall dormitory, 8-9; summer cruises in the early 1920s, 9-15, 18-19; athletics, 15-17; hazing in the early 1920s, 16-17; social life for midshipmen, 18

Naval Reserve
Naval reservists were vital to U.S. victory in World War II, 176-177

News Media
Reporters in Hawaii asked for the replacement of Pacific Fleet public relations officer Waldo Drake in 1944, 140-142; responded energetically to the Navy's fleet hometown news releases in 1945, 144-145; coverage of the invasion of Iwo Jima in 1945, 145-149, 154-155; coverage of the invasion of Okinawa in 1945, 146-147; woman reporter Dickey Chapelle went ashore to cover the invasion of Okinawa in 1945, even though prohibited from doing so, 149-151; newspaper publishers interviewed Admiral Chester Nimitz near the end of World War II, 152-153

Nimitz, Fleet Admiral Chester W., USN (USNA, 1905)
As Commander in Chief Pacific Fleet in 1944, was cautious about having aircraft carrier support from the British, 119; in 1944 Miller replaced Captain Waldo Drake as Pacific Fleet public relations officer because the Secretary of the Navy felt the service needed better publicity, 138-142, 162; kind personality, 142-143, 190; interviews with newspaper publishers, 152-153; concurrence on public relations policy concerning kamikazes, 156-157; made a triumphal tour of Texas and the East Coast in the autumn of 1945, 165-168; in the late 1940s wrote a testimonial for the American Petroleum Institute on the contribution that oil had made to the successful U.S. effort in World War II, 190-191

Northampton, USS (CA-26)
Operation of floatplanes, 34-35, 92; handling of the ship, 93-94

02U Corsair
Vought floatplane that operated from the heavy cruiser Northampton (CA-26) in the mid-1930s, 34-36; plane caught fire on board a heavy cruiser in the mid-1930s because of sparks from the smokestack, 34, 94; Lieutenant Logan Ramsey had a landing accident because he couldn't get his hook down while coming aboard the aircraft carrier Langley (CV-1) in the late 1920s, 40-41

OL-9
Loening amphibian used as an observation plane by the battleship West Virginia (BB-48) in the late 1920s, 31-33

O'Hare, Lieutenant (j.g.) Edward H., USN (USNA, 1937)
Was brought to the United States in 1942 for publicity purposes after shooting down five Japanese bombers in one mission, 157-158; death of, 158

Oil Industry

The American Petroleum Institute's public relations efforts on behalf of the industry, 1948-57, 186-192

Okinawa

News media coverage of the invasion of in April 1945, 146-147; woman reporter Dickey Chapelle went ashore to cover the invasion in 1945, even though prohibited from doing so, 149-151

Osborn, Lieutenant Robert, USNR

Talented cartoonist who made safety drawings for Naval Aviation News during and after World War II, 106-107

PBY Catalina

Patrol plane that essentially replaced the rigid airships in function in the 1930s, 89-90

PB4Y Liberator

Aircraft used for Navy antisubmarine operations out of Britain in 1944, 127-128

See also B-24 Liberator

PM

Martin-built flying boat used by Patrol Squadron 16 in the late 1930s, 57, 94, 97

Pacific Fleet, U.S.

In 1944 Secretary of the Navy James Forrestal felt that the Navy was not doing an adequate job of publicizing its activities in the Pacific and thus sent Miller to replace Captain Waldo Drake, 138-142; public relations efforts in late 1944-early 1945, 143-160

Panama

In the early 1920s, Miller made his first airplane flight from Coco Solo, 14; site of an aviation accident involving Lieutenant Dixie Kiefer in the mid-1920s, 21; base of operations for Patrol Squadron 33 in the late 1930s, 97-101

Pan American world Airways

Many pilots who flew for this airline had received their flight training from the Navy, 42, 180; had close ties with the Navy during World War II, 122, 179-180; flying of crucial materials to Europe during the war, 135-136; Juan Trippe's attempt to make Pan Am the sole U.S. international airline, 184; headed by Trippe for many years, 193-208; history of the airline, 198, 200-202

Parachutes

In the 1930s the Lakehurst Naval Air Station was the site of school for parachute packers, 69; Miller and some shipmates made a jump in the early 1930s, 70-71; Lieutenant Ward Harrigan designed a combination of a parachute and raft, 71-72

Patoka, USS (AO-9)
　　Navy oiler equipped with a mooring mast in the 1920s so it could handle rigid airships, 57

Patrol Squadron 16
　　Operated out of Seattle and Alaska in the late 1930s, 94-96

Patrol Squadron 33
　　Operated out of Panama in the late 1930s, 97-101; received the Schiff Trophy for safety in 1940, 100-101

Pay and Allowances
　　Meager amounts for Naval Academy midshipmen in the early 1920s, 9-10; line officers resented extra pay given to naval aviators in the late 1920s, 26

Pensacola Naval Air station
　　Site of flight training in 1926, 26-31; training in the early 1930s, 41-43, 46-47, 51-52

Photography
　　Navy efforts to facilitate photography of the invasion of Iwo Jima in 1945, 145-146, 154-155

Promotion of Officers
　　Miller received a spot promotion to rear admiral in 1945, 160-162

Pryor, Samuel
　　Long-time vice president of Pan American World Airways, 180, 184, 192-194, 196, 204-207; political connections, 203-204; personality and interests, 204-206

Public Relations
　　In 1944 Secretary of the Navy James Forrestal felt that the Navy was not doing an adequate job of publicizing its activities in the Pacific and sent Miller to Hawaii to remedy the situation, 138-143; Navy fleet hometown news program, 144-145; Navy support of the news media coverage of the invasion of Iwo Jima in 1945, 145-149, 154-155; support of coverage of the invasion of Okinawa in 1945, 146-147; Pacific Fleet approach in 1945 in terms of informing the American public about Japanese kamikazes, 156-157; the Navy brought Lieutenant (j.g.) Butch O'Hare to the United States for publicity purposes in 1942, 157-158; frustration in telling the story of submarine operations, 158-159; efforts to tell the Navy-wide story as World War II was winding down in 1945, 162-163; Navy public relations trips within the United States, 163-168; coverage of postwar events, 169-170; in 1945 the title of the Navy's publicity office was changed from "Public Relations" to "Public Information," 175; the American Petroleum Institute's efforts on behalf of the oil industry, 1948-57, 186-192; for Pan American World Airways, 1957-65, 193-208; for Hofstra University, 1968-74, 208-210

Quarton, Ensign Dale, USN (USNA, 1922)
　　Was friendly to Miller as a midshipman, later advised him in 1924 on seeking his first assignment as an officer, 19

Radford, Admiral Arthur W., USN (USNA, 1916)
While assigned to the Bureau of Aeronautics in the late 1930s, helped Miller get command of a patrol squadron, 96-97; got Miller set up as head of Training Literature in the Bureau of Aeronautics in early 1942, 103, 105-106, 171; was connected with Pacific Fleet public relations assignment for Miller in 1944, 137-140; as a lieutenant, he appeared to be a future Chief of Naval Operations, 178

Radio
Miller was co-recipient of a 1940 patent for a radio direction finder, 92

Ramsey, Lieutenant Logan C., USN (USNA, 1919)
Ended up in the water as a result of a landing accident while flying from the aircraft carrier Langley (CV-1) in the late 1920s, 40

Rescue at Sea
Recovery of survivors from the loss of the airship Macon (ZRS-5) off the coast of California in 1935, 89

Rockets
German V-1 attacks on London in 1944, 126-127

Roosevelt, President Franklin D.
In July 1934, F9Cs from the Macon dropped a package near the cruiser Houston (CA-30), which had President Roosevelt on board, 77-80; presented the Schiff Trophy to Miller in 1940, 100-101

Rosendahl, Lieutenant Commander Charles E., USN (USNA, 1914)
Did missionary work at Pensacola in 1926 on behalf of the Navy's lighter-than-air program, 54-55

Rosenthal, Joseph
Took famous flag-raising photograph on Iwo Jima in February 1945, 154-155

Royal Navy
Worked with the U.S. Navy in escorting Atlantic convoys in World War II, 114-115; desire to get more war materials from the United States in World War II, 115-116, 136; aircraft carrier operations out of Scapa Flow in 1944, 116-118; operations in the Pacific at the end of the war, 118-119

Safety
The Bureau of Aeronautics issued a series of "Sense" pamphlets during World War II on various aspects of aviation safety, 104-105; cartoons by Robert Osborn, 106-107

San Diego, California
Two line handlers were killed while tending the airship Akron (ZRS-4) near San Diego in 1932, 84

San Francisco, California
Operations in the vicinity by the airship Macon (ZRS-5) in the early 1930s, 82-83

San Pedro, California
Visits by ships of the U.S. Fleet in 1908 and later, 2; site of Navy submarine base in the late 1910s, 5; Navy pilots had dogfights over the fleet in the mid-1920s, 21

Scales, Rear Admiral Archibald H., USN (USNA, 1887)
As battleship division commander in 1923, 15; as superintendent of the Naval Academy in 1920, had to deal with an investigation of hazing, 16-17

Schiff Trophy
Award for aviation safety presented to Patrol Squadron 33 in 1940, 100-101

Shenandoah, USS (ZR-1)
U.S.-built rigid airship that crashed in Ohio in 1925, 54, 59; by-products of construction, 90

Sherman, Rear Admiral Forrest P., USN (USNA, 1918)
As a member of the Pacific Fleet staff, briefed reporters on the upcoming invasion of Iwo Jima in February 1945, 148-149; concurrence on public relations policy concerning kamikazes, 156-157; accompanied Fleet Admiral Chester Nimitz on a publicity trip to the United States in the autumn of 1945, 165, 167-168; even as a lieutenant, he appeared to be a future Chief of Naval Operations, 178

Shoemaker, Captain Harry E., USN (USNA, 1905)
Cooperation with the ship's aviators while commanding the heavy cruiser Northampton (CA-26) in the mid-1930s, 34-36

Simpler, Lieutenant (j.g.) LeRoy C., USN (USNA, 1929)
Served in the airship Macon (ZRS-5) in the early 1930s, 74, 84

Simulators
Commander Luis de Florez had a major role in developing aviation training simulators in World War II, 107

Sitka, Alaska
Establishment of a Navy seaplane base in the late 1930s, 95-96

Smith, Richard K.
Author of a book published in 1965 on the history of the airships Akron (ZRS-4) and Macon, 50-51

South Dakota
The Navy sent a delegation of flag officers to the state to celebrate Midwest Farmer Day on 3 September 1945, 163-164

Soviet Union
Soviet military mission contacts with Miller in London in 1943-44, 122-126

Stark, Admiral Harold R., USN (USNA, 1903)
Served as Commander U.S. Naval Forces Europe during much of World War II, 113, 125-126, 132, 137; took a back seat to Admiral Ernest J. King following the attack on Pearl Harbor, 131-132

Steichen, Edward
Famed photographer who worked for the Training Literature section of the Bureau of Aeronautics during World War II, 103, 105, 109-111, 171; work in the Pacific later in the war, 154

Stettinius, Edward R., Jr.
Former Secretary of States whose estate Juan Trippe looked out for in the 1950s, 198-199

Studley, Lieutenant Barret, USN
As a flight instructor at Pensacola in the early 1930s, was trying to find medical correlations to students aptitudes for flying, 51-52

Support Force, U.S. Atlantic Fleet
Operated in the Atlantic in 1941 to protect convoys bound for Europe, 102-103; had topflight staff officers, 102

Symington, Captain Thomas A., USN (USNA, 1907)
As commanding officer of the heavy cruiser Northampton (CA-26) in the mid-1930s, 24, 36, 92

Texas
Fleet Admiral Chester Nimitz made a public relations trip to the state in the autumn of 1945, 166-167

Tirpitz (German Battleship)
Attacked by British aircraft carrier planes in 1944, 116-117

Towers, Captain John H., USN (USNA, 1906)
In the mid-1930s, as Assistant Chief of the Bureau of Aeronautics, got Miller involved in compiling the history of U.S. naval aviation, 49-50, 101; in World War I brought the Yale aviation unit into the Navy, 196

Training
Flight instruction in 1926 at Pensacola, Florida, 26-31; flight training at Pensacola in the early 1930s, 41-43, 46-47, 51-52; Commander Luis de Florez had a major role in developing aviation training simulators in World War II, 107; de Florez made training films in World War II, 174; flight training in Miami in World War I, 196

Training Literature
Established within the Navy's Bureau of Aeronautics in 1942 to assist in training aviators, 103-104, 176; promoted safety within naval aviation, 104-107; relationship with the Time-Life organization, 103-104, 108-109; publication of a recognition journal, 108-109; did publicity on behalf of naval aviation, 110-112, 171; brought Lieutenant (j.g.) Butch O'Hare to the United States for publicity purposes in 1942, 157-158

Transcontinental and Western Air
   Operations of the airline in the late 1940s by Jack Frye and Howard Hughes, 180-183

Trapnell, Lieutenant (j.g.) Frederick M., USN (USNA, 1923)
   Served in the airship Akron (ZRS-4) in the early 1930s, 66; in the airship Macon (ZRS-5), 71, 73-74

Trippe, Juan
   Founder and long-time head of Pan American World Airways, 180, 184, 193-194, 197-202, 207; personality, 194, 197-202; personal background, 195-196, 203

UO-1
   Vought observation plane that flew from the battleship California (BB-44) in the mid-1920s, 20-21; Lieutenant Dixie Kiefer was injured by fellow pilot Dutch Greber, flying a UO in Panama in the mid-1920s, 21; fighter version on board the battleship West Virginia (BB-48) in the late 1920s, 37

V-1
   Used in German rocket attacks on London in 1944, 126-127

Waller, Lieutenant (j.g.) Raymond R., USN (USNA, 1924)
   Helped get Miller assigned to the airship Akron (ZRS-4) in 1932, 55

Weather
   Impact on the Navy's rigid airship operations in the early 1930s, 62; loss of the airship Akron (ZRS-4) in a storm off New Jersey in April 1933, 67; the airship Macon (ZRS-5) was lost amid violent air currents off the coast of California on 12 February 1935, 84-89

West Virginia, USS (BB-48)
   Commanded by gentlemanly captain Wat Cluverius in the late 1920s, 24; relationship between aviators and line officers, 25-26; operation of floatplanes in the late 1920s, 31-33, 37

Wieber, Lieutenant Carlos W., USN (USNA, 1918)
   Served in 1926 as a flight instructor at Pensacola, 27

Wiley, Lieutenant Commander Herbert V., USN
   Commanded the airship Akron (ZRS-4) up to the time of her loss in 1933, 70; was aggressive while commanding the airship Macon (ZRS-5) in the Pacific up to the time of her loss in 1935, 73-80, 82, 84; in July 1934, F9Cs from the Macon dropped a package near the cruiser Houston (CA-30), which had President Franklin D. Roosevelt on board, 77-80; the Macon, under his command, was lost in February 1935, 84-89

Winant, John G.
   Served as U.S. ambassador to Great Britain during World War II, 113, 122

World War I
Wartime aviators still on active duty in the 1920s and 1930s had limited naval experience, 25-26, 38, 93; German zeppelins had limited effectiveness, 59, 80; F. Trubee Davison formed the Yale aviation unit in 1916 and took it into the Navy the following year, 195-196

XJW-1
See JW-1

Yale University, New Haven, Connecticut
Source of a U.S. naval aviation unit in World War I, 195-196

Young, Lieutenant (j.g.) Howard L., USN (USNA, 1923)
Served in the airship Akron (ZRS-4) in the early 1930s, 55, 60, 66; death of, 67; in the airship Macon (ZRS-5), 71, 73-74

www.ingramcontent.com/pod-product-compliance
Lightning Source LLC
Chambersburg PA
CBHW080614170426
43209CB00007B/1431